The Popular Image of the Black Man in English Drama, 1550-1688

Elliot H. Tokson

The Popular Image of the Black Man in English Drama, 1550-1688

G.K. Hall and Co. Boston, Massachusetts

Library of Congress Cataloging in Publication Data

Tokson, Elliot H.
    The popular image of the black man in English drama, 1550–
1688.

    Bibliography
    Includes index.
    1. English drama—Early modern and Elizabethan,
1500–1600—History and criticism.   2. English drama—
17th century—History and criticism.   3. Africans in
literature.   4. Blacks in literature.   5. Slavery and
slaves in literature.   6. Race awareness in literature.
I. Title.
PR658.A4T6   822'.3'093520396   81–17860
ISBN 0-8161-8392-9   AACR2

This publication is printed on permanent/durable acid-free paper.
MANUFACTURED IN THE UNITED STATES OF AMERICA

To Robert Bone of Columbia University, who not only located the funds that enabled me to undertake this book, but also provided the single inspiration and guidance to complete it. To him is due whatever value the study has. Its faults and flaws I claim as my own.

Contents

Preface

My intention in this study is to describe the ways English creative writers of the sixteenth and seventeenth centuries treated the black Africans who had been introduced into their culture in the middle 1550s. With special attention given to the drama of the period from 1550 to 1688, my focus will be on the image of the black man that the writers molded from whatever materials were then available to them. Whether these sources of information were the written works of earlier commentators or the oral and written reports of contemporary travelers, or whether the writers were affected by their own psychological disposition to black skin or by the total cultural climate in which slavery was fast becoming a dominant force, the resulting image tended to be markedly consistent and strongly negative. I am attempting here to analyze the characteristics attributed to the black man and to evaluate the insistence with which creative writers assigned those qualitites to him.

The significance of this literary reaction to a cultural phenomenon becomes evident when we examine its historical context. Put briefly, English dramatists were trying to respond imaginatively to a black African who was a stranger to their land and their consciousness at exactly the same time that English commercial interests were beginning to exploit that same black man as the most suitable material for slave labor. The institution of slavery quickly and emphatically declared the black man a base human being (and frequently not even a human being at all), permitting and endorsing a practice of treating him as a beast of burden. The declaration justified the treatment.

Within a decade of the earliest face-to-face confrontation between Englishmen and black men in the 1550s, the English slave trade was established and, during the next two hundred years, grew to such large proportions as to become a major economic foundation of English prosperity. English ships were to carry millions of slaves, enriching a growing merchant fleet and a variety of English industries. Hundreds of thousands of blacks would pass through Brititsh ports to furnish labor on English plantations, whose prosperity would be reflected in increased productivity in England. The growth of British economy was inseparable from this vastly expanding slave trade.

> For three centuries the principal maritime powers competed with
> one another in the lucrative slave trade, and carried at least fifteen
> million Africans to the New World. . . . As stimulus to shipbuilding,
> insurance, investment, and banking, the slave trade expanded em-
> ployment in a diversity of occupations and encouraged the growth
> of seaports on both sides of the Atlantic. Africa became a prized
> market for iron, textiles, firearms, rum, and brandy. Investments
> in the triangular trade brought dazzling rewards, since profits could
> be made in exporting consumer goods to Africa, selling slaves to
> planters, and especially in transporting sugar and other staples to
> Europe. By the 1760s a large number of wealthy merchants in
> Britain and France were connected in some way with the West
> Indian trade, and capital accumulated from investment in slaves
> and their produce helped to finance the building of canals, factories,
> and railroads.[1]

The author of this passage, David Davis, having summed up the broad
economic reaches of the black trade, traces the moral and philosophical
attacks on its evil that developed in the eighteenth and nineteenth centuries.
That slavery was irreconcilable "with the image of the New World as uncor-
rupted nature," he concludes, was a question men ignored for over two
hundred years.

Yet there must have existed during this time some consciously felt ten-
sions over slavery that could break so vigorously in the eighteenth century
to lead to emancipation. When, in the middle of the seventeenth century,
Thomas Fuller described the "Good Sea-Captain" in his book *The Holy and
Profane State*, he attributed to him an unwillingness to drown Negroes who
were taken prisoner in naval engagements. Fuller went on to insist on the
common fatherhood the English shared with the Negro, although he recognized that the mother, that is, the Church, differed. The passage points to the
inhuman treatment of the black man and the undercurrent of uneasiness that
it produced in a nation that cherished its human liberties.

Whether that tension created by the cultural clash of white with black
extended to any degree into contemporary creative literature can be determined only by a careful study of the plays (and several interesting poems)
of the period. Professor Davis has sharply and provocatively raised the
question of the role of creative literature in this cultural struggle: Did the
literary imagination, he asks, in any way help to bridge the gap that lay
between the races?[2] Constructing such a bridge across the gap would mean,
in part at least, bringing one race to see the other as "men of feeling" who
have a "capacity for a moral life." Were the men of creative imagination men
of deeper insight or were they men of tunnel vision who could see no further,
at least on this issue, than the pressures of their own culture permitted them?

Studies have shown that eighteenth-century writers did succeed in creating greater sympathy for and understanding of the black man.[3] But little close attention has been called to this particular question in the literature of the preceding period (1550-1688) when the racial encounter was fresh and perplexing. The dates here represent, at one end, the first appearance of black men on English soil (early 1550s), and at the other, the publication of Mrs. Aphra Behn's novel *Oroonoko* (1688), which initiated a tendency to ennoble the black man as part of the growing image of the noble savage.

With this broad framework in mind, I should say something about the materials pertinent to this study and the procedure I have followed.

I should emphasize that this book is a study of the *popular* image of the black man in the drama of this period, 1550-1688. By "popular" I mean the image that appeared and reappeared with almost predictable consistency when a black man was paraded across the stage. Now *Othello* may be one of the most important literary productions of the time to present the problem of the black man as he first entered English consciousness. But of all of Shakespeare's great tragic heroes, certainly Othello's character must be ranked as one of the most controversial. Arguments have been raised both for and against the view of Othello as a noble Moor, and, in the light of modern developments, the problem of that nobility—or barbarism—unavoidably has turned attention to the question of Shakespeare's racial tolerance or bigotry. Some critics believe that Shakespeare was uninterested in the racial aspects of the tragic situation altogether, while others hold that Shakespeare was so deeply concerned with Othello's blackness that to miss that theme is to miss the heart of the play.

Whether Shakespeare imaginatively probed more deeply than any other writer of this period into the possibilities of the black man, or whether he basically followed the stereotyped patterns on which he traced the outline of Othello's character, or whether he combined popular notion with original perspective are gritty questions that one could more fruitfully pursue were there available some suitable materials with which Othello could be compared. The image of Othello is already there to be studied for its major identifying characteristics. What we need now is the composite picture of the black man of the period as it appears in other plays. I have attempted, therefore, to provide that picture by omitting *Othello* altogether and concentrating on how the black man fares in the rest of the period's drama.

To make the various facets of the image of the black man more fully understandable and convincing I have followed the procedure of isolating from the individual treatments of black characters several major qualities that appear and reappear and grouping the similar characteristics as a single facet for separate study. The villainy of the black man, for example, can be better understood when it receives a separate investigation, drawing material from the many different characters who, in one form or another, exemplify or reflect the particular quality. What could seem idiosyncratic in one play becomes more generally characteristic if it occurs repeatedly. The white man's belief in and fear of the black man's reputed sexual prowess and attractiveness to white women, to note another example, becomes more evident when we draw together a large number of references to lust and love from many sources for contrast and comparison.

Once we have isolated and identified a basic quality of the black man, we increase the ease of studying that quality and its ramifications by gathering into one section of the book numerous relevant passages from different writers. Furthermore, if we discussed such a quality among other features of the same character, we might tend to identify that quality with that specific character and thus obscure its significance in the larger view of the black image as a whole. The quality would more likely seem a peculiarity of a particular character. Even if we were to discuss the same quality later in connection with another character who also exemplifies it, the fact of its widespread existence, its stereotypicality, would be obscured or lost.

Therefore, in the hope of achieving a clearer picture of what white English writers as a group thought of the alien black man, I have chosen to emphasize patterns of qualitites rather than individual characters.

Chapter 1

The Nonliterary Response

It is often said that the Renaissance discovered man, and that the perplexities associated with the discovery were profound. But even so, the man discovered was a familiar fellow, a white European. When, at about the same time, the explorers threw the spotlight of publicity upon backward, darker-skinned, non-Europeans, when they brought home and told their stories of naked cannibals, there was something more involved than the enlargement of the European sample of the genus *Homo*. Here, or so it seemed, was a different kind of man. Or was he a man? There were those to say he was not.[1]

Englishmen were first asked to face the question of the humanity of the black man when, in the middle 1550s, English traders brought five black men from Guinea to London. These Guineans were kept in London until they could speak English[2] and then four returned to their native land. The one who remained married "a fair English-woman" who subsequently gave birth to a baby "in all respects as black as his father." The reaction to the news was strong, for the phenomenon of a white woman's producing on English soil "a coal-black Ethiopean" was taken as a disparagement of the white race.[3]

Of course the existence of dark-skinned Moors was not unknown even to Englishmen of earlier periods. As early as 1510 Moors had been represented in English masques, and in 1522 they had been portrayed in street pageants.[4] Englishmen certainly knew of the black-skinned lover in the *Song of Songs*, and Richard Eden's *The Decades of the New World*, a work containing descriptions of black-skinned people, was to be published in 1555. The actual face-to-face meetings on English soil, however, began probably in 1554.

In the following century, the problem of conceptualizing a different race and describing it sharpened rapidly as the meeting of the two races spread. Expanding English exploration and involvement in slavery made many more Englishmen aware of the black man. For example, a glance at Hakluyt's *Navigations* shows an increasing number of trading vessels going to Africa in the seventies, eighties, and nineties. Similarly, it has been estimated that from the time John Hawkins initiated the English slave trade in 1563 to the middle of the eighteenth century, British ships carried well over two million black slaves to the West Indies alone, many of whom passed through English ports.[5] The establishment of official relationships with Barbary had been made before the end of the sixteenth century and in the 1580s trading companies had been licensed by the Crown to engage officially in business with African peoples. Among the many forces that shaped the developing conflict between the races—for example, the philosophical, theological, and economic pressures supporting the institution of slavery—there was also the crucial factor of the image of the black man himself as Englishmen conceived it.

During the Renaissance, the term "black man" included in its reference those people called "Moors," "Black-a-Moors," "Negroes," and "Aethiopians." Although Englishmen became increasingly aware of the differences among these peoples,[6] they generally perceived them as black people, even using the terms "black" and "tawny" to describe the same character. To white commentators all nonwhites differed from themselves just as blackness differs from whiteness. As Richard Eden wrote: "Toward the South of this region is the kingdom of Guinea, with Senega, Jalofo, Gambera, and many other regions of the Blacke Moores, called Aethiopians or Negros, all of which are watered with the river Negro called in old time Niger."[7] In another passage he writes that in the old times the people in Africa were called "Aethiopes and Nigritae, which we now call Moores, Moorens, or Negroes. . . ."[8]

The learned Thomas Browne was another early commentator who held that "Aethiopean" is synonymous with "Negro." "By the word Aethiop itself, applied to the memorablest Nation of Negroes, that is of a burnt and torrid countenance."[9] Even as late as 1764 James Grainger, who managed a sugar cane estate for his Creole wife, talks of "Negro-nations" suffering from yaws and worms, the dragon worm especially causing "annual lameness to the tortur'd Moor."[10] The twentieth-century Shakespearean scholar E. E. Stoll accepts evidence offered in *Titus Andronicus, Lust's Dominion,* and *The English Moor* "that the word *Moor* was . . . exactly equivalent to *negro.*"[11]

What may be even more significant about a loose nomenclature is that the black man and the American Indian were often mistaken for each other. In practice these two peoples were treated differently: black men were enslaved for hard labor, while Indians were often freed for reasons of security and eocnomic advantage. However, in the literature that concerned them, as David Davis points out, the distinction between them "had a tendency to dissolve."[12] But Davis adds that "the increasing interchangeability of Indians and Negroes was perhaps less a sign of racial ignorance than of a gradual extension of the primitivistic ideal."[13] Wylie Sypher offers the most detailed discussion of this phenomenon as it appeared in the literature of the eighteenth century, when, in spite of the greater ethnological knowledge that had been collected, the fusion continued. He traces the history of the changing identity of Yarico from 1616, when the legend begins with the famous Yarico-Inkle story in which Yarico is an unnamed Indian girl, to the story of Yarico in *London Magazine* of May 1734, in which she has become an African.[14] Earlier, in the seventeenth century, Thomas Dekker's *Lust's Dominion* (1599) appears to confuse the Moor with the Indian, a detail to be discussed later. And what may be of greatest significance is the possibility that Shakespeare's treatment of Caliban may apply to the black man as well as to the New World "savage."[15]

With the problem of elaborate racial differentiation removed by this widespread practice of fusing identities and interchanging names, the major concern of this study will be the early literary response to the "new man," regardless of what he was called. He was considered black and therefore so acutely different from Western man as to hamper his acceptance into the dominant society. Throughout this study, then, the term most generally used to refer to the central subject will be "black man" unless the author under discussion specifically calls him the "Moor" or the "African," the "Ethiopian," or the "Negro." In all cases the characters are clearly black skinned.

It is a supposition of this study that the literary contribution to the development of an image of the black man can best be understood and evaluated only when compared with the image that grew out of the historical experience itself and that found its expression in the journals, travel books, and geographies that were so widely published in the first periods of feverish exploration. What must be examined first, then, is the picture of the black man as it developed in the words of those writers who claimed "scientific objectivity" in their descriptions of Africa and the people living there. This nonliterary response to an event of high cultural shock would no doubt have an effect on the imagination of creative writers. It is therefore important to look at the geographies and encyclopedias of men like Isidore of Seville (*Etymologies*, 622–623), Bartholomeus Anglicus, who copied Isidore in *De proprietatibus rerum* (1240–1260—a book which the printing press was to see through forty-six editions in six languages, and which was translated into English in 1582 by Stephen Batman), Sir John Mandeville (*Travels*, 1356, with 250 surviving manuscripts, forty of which are in English), Johann Boemus (*Omnium gentium mores*, 1524, which was translated into English as *A Fardle of Facions* in 1555 by William Waterman and which ran through twenty-three editions in five languages before 1611), the highly popular Sebastian Muenster (*Cosmographie*, 1544, appearing in forty-six editions in six languages, first translated into English by Richard Eden in 1553 and reissued in 1572), and in the works of Mercator, Ortelius, and the highly influential Hakluyt and his successor Samuel Purchas. These are the works— popular and often erroneous—that would be the source of fantasy and fact about the black man of Africa.[16]

What the sixteenth- and seventeenth-century travelers, traders, and ethnologists saw and thought when they visited Africa or heard reports of others who had been there was more often than not determined by preconceptions shaped by the earlier writers and by their own impulses to react ethnocentrically to the alien society.[17] During the first century of direct contact between white and black races on English soil, the image of the black man, as seen in the nonliterary reactions, was generally unfavorable. The Renaissance voyagers were "almost unanimous" in their disparaging judgments of the people they found in Africa.[18]

The black man was both verbally and physically mistreated in ways that reflected the English conception of him as an evil, inferior, or even subhuman being. In journals and letters numerous references to his demonism, his bestiality, and his ignorance bear witness to such a belief, as does the brutality of the slave trade, sanctioned and supported by the government.

Perhaps somewhat overly dramatic but not untypical is the passage describing Barbary in the highly popular *Pilgrimes* of Samuel Purchas (1613):

> The Throne of Pyracie, the Sinke of Trade and Stinke of Slavery;
> the Cage of uncleane Birds of Prey, and Habitation of Sea-Devils . . .
> the whip of the Christian World, the wall of the Barbarian, terror of
> Europe, the bridle of both Hesperias (Italy and Spain) Scourge of
> Islands, Den of Pyrates, Theatre of all crueltie, and Sanctuarie of
> Iniquitie . . . Hels Epitome, Miseries Ocean, Christians whirlepoole,
> Tortures centre, Hell upon Earth.[19]

The hysterical nature of the attack aside, the passage hits on some basic conceptions of the Moor and his culture, his paganism, his cruelty, his filthiness, and his demonic quality. Creative writers found it hard to imagine things much different.

Although knowledge of a Moorish civilization did exist—England had already established official relations with Barbary by 1577[20]—not much effort was made to temper harsh reactions when the dark-skinned "strangers" appeared in England. When the Moorish ambassador from Barbary, with fifteen Moors in his retinue, paid Queen Elizabeth I an official state visit in 1600, court officials had great difficulty in obtaining housing and hospitality for them, from either government funds or private generosity.[21] Yet earlier that year Sir Thomas Gerard had readily been able to accommodate a French embassy five times as large (eighty members to be exact) in London at government expense.[22] For seven months these black men, "strangely attired and behaviored," lived alone in a house where it was rumored that they slaughtered their own food animals, facing "eastward when they killed anything."[23] It was said that despite the courteous hospitality they received once they were finally settled, they were hateful and uncharitable, refusing to give money to the needy and selling their leftover food to those among

the poor who could afford it. The rumors, then, were unfavorable to these
envoys, who were considered spies rather than "honorable ambassadors,
for they omitted nothing that might damnifie the English merchants."[24]
Bernard Harris believes that behind the shrewdness and cunning of the
Moors, "if the rumors had any truth, was unsensitivity and cruelness, even
murder."[25] That the ill treatment of the Moors and the rumors about their
aims were symptomatic of broader and deeper racial feelings seems obvious.

Exactly what produced and sustained these feelings will probably never
be fully understood. But students of the problem agree that one basic influence on racial judgments is the force of ethnocentrism, the will to view
one's own culture and race as superior to alien ones. Anthropological studies,
asserts Mrs. Katherine Oakes George, have shown that when two cultures
meet in face-to-face situations, it is the tendency of both, and especially the
tendency of the more technically advanced, to act in the ethnocentric belief
that the other culture is patently inferior:

> To be born into a culture has generally implied being supported by
> it; being upheld, as it were, on a pedestal, from which one might
> look down with varying degrees of disinterest or antagonism upon
> other, alien cultures. Hence the observer of alien cultures has tended
> to be prejudiced, in the simple sense that he has preferred his own
> to all other existent cultures and has viewed the stranger as a mal-
> formed deviant from the familiar. The ego-flattering naivete of the
> Aristotelian division of the world's population into Greek and
> barbarian, or freemen by nature and slaves by nature, has formed
> the usual pattern into which men have fitted their observations of
> human differences.[26]

Thus the sixteenth-century historian William Harrison could write of his
fellow Britons in Holinshed's *Chronicles*:

> The Britons are white in color, strong of bodie, and full of bloud,
> as people inhabiting neere north, and farre from the equinoctiall
> line, where the soile is not so fruitful, and therefore the people not
> so feeble; whereas contrariwise such as dwell toward the course of
> the sunne, are lesse of stature, weaker of bodie, more nice, delicate,
> fearfull by nature, blacker in colour, and some so black indeed as
> anie crow or raven.

He then goes on to eulogize the British population who "do excell such as
dwell in the hoter countries" in their "courtesy, strength of body, sincerity
of behavior."[27]

Even the decorative work of cartographers reflects cultural egoism. In one
of the famous maps of Ortelius in his *Theatrum orbis terrarum* (1570),
Europa, with a scepter in her right hand and a globe under her left, is at the

top of the page; in the middle, on one side, is Asia, adorned with jewels, and on the other, Africa, a naked woman. At the bottom is America, a savage woman holding a club and a bleeding head.[28]

In 1676-77 Dr. Samuel Petty of the Royal Society clearly sanctioned the doctrine of European supremacy in his formal treatise *The Scale of Creations*. There are many other kinds of men, he found, but all inferior to European man.[29]

Winthrop Jordan, quoting Hume, Goldsmith, and others, has shown how this ethnocentric force extended into the eighteenth century. He concluded wryly that "by and large, Europeans were a marvelous race,"[30] if you listened to what a European had to say.

There were, however, some writers of broader views who were able to note that ethnocentrism works in two directions. Peter Martyr in the early 1500s had written: "The Aethiopean thinketh the blacke colour to be fairer than the white; and the white man thinketh otherwise."[31] Thomas Browne also recognized that black would appear beautiful to the black man. What pleases one people need not please all people. "Thus we that are of contrary complexions accuse the blackness of the Moors as ugly. But the Spouse in the *Canticles* excuseth this conceit, in that description of hers, I am black, but comely."[32] The church poet George Herbert, lying in a sick bed and rejecting the sympathy of the healthy who felt that they were better off than the sick, chose the issue of ethnocentrism to make his point that each prefers his own:

> Your state to ours is contrary,
> That makes you think us poor;
> So Black-Moores think us foule, and we
> Are quit with them, and more.
>   Nothing can see
> And judg of things but mediocrity.[33]

Peter Heylyn, the cosmographer, also was aware of the two-way thrust of racial pride when he described some Negroes in 1621: "Of complexion they are for the most part Cole-blacke, whence the name Negroes. . . . the blacks [are] so much in love with their own complexion, that they use to paint the Devil White; which I find thus verified."[34]

Just what connection such ethnocentric tendencies have with the way white society has perenially reacted to the color black itself is difficult to determine. Needless to say, though, black has almost always had negative associations. Harry Levin, in his book *The Power of Blackness* (1958), has discussed the meaning of "blackness" in western culture.[35] His exposition of the mythical and symbolic roles of "blackness" focuses our attention on an important force of erosion that has helped to create and sustain the chasm between the races. The whole play between light and darkness, from the underlying imagery of the book of Genesis, to the metaphoric conceptions of the Greeks "as champions of brightness" leading us "out of Gothic darkness," to the innumerable references to the evil of blackness, the negative associative values of the color persist.[36] Although individuals came to recognize the complexity of this problem—writers like Shakespeare and Melville—"usage is stubborn," and even when Mrs. Aphra Behn tried to ennoble the black man she tended to draw him white.

Studies have shown quite clearly that historically in western culture "black" has "been chiefly connected with thoughts of hell, sin, death, and other manifestations of what is gloomy and forbidding."[37] The examples available are so numerous that a few should suffice here: The significance is explicit in expressions such as *black*list, *black*mail, *black*guard, to look *black, black*out, but its understood inferiority to white can be recognized in such subtle and unconscious expressions such as this from the learned Thomas Browne, who arranges colors, it seems, vertically: "the inhabitants of America are fair; and they of *Europe* in *Candy, Sicily,* and some parts of *Spain*, deserve not properly *so low* a name as Tawney."[38] [italics added] And again, in the same passage, Browne reflects the subtly negative attitude toward "blackness:" "there are many within this zone whose complexions *descend* not *so low* [italics added] as unto blackness."[39] There were, however, some special meanings attributed to "black" color in the Renaissance. Don Cameron Allen has pointed out that black could signify not only sorrow and mourning, but disappointed love, constant love, a love that extends beyond the grave, and constancy.[40] Some of these possibilities may enhance an understanding of some poems about black lovers to be discussed later. But more often, as Winthrop Jordan states categorically, referring his readers to the *Oxford English Dictionary*, "Black was an emotionally partisan color, the handmaid and symbol of baseness and evil, a sign of danger and repulsion."[41]

However deep the significance of black was in view of the Englishman, he tended to find it entirely unattractive. If the standards of beauty in the English world were red and white, blackness was their polar opposite.[42] Sir Dudley Carleton, criticizing the appearance of the characters in Ben Jonson's *The Masque of Blackness* (1605), wrote: "Instead of Vizzards, their Faces and Arms up to the Elbows, were painted black, which was Disguise sufficient for they were hard to be known; but it became them nothing so well as their red and white, and you cannot imagine a more ugly Sight, than a Troop of lean-cheek'd Moors."[43] Another writer, considering the decision of Paris to give the apple to Venus and its aftermath, used the Moor as a paradigm for ugliness: "He should have discovered her to have been a beldame foule as the beast that suckled him, then would her harsh hair (which once he thought finer than flaxe) appeare near allyed to Foxes Furre, her complexion Cousin germane to the servant Indian, or tawny Moore."[44]

In addition to the pressures of ethnocentrism and the general aversion to blackness, a third major influence no doubt greatly shaped the image of the black man as it developed through the reports of travelers and ethnologists during the early decades of confrontation. That influence, and perhaps the major one, was the popular treatment of the dark-skinned people in the works of earlier commentators. From the time of Herodotus and Pliny down even to the eighteenth century of Long and Hume, the commentary on foreign peoples in the distant lands of Africa and Asia—and later of America— was a conglomeration of facts, exaggeration, fantasy, and fabrication. Most of the material after Herodotus and Pliny was borrowed from preceding writers and very little reflected on-the-spot observation. Mrs. Margaret Hodgen, in her prize-winning study of anthropology in the sixteenth and seventeenth centuries, has argued persuasively that legend and imagination more often than not were the central influences that shaped these writers' views of the African.[45] Surprisingly, Herodotus, one of the earliest ethnologists, was also one of the most scientifically objective in his treatment of foreign cultures. Unfortunately, what survived from his works was not the scientific spirit but rather those parts that popularized the fantastic.[46] Mrs. Hodgen writes:

> In dealing with the tribes on the southern shores of the Mediter-
> ranean or around the Black Sea, many Renaissance collectors merely
> took down their copies of Herodotus, or reverted to dimly remem-
> bered passages in other ancient authors. Despite intervening
> centuries of trade with Mediterranean ports, despite recent revela-
> tions by Portuguese and other explorers of the characteristics of
> living Africans, these peoples were called by their ancient names;
> and they were reported as conducting themselves in A.D. 1520, or
> 1620, or 1720, exactly as they had been portrayed in the fifth
> century B.C. Boemus, Muenster, Heylyn, and many other seven-
> teenth-century cosmographers are notably confusing on this score.[47]

The old formulas for description remained staple fare for those who wrote after the confrontation.[48]

The basic formula for those who wanted to describe the new people who had been discovered wearing black skins and doing strange things was to describe them simply and clearly by focusing on a limited characteristic. From Bartholomew's *De proprietatibus rerum* (1240-1260) and Sir John Mandeville's semi-legendary *Travels* (1356), to the work of Johann Boemus, *Omnium gentium more* (1520) and Sebastian Muenster's *Cosmographia* (1544), the most important works of this later period, the tendency to stereotype people and places through simplification was dominant. Again, Mrs. Hodgen gives us a clear and convincing description of their methods of operation.

The medieval encyclopedia with its capsule epitome, its stereotypes
and typologies, became the model. In response to a deep human
need for brief formulae which would express the characteristics
of things and peoples in dichotomies of black and white, virtue
and vice, these general cultural descriptions were short, terse,
apothegmatic.[49]

For example, the famous French jurist Jean Bodin describes the differences
between peoples of the northern and southern climates: "The one hath a
flaxen haire and a faire skin, the other hath hair and skin black; the one
feareth cold, the other heate; the one is joyfull and pleasant, the other sad;
the one is fearfull and peaceable, the other hardie and mutinous; the one is
sociable, the other solitair...."[50] In Muenster's *Cosmographia* the same
practice of stereotyping prevails: he attributes "Disloyalte and unfaithfulnes
to the Persians. Craftines to the Egyptians. Deceitfulnes to the Grecians.
Cruelty to the Saracens."[51] Examples of this method of description can be
found throughout the corpus of ethnological writing of the sixteenth and
seventeenth centuries. Agrippa, Boemus, Mercator, Heylyn—all subscribed to
the ideal of brevity and simplicity, and all produced and helped sustain the
idea of rigid national or racial types.

Aside from perpetuating these restricted views of alien peoples, the same
writers tended to accept unquestionably the existence of monstrous peoples
living in areas near those inhabited by black men. Peter Heylyn, one of the
best-known cosmographers, notes in an early edition of his *Microscosmos* that
the ancients thought Africa hardly populated, and "if at all, with such strange
people, as hardly deserved to be called men." He catalogues some of the
marvels described by the ancients:

> Cynophanes, who had heads like dogs. . . . Sceopode, who with the
> shadow of their foot, could and did hide themselves from the heat
> of the Sun. . . . Blemmye, who, being without heads, had their eyes
> and mouth in their Brests. . . . Eeripane, who had no other humane
> quality to declare them to be men, but the shape and making of
> their bodies.[52]

Heylyn goes on to point out that recent investigation had proved the absur-
dity of these claims which were based on "conjecture" or "more doubtful
hear-say."[53] But the truth is that belief in monstrous beings was widely held.
Sebastian Muenster, in his highly popular work *Cosmographia*, without
question accepted the existence of the monstrosities described by Pliny,
Isidore, and Mandeville, and connected anthropophagi with the newly discovered peoples of distant countries and "drew all savage and barbarian
peoples into the same reference, and confirmed in the minds of many readers
the opinion that this was the right place for them."[54]

It is difficult to estimate the effect of linking real men with purely imaginary creatures, but the consequences were probably considerable. The image of the wild man, for example, so ubiquitous in the Middle Ages, is a strong case in point. Richard Bernheimer's *Wild Men in the Middle Ages*[55] fully describes the tradition of this ugly monster who wears a man's shape but is covered with animal-like fur. Widely depicted in the art, literature, and iconography of the Middle Ages, the wild man, Bernheimer states, was "a creature compounded of intransigence, lust, and violence."[56] He is "raw lust" or "bleak hatred," incapable of gentle love.[57] "Appalling ugliness, cannibalism, frightful temper"[58] expand this image into one that tends to correspond to the later concepts of the black man as erotic and savage. Bernheimer traces this tradition of the wild man back to the ancient Greeks, through the Middle Ages when his popularity was probably greatest, down even to the present.

When history produced a need for white men to react to black men, the already highly developed and persistent tradition of the wild men offered itself as one source of ready-made concepts that would result in the two images of the wild man and the black man sharing "the same essential quality."[59] That quality, a "raw, unpredictable, foreign" force of lust and destruction,[60] Bernheimer suggests, originates in some "basic and primitive impulses" that are "hidden in all of us, but are normally kept under control."[61] The unfortunate consequences of such impulses are not directly felt when they result in the creation of imaginary monsters like the hairy wild man whose existence always has remained a fictive one. But when the fairy tale creature helped shape the image of black-skinned men, his qualities were imposed on real human beings who would enter and remain in the historical experience of western culture, and who would suffer from the unfair transference of such qualities.

Such was the great tragic association of monsters with real people, who were quite often African people. As R. R. Cawley concluded about the widespread interest in the fabled cave-dwelling Troglodytes, who lived on a diet of serpents: "The most significant point of their appearance in literature is that they are so often classifed with regularly recognized historical nations, and indeed a race by that name was known since the time of Herodotus to occupy interior Africa."[62]

With their minds filled with the stories of such creatures roaming foreign lands, cartographers had a field day illustrating their maps. In Ptolemy's *Geography*, for instance, a book that went through thirty-five editions between 1475 and 1600, there are vivid color drawings of man-eating savages, devouring the bloody limbs of their hacked victims. Blood spurts everywhere.[63] The 1535 Lyons edition contains many illustrations of anthropophagi. One map of Asia, "Oceani Occidentalis," has pictures of men with one eye in their chests, described as "Colopedes sive monoculi homines st [i.e., Sunt] grandes negri et horribles." Blackness seemed the most suitable color for such monsters. In addition to these monstrosities, there were also pictures of those men whose faces are squarely built in their chests, those dog-headed men mentioned earlier, and that man with one huge leg. All these men are naked. The effect of these illustrated atlases on the conception of those who read them can only be conjectured. Since Shakespeare's acquaintance with maps has been convincingly demonstrated,[64] it is not unlikely that his own ideas about strange peoples were influenced to some degree by the illustrations he saw there.

Another strong factor in the *denigration* (note the cultural bias of the word itself) of alien races and especially of the black race was the Christian Church, which tended to promote a dualistic view of the world as a place where mankind could be divided into two groups. There were the "heathens" and the "saved."[65] Christian writers made no distinction among peoples who were not Christian and preferred rather to view them as simply heathenish and "therefore monstrosities."[66] They wrote so many reports of the bestiality of the black man that they separately and collectively call into doubt the right to refer to these black people as *men*. "Neither paganism, nor Mohametanism, nor Judaism, nor heathenism, had ever held that communicants of other faiths were less than men. Never before had brown skin, yellow skin, or black skin been allied conceptually with irrationality, beastliness, or ahumanity."[67] Orthodox Christianity, under the pressure of the story of Genesis, with its focus on monogeneity and the tale of Noah's flood to explain the diversification of man, did officially recognize the black man as a man—perhaps as one inferior to white men. However, it also inclined to the view of the world as a battleground of the forces of good and evil.[68] And that force of evil was always considered a darker power, which, in time, was naturally connected with the black man.[69] Professor Levin makes this point about color quite strongly when he says: "Even orthodox Christian ethics would permit Satan, the prince of darkness, to have his frequent triumphs in this world." But the world hereafter founded by Christ would be characterized by His garments, *alba sicut lux*.[70] Christianity, therefore, judged the differences between African culture and civilized life not just as proof of social disorder or technological backwardness, but as signs of moral degradation as well. Without the restraint of reason and Christian ethics imposed on it, the raw nature that Africa and the black man displayed was "fallen nature."[71] The blackness of the Negro was explained not as the result of climatic conditions but as a genetic deformity deriving from Ham, the accursed of God. "The dark skin of the Negro becomes more than esthetically displeasing; it becomes the symbol and the product of a moral taint as well."[72]

Although many people accepted the genetic explanation for the blackness in the skin pigmentation of Africans, there were those who recognized that the problem was too complex to be easily dismissed. There are, said Thomas

Browne, "no satisfactory and unquarrelable reasons, [that] may confirm the causes generally received; which are but two in number. The heat and scorch of the Sun; or the curse of God on Cham and his Posterity."[73] Here were the two ways to explain the Negro's color. Many people recognized the existence of both alternatives. As late as 1674, John Josselyn wrote, "It is the opinion of many men, that the blackness of the Negroes proceeded from the curse upon Cham's posterity, others again will have it to be the property of the climate where they live."[74] What seems to have been overlooked is that each of these views had an implicit judgment of the status of the Negro in human society.

The climatic theories of the cause of dark skin—from the myth of Phaethon's scorching the earth to more pseudoscientific explanations—attributed to the sun's rays the pigmentation of Negroes. John Lok, in the middle of the sixteenth century, guessed that Africans were "scorched and vexed with the heate of the sunne." Thomas Newton, in his *The Touchstones of Complexion* (1565), stated that "curled and crooked hayres proceed of a drynesse of Complexion, caused through immoderate heate." People living in hot, dry lands, therefore, have black and "small growing" hair.[75] Much earlier, Caxton translated *The Mirrour of the World*: "In this centre of Ethiope the people ben blacke for lite of the sonne; for it so hot in this contre that it seemeth that the erthe sholde breene."[76] Another important advocate of this theory was Jean Bodin, who attributed the differences among people not to divinely ordained genetic causes such as curses, nor to rapid migration after the flood, nor to a process of universal degenerations, but rather to climate and topography.[77] This theory implicitly accepted the original whiteness of the black-skinned races and enabled those who held it to accept the Negroes as human beings. "The popularity of this theory helped to keep the Negro and other dark-skinned peoples theoretically in the family of Adam, thus upholding their dignity as human beings."[78]

But it was not long before reports came back that there were people without black skins living in the same types of climate as that of the black-skinned races. The theory of climatic cause became questionable and although many people still held to it—including, as we shall see, the men of literary pursuits—the pigmentation issue burst forth again. Richard Eden noted that in the West Indies, where the regions "are under the same line" as those in Africa, the people are "neither blacken, nor with curlde and short wooll on their heads, as they of Africke have, but of the colour of an Olive, with long and blacke hear on their heads."[79] George Best, a voyager and "speculative geographer," wrote that he had seen the result of a marriage between a black man and a white woman—a coal black child: "Whereby it seemeth this blackness proceedeth rather of some natural infection of that man, which was so strong that neither the nature of the clime, nor the good complexion of the mother concurring, could anything alter, and therefore, we cannot impart it to the nature of the Clime."[80] Thomas Browne, too, rejected the theory that the sun had anything to do with the Negro's blackness because he observed that a change in climate did not produce any change in the Negro's coloring.[81]

The climatic theory, which attributed to the black man a humanity in common with Europeans, thus had its flaws, but there was still the other explanation which tended to have few—perhaps because it could not be put to similar tests of experience and logic. This theory rests on the curse laid by God on Ham (Cham), the son of Noah, and the reputed founder of the black races of Africa. Although Johann Boemus in the very popular *Fardle of Facions* did not accept the idea of black skin as a product of a curse, he did assert the descendancy of black people from Ham, who failed utterly to teach his offspring any of the religious or social values held by his faith. Black men, therefore, developed in a milieu of uncivil and nonreligious habits. "With this process of degeneration, a state of barbarism descended upon the sons of Ham, and the culture of men was divided into two categories, the civil and the uncivil, the advanced and the barbarous."[82] Peter Heylyn was also unwilling to accept a curse as the explanation, which he considered ridiculous. But unable to find any other reasonable explanation he attributed blackness to "God's secret pleasure," and then, as if to reflect the difficulty people were having with this problem, he ended by admitting the possible validity of the story of the curse. "Possibly enough the Curse of God on Cham and on his posterity (though for some cause unknown to us) hath an influence on it."[83]

To George Best, however, the story was clear and simple. Cham disobeyed Noah's commandment to his sons not to copulate with their wives out of reverence for and fear of God. Cham, however, knew that the first-born after the flood would inherit the dominion of the earth and "used company with his wife and craftily went about thereby to dis-inherite the off-spring of his other two brothers." As a punishment for this disobedience God willed that "a sonne should be borne whose name was Chus, who not only it self, but all his posteritie after him should bee so blacke and loathsome, that it might remain a spectacle of disobedience to all the worlde. And of this blacke and cursed Chus came all these blacke Moores which are in Africa."[84]

Black men, then, according to this view, were more than superficially different from white. There might be some basic genetic difference that could relegate them to another species. If they were men at all, they were men of a substandard type, or they were beings too closely connected with the powers of darkness to grant them equal standing with the European, especially with the fair-skinned, highly developed Englishman. Best had explained that it was "our great and continuall enemie the wicked Spirite" who had prompted Cham to disobey.[85] And so, through this connection, the spirit of evil had some special interest in those peoples who were said to be Cham's descendants. The black inhabitants of Angola, Peter Heylyn reported, are "said to be much given to *sorcery* and *divinations* by the flight of birds; Skilful in medicinal herbs and poysons, and by familiarity with the Devil able to tell things to come. Permitted as most Pagans are, to have as many wives as they will."[86] The connection between the black man and the devil became a strong likelihood. William Strachey put the matter quite plainly, summarizing the importance people put on the knowledge and acceptance of the Christian faith as the sine qua non of goodness: "what country soever the children of Cham happened to possesse, there biganne both the Ignorance of true godlinesse . . . and Ignauraunce of the true worship of God . . . the Inventions of Heathenisme, and adoration of falce godes, and the Devill."[87]

Thomas Herbert was likewise unequivocal in identifying the Devil with the black man. "Negroes," he wrote, "in colour so in condition are little others than Devils incarnate."[88] "The Devil . . . has infused prodigious Idolatry into their hearts enough to rellish his pallet and aggrandize their tortures when he gets power to fry their souls, as the raging Sun has already scorcht their cole-black carcasses."[89] Herbert was unaware of the inconsistency in asserting the nonhumanity of blacks as devils and then explaining their blackness by declaring their original whiteness (and humanity) by invoking the climatic theory to explain their blackness. This fantastic product of a manichean tendency to identify the heathen with an anti-Christ, a spirit of Evil, can nowhere be seen better than on the Elizabethan stage where, as we shall see in a later chapter, the Satanic image of the black man received such a full scale treatment that hardly a play with a black man in it avoids the innuendo.

Unlike David Hume, who in 1748 based his suspicions of the basic inferiority of black men to whites on their failure to produce anything of eminence either "in action or speculation" by the nation as a whole or by any individual, earlier writers were reacting to personal observation or to reports of the discrepancies found existing between black society and its English counterpart. The fact that blacks were not Christians, that they had different concepts of law and religion or what appeared to be no law or religion, and that their economies differed, seemed to suggest to the anglophilic mind that they were not men at all. Richard Eden observed that in the old times people in Africa were called "Aethiopis and Nigritoe, which we now call Moores, Moorens, or Negroes, a people of beastly living, without a God, love, religion, or common wealth, and so scorched and vexed with the heat of the sunne, that in many places they curse it when it riseth."[90]

In *A Fardle of Facions*, Boemus wrote that the southernmost Africans absolutely lacked a capacity for human feelings and a moral sense, as their practice of incest and polygamy showed. They "carry the shape of men, but live like beasts: they be very barbarous and go naked all their lives long, using both wives and daughters common like beasts: they be neither touched with any feeling of pleasure or griefe, other than what is naturall; neither do the [sic] discerne any difference betwixt good and bad, honesty and dishonesty."[91] (Boemus' English translator, Ed. Ashton, was inspired by this denunciation to show how much better Englishmen were and added at this point twenty-eight pages of his own eulogy of England and its customs.)

Other writers attributed the peculiarities of the black man to what surely tended to deny him human status—a lack of reason. John Leo Africanus, certainly known to many of the Elizabethans, wrote in his treatise on Africa that Negroes led a beastly life and "were utterly destitute of reason."[92] The inhabitants of Terra Nigritanum, said Heylyn, "till the coming of the Portugals thither, were for the most part rude and barbarous, that they seem to want that use of Reason which is peculiar unto man; prone to Luxury, and for the greatest part Idolaters, though not without some small admixture of Mohometans."[93]

What heightened the tendency to see a bestiality in these people was their association and even identification with the monstrosities so vividly described by medieval encyclopedists. Hakluyt, for instance, lent credence to the fanciful by reporting the existence of the legendary Troglodytes "whose inhabitants dwel in caves and dennes; for these are their houses, and the flesh of serpents their meat, as writeth Pliny and Diodorius Seculus. They have no speech, but rather a grinning and chattering. There are also people without heads, called Blenunes, having their eyes and mouth in their breast." He continues to name other creatures who have nothing of men but the shape, and points out that there are "Aethiopeans called Rhopsii, and anthropophagi, that are accustomed to eat man's flesh."[94] Others, too, liked to note in the land of Negroes there were "greedy devourers of man's flesh, which they prefer before that of Beeves or Muttons."[95] As a matter of fact, "it became common belief among Europeans that Africans habitually ate men from taste and preference. But it became just as common belief among Africans that Europeans did the same."[96]

Evidently, the reports that reached the ears and eyes of Englishmen were monotonously similar, cataloguing in the most condemning ways what the commentators considered the shortcomings of the African when compared to the Englishman; his bestiality, lawlessness, ignorance, barbarity, and, what Winthrop Jordan considers the underlying basis that divided the two races, his heathenism.[97]

Of the many traits in the African that Englishmen found particularly distasteful, two qualitites drew especially close attention: his sexual prowess and his fierce jealousy. From the earliest confrontations, white travelers took special interest in the sexual equipment and activities of the black man. The nakedness of the people, of course, was what first captured the eyes of foreigners. The unashamed display of genitalia, instead of striking the visitors as a sign of innocence, more often than not seemed to them downright depraved and corrupt. As early as 1555 William Towrson wrote of the

Guineans that "the men and women goe so alike that one cannot know a man from a woman but by their breasts, which in the most part be very foule and long, hanging downe low like the udder of a goate."[98] Heylyn described the women and added a touch of erudition: "The women said to be of such great brests in the former times, that they did suckle their children over their shoulders (as some women are now said to do near the Cape of Good Hope), the Dug being bigger than the Child. Of which Juvenal 'In Meroe the Mothers Pap/Is bigger than the child in lap.'"[99]

Richard Jobson described the large propagators of black men who were observed to be "furnished with such members as are often a sort burthensome unto them." In order to avoid injuring a pregnant wife, such an endowed man had "allowance of other women, for necessities sake,"[100] Jobson went on to explain the unusual dimensions of genitals by referring to the curse placed on Ham "who discovered his father Noah's secrets" and who was thenceforth marked in that "same place, where the originall cause began."[101] This practice of having "women in common" caught the interest of writer after writer. Boemus noted that the Ethiopians go naked except for their genitals and that "they have many wives a peace with whom they lye openly in all men's sight." When one gets married all the guests lie with the bride "to performe the act of generation."[102]

Among other people, he said, a man gives a woman he has slept with a welt from an animal skin which she uses to decorate her garment. The woman who has "the most welts upon her garment is accounted the best woman, as beeing beloved of most men."[103] Some blacks were so sexually driven, a report asserted, that "boys who are twelve and girls who are ten seek to lose their virginities. Some lose their maidenheads so early that they can't recall ever having been virgin."[104]

The freedom of these people in their sexual unions was so greatly different from the limitations imposed on the sexual activities of the strictly monogamous European societies that it shocked white sensibilities and produced remarks such as this from John Leo Africanus: "They have great swarms of Harlots among them; whereupon a man may easily conjecture their manner of living."[105] Francis Bacon, erudite and obviously aware of many of these reports, used the black man as a symbol for fornication when he wrote of "an holy hermit" who "desired to see the Spirit of Fornication; and there appeared to him a little foul ugly Aethiop."[106] John Davies of Hereford versified this reported quality of the black man:

> For South-ward, Men are cruell, moody, madd,
> Hot, blacke, leane, leapers, lustful, use to vant,
> Yet wise in action, sober, fearfull, sad,
> If good, most good, if bad exceeding bad.[107]

Regardless of which aspect they noted, most commentators could only look with condescension or condemnation on black promiscuity. "Yet is there no nation under Heaven more prone to Venery; unto which vice also the Libyans and Numidians are too much addicted."[108] This pervading interest in the sexuality of the black race, which, according to Jordan, [109] had no comparable force when observers examined other alien peoples, was certain to find its reflection in the literary treatment of the black man, especially in the popular form of entertainment, the stage. What playwrights would make of the sexual reputation of the black man will require a separate chapter, but suffice it to say here there is hardly a black character created for the stage whose sexuality is not made an important aspect of his relationships with others. For whatever reason, blackness and lust went handily, inextricably together, and writers made the most of the link. The literary men, as we hope to show, used what was currently and popularly thought of the black man's libido and so helped to perpetuate and even enlarge these conceptions of his extraordinary sexuality.

Yet, excessive sexuality was not to be considered as an isolated characteristic affecting no other quality of the black man's character. Strangely enough, although much was made of the free sharing of women by the men in black society, many commentators declared that black men were prone to excessive jealousy. Writing of the black world, John Leo Africanus unreservedly announced, "No Nation in the World is so subject unto Jealousie; for they will rather lose their lives, than put up any disgrace in the behalfe of their women."[110] This view of the jealousy of the black man was so widely held that it got its analytical treatment in a treatise on jealousy translated into English in 1615:

> Lastly Jealousie commeth in respect of a man's Reputation and
> Honour, according as his nature is, or as his Breeding hath beene, or
> after the fashion and manner of the country, in which hee is borne
> and liveth, because (in this point) divers are the opinions of men,
> and as contrary are the Customes of Countries, whereupon they
> say, that the Southern Nations, and such as dwell in hot Regions are
> very Jealous; eyther because they are much given and inclined unto
> Love naturally; or else for that they hold it a great disparagement
> and scandall, to have their Wives, or their Mistresses taynted with
> the foule blot of Unchastitie.[111]

Peter Heylyn, who had so much to say about the images of black people, is unfailingly true to the current tendencies of his day once again. Of the Barbarians he writes that they are "exceeding distrustful, in their hate implacable, and jealous of their Women beyond all compare." Of other black peoples, he continues: "The people extream black, much given to lying,

treacherous, very full of talk, excessively venerous, and extream jealous."
Still others, he says, are "implacable if once offended, their thirst of Revenge
not to be quenched but by Bloud."[112] Once the jealousy of the black man
was provoked, the consequences, as these reports suggest, could be disastrous
for all those involved.

Although the case against the black man would prove insurmountable in
the final balancing of testimony, there were those travelers who could find
positive traits among these newly discovered peoples. Most frequently praised
were the gentle openness and friendliness of the black people and their
physical beauty and hygiene. "We found the people most gentle, loving, and
faithful, void of all guil and treason, and such as live after the manner of the
golden age,"[113] wrote one traveler quoted in Hakluyt. "They are a people
of a tractable, free and giving nature, without guile or treachery," wrote
another.[114] Two other traders in Africa in 1591 wrote that when the English
met trouble with European competitors the king of the Negroes promised
"that his subjects the Negroes should be ready to ayde, succor and defend
us. In which people appeared more confident love and goodwill toward us,
than ever we shall finde either of Spaniards or Portugals, though we should
relieve them of the greatest misery that can be imagined."[115] Even John Leo
Africanus, whose work contained so much negative opinion of the black
man, found that in Barbary the people were completely guileless and were
"not only embracing all simplicitie and truth but also practising the same
throughout the whole course of their lives."[116] And in 1577 Edmund Hogan,
ambassador to the court of Mully Abdelmelech, Emperor of Morocco and
King of Fez, wrote of the king's humanity, of his interest in music, and of
the fair trade agreement Mully had made with England.[117] One writer
summed up this positive view of the black people when he exclaimed: "If
there is one corner of the earth where decency of conduct and morality
is still honored, it finds its temple in the heart of the desert among the
Negroes."[118]

How these comments on the "open and free" nature of black men helped
shape Shakespeare's concept of Othello may prove fruitful to consider at
some other time. What they did say, in any case, was that there appeared to
be evidence that blacks could be considered bona fide members of the human
race. Generally, however, when the literature tended to a favorable view of
the African, his physical features were the subject of admiration, his teeth
and strength, his well-shaped eyes, and physique.[119] One writer, for example,
expounded at length on the beauty of the black mistress of the governor of
St. Lugo and on the well-developed, shapely figures of the black women in
general. He reported that the black men he had seen in the Barbadoes were
"shaped exactly in accordance with Albrecht Durer's rules on proportion."[120]

Similarly, some observers noted the cleanliness of African Negroes,
although most saw only filth. These few told of the habit of Africans to

bathe daily, and to care for their teeth. One mentioned their delicacy of bodily habits, considering it a shame to "let a fart" in front of others.[121] In this same writer there is a plea for an acceptance of the brotherhood of all men regardless of skin color: "We might also serve that one-most God; that the tawne Moore, blacke Negro, dusky Libyan, ash-coloured Indian, olive coloured American, should, with the whiter European become one sheepe-fold under one *Great Shepheard*."[122] He went on to pray that all men regardless of race, color, language, sex, or condition would be one "in him that is One, and only blessed forever, Amen."[123]

But his prayers by and large went unanswered. The "evidence" against the black man for failing to meet white—or English—standards of virtue, religious truth, and social life was too heavy to be offset by these favorable but lightweight minority reports. Regardless of what the Church might say officially about the common humanity of the black man, people still thought of him "either as an inferior man or a superior animal."[124]

Against a backdrop of such widely accepted concepts which were reported as empirically proved, the image of the black man that emerged from the pens of imaginative writers can best be understood. Did these creative writers of the period simply adopt these views, which were so strongly antiblack in effect? Or did they imagine greater possibilities for the black man than the nonfictional works projected? Did they parade on the stage and in their poetry stereotypes that could do little to bring the opposing cultures closer together? Did they expand this image into something more human, that is, into something that contained human qualities in common with those of white Englishmen, providing a footing, at least, to permit the black man to appear as a fellow man and common brother?

Of course, not all writers did the same thing, nor did one writer do one thing consistently, but each writer who decided to bring the black man onto the stage or into his lines of poetry had to decide, first, what to make of him generally, and then, what specific qualities to bring out in his speech and act. The impact of the total material would determine just how the black man fared—as a human being capable of being sympathetically understood and met as a man, or as a bestial creature deserving only exploitation and abuse, or perhaps even as a literal agent of the Devil, to be denounced and excoriated. Were black men just men of another color, or men of inferior class, or "Devils incarnate"?[125] Although there were evidently creative writers to dramatize each view, those who took the sympathetic view were, sadly, in the small minority.

Chapter 2

A Model of Literary Response in Four Love Poems

When we turn to study the image of the Negro as it emerged from the literary production of the late sixteenth and seventeenth centuries, we immediately discover, not surprisingly, that dramatists were more often drawn to the figure of the black man than other writers. This occurred perhaps because the drama more readily makes use of contemporary incidents and issues, perhaps because the Negro in himself offered a potentially dramatic effect on stage, perhaps because the dramatist could depend on a storehouse of expected audience responses to the appearance of a black man and could work that response for his own end. Whatever the reason, Peele, Chapman, Shakespeare, Dekker, Jonson, Heywood, Webster, Middleton, Brome, among others, all created black characters in their plays or masques. The image that develops from this dramatic corpus is rich and complex and will constitute the major concern of this book. But before we turn to that more extensive body of material, it will be helpful to look first at a kind of miniature quasi-drama that slipped into the nondramatic literature during the first half of the seventeenth century in the form of four short dialogue poems. In three of the poems Negroes are central characters and in the fourth a Negro is addressed by a white youth.

The pertinence of these poems is that they reflect in brief some major trends of early literary reaction to a growing awareness in white society that black-skinned peoples existed and had to be accounted for. Hence, it seems likely that the poems can offer some illumination of the more complex work of the playwrights by offering a brief but clear overview of the situation. Unacclaimed, and until recently hardly noticed, the four poems, written by George Herbert, Henry Rainolds, Henry King, and John Cleveland,[1] could be considered as a model in miniature of early imaginative treatment of the Negro. The poems express some broad racial attitudes which, while avoiding the extreme polarities of demonization or ennoblement, include some of the other major modes of reaction.[2]

Sometime between 1612 and 1626, George Herbert, whose life was to be dedicated to the Church of England, and whose poems were to dwell almost exclusively on God, the Church, and his own relationship to both, wrote in Latin what might have been his only pure love poem.[3] Other clergymen or men who would later enter the clergy have also written amatory verse of one kind or another. But the astonishing fact here is that Herbert's love poem concerns an interracial relationship in which a Negro maid voices her grief over the coldness a white man has returned for her proffered love. To be the only love poem of a religious poet living in any age would make this poem unique; to be written in a period in which the very nature of the Negro as a human being was questionable (as the drama will make clear) makes it remarkable.

Contemporaries of Herbert must have thought so also, for Henry King's *Poems*, written during the 1630s and published in 1647, contain two curious poems related to Herbert's "Atheiopissa."[4] The first was called "A Black-moor Maid wooing a fair Boy: sent to the author by Mr. Henry Rainolds." The second poem was King's own "The Boys Answer to the Blackmoor." Rainolds' poem is closely related to Herbert's Latin one, but contrary to the opinion of Gerard Previn Meyer, who calls it a translation, it is really a different poem, obviously adapted from Herbert, but unique in itself.[5] It contains five images not found in Herbert, who, in turn, uses seven images that Rainolds avoids. No matter how the idea of free translation is stretched, it hardly seems fair to say in the case of two twelve-line poems with these differences that one is merely the translation of the other. King's poem is a firm reply to both Herbert's and Rainolds' liberal conceptions of the Negro as a human being. On philosophical grounds King argues that such a mixed union is impermissible.

Extending the possibility of combinations in interracial courtship, John Cleveland entered the scene by creating a reversal of the other situations, this time involving a black youth pursuing a white girl. Published in 1647 also, his poem entitled "A Fair Nymph Scorning a Black Boy Courting Her," is directly connected with the other three, not only making use of the same subject matter, but also employing similar imagery and dramatic presentation.[6] Although his poem takes the form of a dramatic dialogue and the other three are dramatic monologues, all four poems present characters who are allowed to reveal themselves through their thoughts and feelings, and through their choice of language, imagery, and tone of voice. The images that emerge here—two Negro girls in love, a Negro boy in a more or less sexual mood, and a white girl, disdainful of her black wooer—dramatize several trends of literary response to the nature of the Negro that characterized the period prior to 1688, when the influence of Mrs. Behn's novel *Oroonoko* changed the literary climate of this racial question.

Since it is obvious that the complex nature of a man's moral views and social judgments are not likely to be contained in one short poem, the following discussion will not try to define each writer's racial attitudes. Furthermore, in the metaphysical tradition of seventeenth-century poetry, the unusual subject or the extravagant idea frequently found its way into verse as a challenge to the poet's skill and wit. To believe, therefore, that each poem of the period literally expresses the real opinions and attitudes of the poet himself is to be just as mistaken as to believe that each character in a play expresses a dramatist's views. The emphasis here, then, is on the image itself as it might represent general tendencies of the period rather than on the private view of the poets. As the poems are not readily available in anthologies, they are included in their entirely below.

II

A Negro maid woos Cestus,
a man of a different color

What do I care if my face is black?
Dark, O Cestus, has this color too, but love
Wants it anyway. You are aware that always
The forehead of the traveler is scorched.
Ah, the girl who perishes for love of you
Has a long way to go. Who despises
The furrow if the land is black? Shut your eyes,
And all you see is black. Open them,
And you will see the shade the body makes.
I will do at least this service
Out of love for you. Because my face is smoke,
What fires do you think have hid within my heart
So long in silence now? O stony man,
Do you say no? O Fates who gave me
Mournful checks, foretelling my affliction!

> *The Latin Poetry of George Herbert*,
> translated by Mark McKloskey and
> Paul R. Murphy (Athens, Ohio: Ohio
> University Press, 1965), p. 171.

A Black-moor Maid wooing a fair Boy: sent
to the Author by Mr. Henry Rainolds

Stay, lovely Boy, why fly'st thou mee
That languishes in these flames for thee?
I'm black 'tis true: why so is Night,
And Love doth in dark Shades delight.
The whole World do but close thine eye,
Will seem to thee as black as I;
Or op't, and see what a black shade

Is by thine own fair body made,
That follows thee where e're thou go;
(O who allow'd would not do so?)
Let me for ever dwell so nigh,
And thou shalt need no other shade than I.

Mr. Hen. Rainolds

Henry King, *The English Poems of
Henry King, D. D.*, edited by
Laurence Mason (New Haven: Yale
University Press, 1914), p. 16.

The Boyes answer to the Blackmoor

Black Maid, complain not that I fly,
When Fate commands Antipathy:
Prodigious might that union prove,
Where Night and Day together move,
And the conjunction of our lips
Not kisses make, but an Eclipse;
In which the mixed black and white
Portends more terrour than delight.
Yet if my shadow thou wilt be,
Enjoy thy dearest wish: But see
Thou take my shadowes property,
That hastes away when I come nigh:
Else stay till death hath blinded mee,
And then I will bequeath my self to thee.

Henry King, *The English Poems of
Henry King, D. D.*, edited by
Laurence Mason (New Haven: Yale
University Press, 1914), p. 16.

A Fair Nymph Scorning a Black Boy
Courting Her

Nymph   Stand off, and let me take the Air,
        Why should the smoke pursue the fair?

Boy   My Face is smoke, then may be guest
        What Flames within have scorch'd my breast.

Nymph   Thy flaming Love I cannot view,
        For the dark Lanthorn of thy Hue

Boy	And yet this Lanthorn keeps Love's Taper Surer than your's that's of white Paper. What ever Midnight can be here, The Moon-shine of your Face will clear.
Nymph	My Moon of an Eclipse is 'fraid; If thou should'st interpose thy Shade.
Boy	Yet one thing, Sweet-heart, I will ask, Take me for a new fashion'd Mask.
Nymph	Done: but my Bargain shall be this, I'll throw my Mask off when I kiss.
Boy	Our curl'd Embraces shall delight To checker Limbs with black and white.
Nymph	Thy Ink, my Paper, make me guess Our Nuptial-bed will prove a press; And in our Sports, if any come, They'l read a wanton Epigram.
Boy	Why should my Black thy Love impair? Let the dark Shop commend the Ware; Or if thy Love from black forbears, I'll strive to wash it off with Tears.
Nymph	Spare fruitless tears, since thou must needs Still wear about thy mourning Weeds. Tears can no more affection win, Then wash thy Aetheopian Skin.

John Cleveland, *The Works of John Cleveland* (London, 1687), pp. 16-17.

A close reading of the poems shows both Herbert's and Rainolds' poems depicting a human being in poignant moments of sadness and frustration. The girls' deep and sincere expression of love and pain render them familiarly human. They are women in love, rejected and forlorn, each making the best effort she can to overcome the man's objections. The emphasis that each girl puts on racial difference as the cause of failure produces two different characters, to be sure, but each figure is a successful break from the less sympathetic images of the Negro that tend to pervade the literature of the stage.

King and Cleveland, on the other hand, present more conventional reactions to the idea of miscegenation. King's poem projects a white man, fully conscious of his superiority, in a state of natural repulsion to the thought of a mixed union, and Cleveland's somewhat more artificial work depicts the black man as a lascivious courter and the white girl as the caustic-minded, unwilling object of his hated attentions. Like the boy in King's poem she is revolted by the thought of a sexual encounter with him, although her free language suggests that she is not an ideal of pristine innocence. It is the color that sickens, not the proposal itself. The language of these two poems and the tones of the speakers expand the repudiation of the Negro as lover into a broader rejection of the Negro as human being, and so taken together do constitute one model of response to the Negro that differs considerably from the feelings so implicit in the poems of Herbert and Rainolds.

Before examining Herbert's poem in detail, however, we might find it informative to pause for a moment over the poetic work of his older brother, Edward Herbert of Cherbury. Although Lord Herbert is perhaps better known for his autobiography and his contributions to rational theology than for his poetry, several of his poems are, nevertheless, as unique in his period as is Herbert's single love poem. Their relevance to this study is based on the assumption that George Herbert knew his brother's poetry in one form or another. We know it was customary then for nonprofessional poets to keep their work in manuscript form and circulate it among friends and acquaintances just as John Donne did to enable both Herberts to read his poetry. This assumption that George did know his brother's work or was at least familiar with its informing spirit might help to account for that lonely love poem from a Negro girl.

Much has been written about the meaning of the black skin of the Negro in a white world. The mythical attribution of blackness to death, the devil, chaos, evil magic, melancholy, and other phenomena too numerous to mention, Harry Levin's book details precisely.[7] (Chapter III of this study will detail the significance of blackness as Renaissance playwrights used it.) Lord Herbert, however, emphatically refutes these negative symbolic meanings of blackness by being, instead, attracted to its beauty. In poem after poem he pays tribute to the color black, while he clearly avoids showing any fascination that borders the morbid.[8]

At first, Herbert praises blackness where he finds it in white women:

> Nor is thy hair and eyes made of that ruddy beam,
> Or golden-sanded stream,
> Which we find still the vulgar Poets theme,
> But reverend black, and such as you would say,
> Light did but serve it, and did shew the way.
> By which at first night did precede the day.[9]

In the poem that follows immediately in the text, "To her Eyes," he writes:

> Black eyes if you seem dark,
> It is because your beams are deep,
> And with your soul united keep.

The poem identifies the beauty of blackness with its existence prior to the creation of light. "The veil of an eternal night," is linked with that "first cause," for that first cause had within it that very veil of darkness, from which there was created a second light by which to see. Darkness is the original principle of existence. Herbert concludes, then, that the divine lies within the mystery of blackness:

> He must yet at the last define,
>   That beams which pass
> Through black, cannot but be divine.[10]

Lord Herbert is not, to be sure, talking about Negroes. But still his interest in black, even in abstract terms, differs radically from popular perception and myth. In "To her Hair," he questions why blackness so perplexes man:

> It is, because past black, there is not found
>   A fix'd or horizontal bound?
> And so, as it doth terminate the white,
> It may be said all colour to infold,
>   And in that kind to hold
>   Somewhat of infinite?[11]

Again we see that he finds something mystically divine about blackness, linking it with the infinite.

In his "Sonnet of Black Beauty," Lord Herbert ascribes to blackness immutability, a quality possessed by no other color. Black, he says,

> Art neither chang'd with day, nor hid with night;
> When all these colours which the world call bright,
> And which old Poetry doth so persue,
> Are with the night so perished and gone,
> That of their being there remains no mark,
> Thou still abidest so intirely one,
> That we may know thy blackness is a spark
> Of light inaccessible, and alone
> Our darkness which can make us think it dark.[12]

Only man's ignorance prevents him from seeing the real beauty of blackness. "Another Sonnet to Black itself" defines blackness as the source of all color and connects it with divine ordination of life. Under the veil of darkness, he writes, do the Heavens reveal what they have ordained. Although the conceit is from the field of astrology, the association of blackness and heaven continues to be a central idea of Lort Herbert's.

Finally, in two poems he addresses himself to dark-skinned beauties, and values their color as far superior to that of the English woman. In a poem called "The Sun-burn'd Exotique Beauty," there is strong evidence that he is addressing a Negro woman whose skin is the color of burnished gold. He calls her "child of the Sun," attributing her coloration to climatic conditioning. Then he compares her color with the color of hair he calls most beautiful. We remember that he has already acclaimed the supreme beauty of black hair. In addition he refers to the beauty of diffused light in almost exactly the same way that he wrote about blackness. When he writes of her color:

> When thou art so much fairer to the sight,
> As beams each where diffused are more bright
> Then their deriv'd and secondary light

he reminds us of other references to black, such as "black beamy hairs," or "Black beauty, which above that common light" or

> Black eyes if you seem dark,
> It is because your beams are deep
> . . . .
> By you doth best declare
> How he at first b'ing hid
> Within the veil of an eternal light,
> Did frame for us a second light,
> And after bid
> It serve for ordinary sight.[13]

When he praises not only the woman's outward beauty but even the odor of her body as being fragrant and appealing, he seems to reverse the traditional habit the white man has had of turning his nose away from the dark-skinned man.

The culmination of Lord Herbert's interest in the beauty of another race is found in the poem "The Brown Beauty," which is addressed to one whose skin color stands midway between the "whitely raw" of Northern beauties and the "adust aspect" of Moors and Indians. This brown beauty, however, is the perfect balance between two extremes (see footnote 18 for a remarkably similar thought expressed by his brother), and her external proportion signifies, from a platonic point of view, the beauty of her inner being. Herbert's world view, it seems safe to say, includes the possibility that other races can exist on a human level equal to and even higher than his own. He offers this concept of womanhood as a model of womanly perfection:

That when the World shall with contention strive
To whome they would a chief perfection give,
They might the controversie so decide,
As quitting all extreams on either side,
You more than any may be dignify'd.[14]

In Lord Herbert the impulse to judge other races as substantially inferior to his own white English Christian one seems to have been inoperative. His importance lies in his differing so drastically from most of the ancient and popular ideas as to permit a more just judgment of a people whose central differentiating feature was considered at that time to be a black skin. That George Herbert may have been moved by his brother's poems and the ideas embodied in them cannot be proved, but certainly the possibility of that connection exists.

George Herbert's poem shows the Negro girl painfully replying to a white man who evidently, because of her color, has just refused her offer of love. Her opening line, therefore, is the beginning of a defense of blackness itself.

What do I care if my face is black?
Dark, O Cestus, has this color too, but love
Wants it anyway. . . .
           . . . Who despises
The furrow if the land is black?

She accepts what she is and accepts it proudly, associating blackness with the two vital forces perpetuating life itself: the act of love and the plowed earth. Moreover, physical darkness, she claims, is universal. Only the presence of light distinguishes black from other colors: ". . . Shut your eyes, / And all you see is black."[15] When you open them, she continues, you become aware of the link between all bodies and darkness, for the presence of shadows is inescapable: ". . . Open them, / and you will see the shade the body makes." Blackness, then, is the very product of material existence. What her argument pleads for is an understanding that blackness, so natural and ubiquitous, and so acceptable in most sources, ought not be condemned in the coloration of a person's skin.

Furthermore, she divorces skin coloration from moral stigma by attributing her blackness to climatic conditions.

The forehead of the traveler is scorched.
Ah, the girl who perishes for love of you
Has a long way to go.[16]

The metaphor of the traveler in the sun serves a double purpose: first, it measures the strength of her love, and second, it implies her claim to a humanity equal to his. Her love, she claims, has until now persevered silently, but she can no longer restrain herself. In desperation she utters her plea, and when scorned again, she denounces the man and resigns herself to her misery.

> . . . Because my face is smoke,
> What fires do you think have hid within my heart
> So long in silence now? O stony man,
> Do you say no? O Fates who gave me
> Mournful cheeks, foretelling my affliction!

In this last anguished apostrophe to Fate, her reference to her black face as a sign of "affliction" has, in the light of the symbolic meaning of blackness in Renaissance England, considerable force behind it. Blackness, if we recall Allen's explication (see p. 7), often stood for sleep, sadness, unrequited love, constancy, and even eternal love.[17] The first two meanings are explicit in the poem. If the last two can be inferred, as the ending suggests they could, a touch of nobility begins to develop in the girl's character. At the least, she invokes compassion. As it is, she stands there, feeling pride in her own racial identification and suffering universal human emotions.[18] There are few comparably sensitive portraits of the black man in the drama of this period.

In addition to all this, there is a faint hint of a Christian quality in the maid's earlier suffering in silence and in the perseverance of her love that moves her to a willingness to serve unrewarded as the shadow of her lover. "I will do at least this service / Out of love for you." But this selflessness is only a trace, and it tends to be obscured by her more fervent defense of blackness and her tearful appeals to his pity. In Rainolds' poem, however, that quality of steadfastness in the face of rejection, the willingness to serve without hope of reciprocal devotion, the submerging of self in an unselfish love, is the central characteristic of the black maid. Herbert's Negro maid resigns herself to grief and self-pity, but Rainolds' maid displays little of such overwhelming despair. Her love is stronger than her sense of rejection. Herbert's maid calls out in bitterness, "O stony man, / Do you say no?" But Rainolds' girl is more lovingly gentle in her appeal.

The tone of her language in the phrases "lovely boy," and "thine own faire body" and the parenthetical "O who allow'd would not do so?" indicates the triumph of devoted love over self-pity. (Only in one line—"That languishes in these flames for thee"—does she focus on her own misery.) Hers is a sympathetic picture of a woman who has been disappointed in love. Whether she realizes that there are racial reasons for her rejection is ambiguous. Unlike Herbert's maid, who knows the cause, she begins her brief monologue by asking *why* she is being shunned. In softened tones that contrast with the defiantly proud ones of Herbert's opening lines, she asks: "Stay, lovely Boy, why fly'st thou me / That languishes in these flames for thee?" Then in the next line, after this profession of her own love, she suggests a possible cause of his unwillingness. "I'm black 'tis true" she admits, as though in her innocence she is uncertain if this is what bothers him. Considering that her color might be the reason, however, she tries to persuade him, in language similar to that of Herbert's girl, to accept her darkness for its universal quality.

> . . . why so is Night,
> And love doth in dark Shades delight.
> The whole World do but close thine eye,
> Will seem to thee as black as I.

And finally she offers herself selflessly as his shadow, demanding nothing but to be near him. Unlike the offer made by Herbert's girl this maiden stresses her unique devotion that needs no returns.

> Or op't, and see what a black shade
> Is by thine own fair body made,
> That follows thee where e're thou go;
> (O who allow'd would not do so?)
> Let me for ever dwell so nigh,
> And thou shalt need no other shade than I.

Her simplicity, frankness, and above all her steadfastness all appear to her credit as a human being and render insignificant any color difference that traditionally might stigmatize her as subhuman.

Rainolds and Herbert, in these poems at least, see Negroes as human beings who happen to have black skins. Had the emotional and psychological qualities of the images of these two Negro maids been more widely understood and accepted, that gap between the two races would, to some degree, have been lessened.

On the other hand, Henry King's "The Boyes answer to the Black-moor" contains the philosophical thought and emotional attitudes that work to sustain the complete separation of the races. In the opening lines of the poem, the boy coldly rebukes the Negro maiden by denying any role of individual will in his decision. "Black Maid, complain not that I fly, / When Fate commands Antipathy." His rejection of her, he asserts, is not peculiar to him. He flies from her because the superior power of Fate has decreed their contrariety, and hence his repugnance is uncontrollable and irremedial, representing as it does a fulfillment of nature. Yet, in view of her lack of reciprocal disgust, it would seem that Fate intended only that the white race hold the black in aversion, and not that a mutual hatred be established. Quite clearly, what underlies this implication is his strong sense of superiority.

As the white youth proceeds, the philosophical argument implicit in the reference to Fate surfaces in the metaphorical language he chooses. Their union, he says, would be comparable to a union between day and night, an absolutely unnatural conjunction of naturally separated phenomena. The result of miscegenation would be "prodigious," that is, it would be an abnormal union made outside of the bounds of nature.

> Prodigious might that union prove,
> Where Night and Day together move,
> And the conjunction of our lips
> Not kisses make, but an Eclipse;
> In which the mixed black and white
> Portends more terrour than delight.

White and black are mutually exclusive types of beings and need to be kept separated. A kiss between them would be as threatening to the natural order of the universe as (so popular conception would have it) the eclipse is. The submission of light to darkness produces only terror and forbodes ill, not good. His repudiation of her offer of love, therefore, is grounded in the philosophical belief in an orderly universe in which each thing has its place and function in a great scheme: any part that thwarts its own prescribed function produces the threat of disaster. Miscegenation is no less dangerous than the eclipse. His image of the eclipse, furthermore, could very well be one of the earliest expressions of the unconscious fear the white man has traditionally had of losing his racial characteristics through intermingling with colored races. An eclipse, after all, does mark the obscuration of one body by another, resulting in the domination of shadow over light.

As the philosophical rationale in the denial of love suggests the boy's sense of superiority, the tone of his language confirms it. His speech opens with the blunt words "Black Maid, complain not that I fly . . . ," apostrophizing her by color and forcing her to acknowledge that racial difference. A kinder, less supercilious persom might have said, "Young Maid," or "Strange Maid," or "Sad Maid," but the phrase "Black Maid," appearing in an opening spondee, hammers home his sense of scorn. In the image of the eclipse, the tone of disdain and haughtiness lies just beneath the surface of the words, but in the remainder of the poem it resounds more fully.

> Yet if my shadow thou wilt be,
> Enjoy thy dearest wish: But see
> Thou take my shadowes property,
> That hastes away when I come nigh:
> Else stay till death hath blinded mee,
> And then I will bequeath my self to thee.

He teases her with permission to be his shadow—only if she acts like a real shadow and leaves as he approaches. What she has said figuratively, he taunts her with literally. And finally, in a vein of bitter humor, he offers himself to her when he is dead and can not look at her. The sight of black skin is that repulsive.[19]

As an expression of another kind of reaction toward the Negro one can expect to find in this period, Henry King's poem is unambiguous and precise. The Negro belongs to an inferior race which, according to the great natural order of the universe, is destined to remain separated from the white race. Any attempt toward miscegenation is a denial of that natural order and can only produce chaos. Morally speaking, therefore, the rejection of a Negro, because it tends to sustain the natural order and the racial gaps within it, is a desirable good. Whether this is King's personal view it is impossible to determine. What can be said, though, is that it frames the attitudes of the person he has created and reflects a popular mode of thought of the times, more fully expressed on the stage.

In the fourth scene of this little "closet" drama, John Cleveland wryly inverts the sexes and colors so that the dialogue is an exchange between a white girl and a black boy. But because he uses similar poetic devices and the same situation (the black fruitlessly courting the white), his "A Fair Nymph Scorning a Black Boy Courting Her" is still quite clearly linked with the other three poems. It too contains implicit and explicit philosophical and emotional responses to the Negro, illuminating some aspects of his image and introducing new ones. For example, the abnormality of an interracial union is explicitly made clear in the poem as are the dangers of such a union. Cleveland, like many others of his time, believed deeply in a natural order long established in the universe, and he was disturbed whenever he found what he considered a breach in that order. Although this concern finds its most artistic expression in his political satire where, according to recent commentators, his dominant theme is the "monstrous reversal of the natural order by unnatural alliances,"[20] Cleveland also, in some minor poems, passed judgment against more private unnatural alliances between two people. Even the editor of the 1687 edition of Cleveland's works seized on Cleveland's interest in such unions to add a number of spurious poems on that subject to the two that are authentically his. In that early edition, described by Saintsbury as the "omnium gatherum" of poems attributed to Cleveland, there is a whole section of poems about abnormal relationships, but only two are genuinely his: "A Young Man to an Old Woman courting him" and "A Faire Nymphe scorning a Black Boy Courting Her."[21] A brief look at the first of these can enlarge the significant point of the second.

In "A Young Man to an Old Woman courting him," which immediately follows the "Fair Nymph's Reply" in the *Collected Poems*, the young man rejects the older woman on the grounds of the sinful unnaturalness of such a union:

> Thy Stock is too much out of Date
> For tender Plants to 'innoculate.
> A match with thee the Bridegroom fears
> Would be thought Incest in his years.

The regular order of the universe must be upset to permit such a marriage.

> When Aetna's fires shall undergo
> The Penance of Alps in Snow
> . . . .
> When the Heaven shuffle all in one,
> The Torrid with the Frozen Zone,
> When all these conditions meet,
> Then Sybil, thou and I will greet.

Even in a sensual, mocking poem like this, Cleveland expresses a belief in the disruptive function of an abnormal mating. Human beings have to mate in an arrangement that accords with a broader scheme of universal order. In spite of Cleveland's cavalier treatment, the references in this poem to natural phenomena like light and darkness, heat and cold, and their mutual incompatibility, illuminate a reading of "A Fair Nymph's Reply."

Although the latter poem itself is disjointed and artificial, an unsuccessful exercise in metaphorical conceit, it still contributes to our understanding of ways in which people viewed the Negro. As in King's poem the Negro is immediately and harshly rebuked in language similar to that of the earlier poem.

> Nymph   Stand off, and let me take the Air
> Why should the smoke pursue the fair?

Unlike the logical way in which Herbert's maid related her own smoky complexion to the fire of love, the reference to "smoke" here is gratuitous and therefore denigrating. As he attempts a witty response by extending the metaphor into one like Herbert's, she turns his imagery against him:

> Boy   My Face is smoke, then may be guest
> What Flames within have scorch'd my breast.

> Nymph   Thy flaming Love I cannot view
> For the dark Lanthorn of thy Hue.

This sarcastic jest strongly suggests that his dark skin disables her from acknowledging the presence of such an intimate human emotion within it. Actually her objections to him are threefold. First, as in the lines above, she abhors the color of his skin, and finds his presence stifling. His blackness haunts her throughout the poem. When he offers to shed his blackness through the cleansing agent of tears, she turns him off coldly by saying that no degree of his grief could ever change his blackness, that is, nothing could move her to suspend her consciousness of his color.

> Boy   Why should my Black thy Love impair?
> Let the dark Shop commend the Ware;

> Or if thy Love from black forbears,
> I'll strive to wash it off with Tears.

Nymph   Spare fruitless tears, since thou must needs
Still wear about thy mourning Weeds.
There can no more affection win,
Than wash thy Aetheopian Skin.

A second objection is her fear, similar to that of King's boy, of being subjected to an eclipse, with its inherent threat of the triumph of darkness over light. When he expresses the hope that her fairness could, figuratively, brighten him (perhaps even literally modify his blackness through offspring),

Boy   What ever Midnight can be here,
The Moon-shine of your Face will clear,

her answer, although metaphorically consistent, strongly suggests a psychological inhibition to mate with someone whose qualities may very well obliterate her own.

Nymph   My Moon of an Eclipse is fraid;
If thou should'st interpose thy Shade.

The abnormality of such a threatening union is one that she cannot brook.

Finally, she knows that their union can only result in a scandal and develop into a licentious lesson for others.

Nymph   Thy Ink, my Paper, make me guess
Our Nuptial-bed will prove a Press;
And in our Sports, if any come,
They'll read a wanton Epigram.

In the last two lines there is also a suggestion of interpreting a "wanton Epigram" as a child (the "any" of "if any come") whose birth would be read only as a consequence of sexual libertinism. In any case, theirs could be no more than a sexual union, recognized by society as no more than that, and one that she firmly condemns. Instinctively, intellectually, and socially, such a mating is anathema to her.

Neither of the two figures comes through with any force of reality. Both seem wooden and hollow, lacking any convincing human qualitites. Nevertheless, what they say does fill out one image of the Negro and typifies some feeling in the seventeenth century toward it. His belief that his blackness and its negative qualitites can be beneficially modified by her whiteness and, conversely, her shrinking from fear of contamination by him, subject him from the white point of view to a position distinctly lower in the scale of being. His image as a black seducer of white women (his most vivid line is the sexual picture of "Our curl'd Embraces shall delight / To checker Limbs with black and white"), his willingness to surrender his racial blackness, and their mutual tendency to see him as anything but a man—smoke, a lanthorn, midnight, a shade, a mask, ink, a shop—further tend to negate any claims to equal human stature he may have had. The whole game of inventing metaphorical conceits is a systematic dehumanizing of the black lover. Not that the white girl emerges as anything more than a shell. That is the result of artistic shortcomings in the poem generally. Still her arguments against her black wooer and her total rejection of his pleas (often self-disparaging) provide another example of ethnocentric attitudes similar to those of Henry King's boy.

Against a background of racial confrontation, these four poems dramatize in brief several major outlooks on the new experience. Those of Herbert and Rainolds contrast sharply with the popular view of the Negro as unfeeling, ugly, inferior, savage, and subhuman; the replies of King and Cleveland merge into the background, adding to the texture of the conceptions that divided the races then, and still to some degree keep them apart today.

With these poems as an example of a literary response to the black man, limited as that response is in depth and scope, a study of the larger body of literary material, especially the drama of that day, will reveal other facets of the black man's image to produce a fuller, more vivid and impressive portrait. It is through this more richly detailed assessment of the black man, effectively dramatized on the stage and doubtlessly injurious to the future of his race, that Englishmen could answer their consciences regarding the legitimacy of slavery.

Chapter 3

Blackness in the Plays:
A Variety of Aspects,
a Consistency of Opinion

Several writers have already discussed the general significance of blackness in the dominant white culture of the western world,[1] and others have studied its particular meaning in Renaissance England.[2] But just what special uses English dramatists of this period made of blackness of skin pigmentation has not been detailed for separate consideration.[3] Especially in plays where black characters were to figure either significantly or even only slightly as peripheral interests, their blackness seldom went unnoticed or unmentioned. Both white and black characters sometimes call attention to it gratuitously, simply because it is there and they are very conscious of it. Sometimes secondary racial traits are also mentioned, but the primary importance of skin color can be inferred not only from the sheer weight of references to it but also by the habit of confusing racial distinctions under the single index of blackness. That is to say, the national identity and geographic origins of the black man are sufficiently blurred by the characters so that a black man, be he Moor, Negro, or Ethiopian, was simply considered to be a black man. The vocabulary designating him and his color, though varied, had this single point of reference. Regardless of what shades of colors were known in fact to exist, in the plays these non-Caucasian figures—as will be shown—were regarded as members of a black race.[4]

Just as writers concurred about blackness as the dominant and broadly inclusive trait of these Africans, they also were ready to agree to a common interpretation of its deep moral significance. There is a whole body of explicit statement directed at the question of the moral condition of the black-skinned foreigner, and most of it is shaped by a cultural prejudice toward the color black itself. Fundamentally, the black man's image rests on his dramatization, on what he does and says and on how he is used physically and verbally by the white characters around him. But of great importance, also, are these critical passages that contain clear, emphatic expressions of white beliefs. A close reading of these verbalized concepts reveals an image of the black man quite consistent with the one that develops through the dramatic action.

Another characteristic concern of the dramatists was to offer traditional explanations of the source of the stranger's blackness. Surprisingly, though, the writers failed to make much of the genetic theory, which would have supported the moral judgments stretching through the plays, and instead tended to rely on the climatic explanation. The sun seemed to be a more poetically useful object to invoke in accounting for a dark skin than the Book of Genesis. And though a climatic theory should have precluded the idea of a permanence to the blackness, the writers still made much of the inability of the black man to change his color, and of his sensitive awareness of his appearance and its reputed ugliness among a white population.

No single factor can account for the degree of consistency in the treatment of black figures. The descriptions of travelers and ethnologists no doubt influenced some imaginations, and so probably did the views of one playwright affect the perspectives of another. Psychological predispositions of the writers themselves cannot be overlooked as another likely force modifying cultural attitudes. And the simple materialistic aim of profiting at the box office from the popularity of a dramatic type could have produced more of the same. Furthermore, the total cultural climate of a society deeply and profitably engaged in trafficking in slaves and slave labor just as certainly affected the writers, for the black man in their hands suffered a debasement that made slavery seem a reasonable fate for such beings.

However, one popular philosophical idea of the period deserves more than passing mention, explaining in part, at least, why so many black characters displayed similar moral traits. That was the Neoplatonic idea that associates inner being with outer appearance. Villains were far more often physically unattractive than handsome, while heroes were always pleasing to the eyes. If black was considered ugly, theatergoers could hardly expect those people on the stage sporting black faces to be inwardly beautiful. "Nearly always the physical trait [of a character] is also a moral symbol . . . in extreme cases, a stigma like Richard the Third's hump."[5] Nemmer discusses this point historically.

> In the old morality play, the moral tone was obvious, and characters
> were simply vices or virtues; but with the development of secular
> drama, characters became more individualized, and yet the element
> of allegory continued to prevail. Instead of being labeled as virtues
> or vices, characters were often morally distinguishable by their
> particular physical distinctions. . . . Traces of the old vices could
> be recognized in deviating physical types, such as fat knaves, thin
> rogues, black Moors, and deformed hunchbacks.[6]

Spenser's version of the neoplatonic idea is one of its best poetic statements. In his "Hymne in Honour of Beautie," he writes:

> So every spirit, as it is most pure
> And hath in it the more of heavenly light,

So it the fairer bodie doth procure
To habit in, and it more fairely dight
With chearfull grace and amiable sight.
For of the soule the bodie forme doth take.[7]

If this were true of the beautiful soul, the converse would be also true with a morally ugly one. "An evil favoured and crabbed counteance doth evermore yielde untoward condicion," wrote Hill in the *Epistle of Melampus*.[8] The characters in Shakespeare who voice an opinion about the moral or psychological significance of external appearances by and large tend to accept its validity. Of the sixteen passages in which Nemmer observes them mentioning this idea of the reflection of inner character by outer appearance only two deny a connection: the famous observation of Duncan that there is "no art / To find the mind's construction in the face"[9] and Viola's comment "that nature with a beauteous wall / Doft oft close in pollution."[10] The other passages either assert or tacitly accept the likelihood of its truth.[11]

The physical appearance of the black man, therefore, as he took the stage in the late sixteenth century must be taken into account before analyzing the traits of his character that were developed dramatically. His physical features would be used to create in the audience a readiness and an expectation for him to act in certain ways.[12] Naturally, his black skin was the critical discriminating feature that writers could not avoid. However, the lips and hair of the black man were also observed as distinct features of this new race, and probably unattractive ones. In Massinger's *The Parliament of Love* (1624) Chamont gives to his ward Bellicent the gift of a servant, Beaupre, who has disguised herself as a Moorish slave. When Bellicent sees the disguised girl, her attention is immediately caught by the absence of physical features which she had evidently expected in a black person. Her illuminating remark singles out those features as distasteful and unappealing to a white woman.

> Bell   Tis the handsomest
>   I e'er saw of her country; she hath neither
>   Thick lips, nor rough curl'd hair.[13]

The comment also argues the availability of Moors in England with whom comparisons could be made.[14]

Much earlier, in Chettle and Munday's *The Death of Robert, Earl of Huntington* (1601), King John calls Queen Isabella a "thick lipt Blackamoor."[15] And a decade before that, Shakespeare had Aaron warmly calling his endeared newborn son a "thick-lipped slave."[16] In the same play there is also the famous reference of Aaron to his "fleece of woolly hair that now uncurls," with its subsequent phrase symbolic of evil: "Even as an adder when she doth unroll to do some fatal execution."[17] Also in the play is the single reference in this period to the peculiarity of the black man's eyes—the seeming predominance of their whiteness. Lucius is aware of this peculiarity, which may be only Aaron's, when he sees Aaron holding his black infant: "Say, wall-ey'd slave, whither wouldst thou convey / This growing image of thy fiendlike face?"[18]

These physical qualities, of course, receive only marginal attention, perhaps because of the difficulty of reproducing them on stage, but more probably because of the greater fascination with the inescapable polarity between the black skin of the African and the white skin of the Elizabethan. On this point Winthrop Jordan, considering the total body of nonfictive reports, states confidently:

> In the more detailed and accurate reports about West Africa of the seventeenth century, moreover, Negroes in different regions were described as varying considerably in complexion. In England, however, the initial impression of Negroes was not appreciably modified: the foremost fact about the Negro was that he was "black."[19]

Although there was an awareness of different skin color ranging from near white to "coal-black," "blackness became so generally associated with Africa that every African seemed a black man."[20] This same reluctance or incapacity to distinguish among African peoples operates throughout the drama. The African character is described as "swarty," "sooty," "tawney," and black."[21] Sometimes the same character is described by several of these words; Aaron, for example, calls his child both a "tawney slave" and a "coal-black calf."[22] In a stage direction Shakespeare names the child a "blackamoor," and Aaron himself is called the "swarth Cimmerian."[23] Obviously the terms "tawney," "swarth," and "black" are freely interchangeable here. Furthermore, in Rowley's *All's Lost by Lust* (1619), Africans are described by Roderick as "the barbarous and tawney Affricans." A few lines later he talks of "their swarty looks."[24] Another instance of this liberty appears in Heywood's play, *The Fair Maid of the West,* Part I (1600-1603), when Clym, the clownish servant of the heroine Bess, refers to Mullisheg, King of Fez and Morocco as "the black-a-morian king,"[25] and adds, "mayst thou never want sweet water to wash thy black face in."[26]

Contrary to Eldred Jones's claim that some Moors were portrayed as white Moors in contrast to black ones,[27] there is little evidence from the texts to support that idea. If one Moor is described as black and another is not described by color at all, it hardly seems safe to conclude that the second appears as a white man. (See Jones's discussion of Muly Mahamet and Abdelmelec as they appear in Peele's *The Battle of Alcazar* [1588-89].) It seems more likely that Moors in general were considered to be black men,[28] and that Peele's reference to Muly as the "Negro Moor" indicates Peele's intention to closely follow his source (*The Second Book of Battles* describes Muly's mother as a Negro) and to emphasize the degree of Muly's blackness and hence his evil. Actually, he is called "the Moor," "this Negro moore," and "this Negro," the terms evidently intended to be used interchangeably. Abdelmelec, on the other hand, is only referred to as a Moor.[29] Since he is a good Moor, he may have been thought to be white inside, but his external appearance was probably intended to be shaded to some degree.

In addition to this tendency to subsume any physical differences within the single quality of blackness, there was little effort to distinguish among Africans of different origin just as there had been in the "factual" accounts of Africa. Moor, Negro, Ethiopian, Blackamoor (and in some cases even Indian) were considered the same man. In *The Masque of Blackness* (1605), Jonson provides a classical example of ethnological blending when he describes the geography of the river Niger in Aethiopia. Here, he says, the inhabitants are called Negroes; a few lines later he adds that the masque is set in that land because Queen Henrietta wanted the characters to be "blackmoors." The character of Nigir was to be "in form and colour of an Aethiop; his hair and beard curled."[30] Here, then, are the Negro, Blackmoor and Aethiopian united in one figure—and that one characterized by blackness and curly hair. Thomas Campion, in a *Masque at Whitehall* (printed in 1614), had little problem with a portrayal of Africa personified. She appeared "like a Queene of the Moores with a crown."[31] This practice of obliterating ethnic distinctiveness within a single embracing figure can be found almost anywhere, in a remark of a character in Marston, who talks of a Moorish slave as "a Deere Ethiopian Negro"[32] or in a passage in Shakespeare, who uses the word "Negro" just once in all of his works, and uses it synonymously with the word "Moor." When Lorenzo accuses Launcelot of lechery he talks of "the getting up of the Negro's belly. The Moor is with child by you, Launcelot."[33]

An even more interesting and perhaps just as significant confusion of racial identities is that found in Dekker's *Lust's Dominion* (1599), where the Indian and black man are fused in one image. This problem has been carefully described by the editor Fredson Bowers and need only be outlined here. In Act I, scene 2, Cardinal Mendoza, the Moor's enemy, threatens to banish the black Eleazer "to beg with Indian slaves." Later Eleazer in adoration addresses himself to the sun: "By heavens great Star which Indians do adore." And in Act IV, scene 2, Eleazar swears by "all our Indian gods."[34] Throughout the rest of the play the references to him are definitely those to a black man. This confusing of the black man and the Indian is even more fully developed in the literary treatments of the story of Thomas Inkle and the Indian maid Yarico, who in the New World helped him to survive capture, bore his child, and finally suffered the anguish of being deserted when he took ship back to England. As the story was retold repeatedly in the literature of the seventeeth and eighteenth centuries, the color of Yarico's skin changed from red to black. Although she was still called an Indian she had become a black Indian.[35] This phenomenon of blending alien peoples of different skin colors into a single figure suggests a broader view of Shakespeare's conception of Caliban and the whole racial relationships developed in *The Tempest*. Some readers have identified the savage Caliban as a being representative of the black man as well as the American Indian.[36]

The terminology designating the blackness of skin was varied, as were references to the geographical origins of black people, but the moral significance of their black appearance offered few alternatives to a white-oriented culture. Simply stated, black skin almost invariably suggested the idea of sinfulness in one form or another.[37] A black-skinned man was an alien; and worse than that, a paganistic or atheistic alien, living totally outside of the grace offered by Christianity. He symbolized the damned. And even worse, he shared the same color with Satan and all agents of hell. Even in the most superficial function of this blackness—its capacity to conceal a blush—men found evidence of its inherent compatibility with sin. This inferred knowledge of the alliance between sin and its concealing shield of blackness is held by both blacks and whites. When a black man voices it, it can heighten his evil, as in the words of the archvillain Eleazer in *Lust's Dominion* (1549):

> Ha, ha, I thank thee provident creation,
> That seeing in moulding me thou dids't intend
> I should prove villain, thanks to thee and nature
> That skilful workman; thanks for my face,
> Thanks that I have not wit to blush.[38]

When a white man alludes to a blush in a black character, he intensifies his contempt, as when Gomera, in Fletcher's *The Knight of Malta* (1616) excoriates Zanthia, the treacherous black bawd of the villain Mountferrat:

> . . . Thou sinful usher
> Bred from that rottenness, thou baud to mischief.
> Do you blush through all your blackness?
> Will not that hide it?[39]

If her blush is visible it is a rare case. In Ravenscroft's version of *Titus Andronicus* (1686) Aron [*sic*] knows that his blushes are hidden:

> If Blushes could be seen thro this black Vayle,
> These undeserved praises, from your Mouth
> Would dye my Vizage of another hue;
> Quick mounts the blood up to my swarthy Cheeks
> Tho' not perceiv'd, the Oven glows within.[40]

Aron admits that he can blush, but he knows his emotional condition remains hidden from view. Abdelazer, on the other hand, in Mrs. Behn's *The Moor's Revenge* (1677), believes it is his incapacity to blush that prevents one from appearing through his blackness. "If I could blush, I shou'd thro all this Cloud / Send forth my Sense of Shame into my Cheeks."[41] Regardless of the reason—inner hardness or outer veil—black people did not give themselves away through a blush, and white writers were quick to note what an advantage to a villain this protection could be.

When more bluntly explicit statements about the color attributes of evil are made in plays containing black characters, the image of these people crystalizes into sharper features with clearly marked boundaries beyond which the moral possibilities of black men could not go. The physical equivalent of sin is blackness. The equation is clearly and repeatedly pronounced. One of its earliest expressions comes in *Titus Andronicus* (1592) as Bassianus accuses the Gothic queen Tamora of lechery and denounces her adulterous relationship with her black paramour Aaron:

> Believe me, Queen, your swarth Cimmerian
> Doth make your honour of his body's hue,
> Spotted, detested, and abominable.[42]

Her dishonor carries the color black, and that color itself evokes detestation in those who are white. Aaron (as he contemplates his own evil) himself admits that "Aaron will have his soul black like his face."[43]

Elsewhere there are other souls colored to match the skin of the black man. Eleazer in Dekker's *Lust's Dominion* (1599) has quite accepted the moral significance of blackness when he adjures the venal Cardinal Mendoza: ". . . Cardinall, this disgrace / Shall dye thy soule, as Inky as my face."[44] Later he reiterates this identification of black and evil in his exhortation to his Moorish servants ordering them to murder some Christian friars: "Your cheeks are black, let not your souls look white."[45] His obsession with the blackness of sin dies hard in this same passage. He encourages his assassins by reminding them of the nature of hypocrisy where the effectiveness of pretended faith is the perfect mask of concealment: ". . . sin shines clear, / When her black face Religions masque doth wear."[46] This black face of sin contrasts definitively with the whiteness of virtue, expressed in the next scenes as the "fair complexion of mine honour."[47]

The sources and history of this symbolic relationship between blackness and evil and hell are evasive and uncertain. However, the symbolism did evolve in a society of white domination, and it is from the pen of Dekker, a man who seems to have known London and its cultural attitudes as well as almost anyone, there comes once again one of the memorable lines on this subject. Isabella, the young princess, embodying the only sure virtue in the play, deceives her Moorish guard into releasing her imprisoned brother and her lover. She then stands by while the Moors, servants of the villain Eleazer, are slain by surprise. She suggests that her companions disguise themselves as Moors so as to catch Eleazer off guard, and directs them to strip the dead bodies of their robes and to blacken their faces. Her metaphor states concisely and definitively the color of evil. "Once rob the dead, put the Moors habit on / And paint your faces with the oil of hell."[48] The line has been quoted frequently by commentators as strong evidence of what blackness meant to the white English world of the Renaissance.

If blackness is the color indigenous to hell, it was not likely that the black man could escape the consequences of inevitable associations. He did not escape, of course, and the extent to which he was made to play the role of hell's agent will be measured in the next chapter.[49]

First, however, there are several other aspects of blackness that figure significantly in plays involving black men. One such feature is the source of a character's blackness. Writers seemed compelled to raise this question directly or indirectly. Strangely enough, though there existed a genetic explanation for black skin that could, through a system of logical manipulations, justify conceiving black men as Satan's agent, there appear to exist few explicit passages in the drama to exploit it. Several passages, however, do reveal the author's awareness of the belief that black skin was a punishment inflicted by God on an evildoer.[50] In Elkanah Settle's late-seventeenth-century drama *The Empress of Morocco* (1687), for example, the satanic Moorish empress, well-skilled in the art of heinous crime, tricks her daughter-in-law into killing her own husband, the empress's son. She then orders the hapless girl to be physically stigmatized:

> First, let her Face with some deep Poys'nous Paint,
> Discolour'd to a horrid black be stain'd.
> Then say 'twas as a mark of Vengeance given,
> That she was blasted by the Hand of Heaven.[51]

Lust's Dominion, which probably contains the most complete set of explicitly stated popular concepts of the black man, as well as a dramatic prototype in Eleazer, provides another instance of this genetic idea. One character says: "Thou left'st me to the mercy of a Moor / That hath damnation dy'd upon his flesh."[52] This implicit explanation of blackness as the stigmata for evil apparently has its source in a Talmudic commentary on the Biblical passage which describes the curse Noah inflicted on his son Cham for looking on his nakedness. According to these interpreters the punishment of slavery was only one penalty to be suffered by Cham's descendants. Blackness was to be another.[53] In the drama the black man is often viewed as a demon—and frequently views himself as one. However, no playwright either literally or metaphorically invokes the story of Noah's curse on Cham to account for the black man's state of condemnation or to affiliate him through damnation with the devil. Literary men somehow either were unaware of the theological exegesis of the Noah story,[54] or knew it and rejected it.

On the other hand, they fostered and strengthened the belief that exposure to the sun's rays produced the black skin of the African. Whenever an explanation of black skin is included in somebody's remark, what usually serves the purpose is the idea of the darkening effect of equatorial life so close to the sun. Sometimes the idea is expressed indirectly, by inference, and for no deeper purpose than to add color or a touch of exoticism to the scene, as in the comment of the King of Fez in Heywood's play: "And when thou'st weary of our sunburnt clime . . ."[55] Sometimes the point wittily and relevantly makes its way into the text, as when Margaretta, in Rowley's *All's Lost by Lust* (1619), has slain her supposed husband and now feels concerned for the safety of her black servant Fydella, who has loyally assisted her in the crime. She urges Fydella to flee, for "this place will be—," and Fydella interrupts her: "Not too hot for me Madam; my complexion is natural to it."[56] Webster, in *The White Devil* (1611), has Flamineo gratuitously referring to Francesco who has dressed and painted himself as a Moor, as "a sunburnt gentleman."[57]

But once again it is the racially conscious Eleazer who points with pride to the source of his blackness. Although the charge of Satanism is hurled again and again at him, eventually forcing him to confess its truth, he too attributes his blackness not to a curse of God but to a blessing from the sun. Yet even in his mind blackness, despite its innocent source, gets coupled with an act of bloody revenge. As he is about to stab King Ferdinand to avenge the death of his wife, Maria, he announces his intention in the name of his blackness: "Now by the proud complexion of my cheeks / Tan'd from the kisses of the amorous sun."[58] Unwittingly he has created a noticeable tension between the amoral nature of a blackness derived from natural processes of the sun and the immoral connotation of blackness construed by men. To invoke a blackness untainted by evil in order to commit an evil act is not logically explicable. Yet perhaps what is really significant here is the very absence of logic in the emergence of cultural beliefs and attitudes. A scene like this can only contribute further to stigmatizing a black skin, whatever its source may be.

There were, however, some writers who apparently were aware that the climatic theory of explaining black skin, with its presupposition of an original white skin, permitted a more favorable approach to the black man. Perhaps he could even be accepted as a part of the human family with little to demean him other than his unattractive color. Ben Jonson recognized that basic assumption of the climatic theory when, in *The Masque of Blackness* (1605), he makes the African spokesman Niger recite the mythological version of the sun theory:

> As of one Phaeton that fir'd the world,
> And that, before his heedless flames were hurl'd

> About the globe, the Aethiops were as fair
> As other dames; now black, with black despair;
> And in respect of their complexion chang'd,
> Are each where since for luckless creatures rang'd.[59]

Niger explains that the Aethiopian women revile the sun each morning because he has scorched them so "with such intemperate fires." He has tried to cheer them up but has failed. If white is beautiful, how can women who have been denied its rewards be lighthearted?

The poet William Bass alludes to this same version of the Greek story when he tries to account for the Aethiopians, and he, too, implicitly grants them a human status:

> The Aethiopian's then were white and fayre,
> Though by the worlds combustion since made black
> When wanton Phaeton overthrew the Sun.[60]

John Davis of Hereford, in his poetic volume of ethnology *Microcosmos*, not only accepts variety of climate as sufficient cause of different temperaments and appearances of people but also rates blackness as a deformity of human beauty:

> From Regions, Winds, and standing of the place,
> Where we abide, come the Aires qualities;
> . . . .
> And in the Torrid zone it is so hott
> That flesh and Blood (like flaming fire) it fries,
> And with a Cole-black beautie it doth blott,
> Curling the Haires upon a wyry knott.[61]

Late in the seventeenth century, therefore, African women in John Crowne's masque *Calisto* (1675) are still complaining of having lost their beauty when their fair complexion disappeared under the heat of the merciless sun. Their only hope is that love may still be theirs in spite of their color. At the same time, as other nations offer their gifts to England, the figure of Africa makes its offering, a gift significant in its typicality: "Thou for thy slaves shalt have these / Scorched sones of mine."[62]

The trouble with the climatic explanation was that it could not be reconciled with the fact that black men who were brought to northern climates failed to lose their blackness, nor did white men turn black (except to a degree, and only temporarily) in the equatorial climates. Observers eventually concluded, in agreement with the Biblical allegation of an Aethiopian's incapacity to change his color, that blackness in skin pigmentation was immutable. Writers, too, found the belief in the immutability of this blackness highly useful as a metaphor for the categorically impossible. For example, a despondent Cleopatra, in Shakespeare, discourages her servant's efforts to cheer up by saying: "But your intents / Are to delight us: alas you wash an Ethiop!"[63] Massinger uses the image several times, but he invests it with additional overtones of the reputed eroticism and jealousy of black men. In *The Parliament of Love* (1624), Cleremont admits that to excuse his guilt in lusting after Leonora "were but to wash an Ethiop."[64] And in *The Bondsman* (1623), also by Massinger, Pisander says of his rival that he suffers irremedial jealousy "Of which, when he can wash an Aethiop white, / Leosthenes may hope to free himself."[65] Through a subtle process of association within a phrase, the ideas of lust, jealousy and Aethiopians are linked.

Perhaps because the Ethiopian could not be washed white—even though a reasoned climatic explanation should have included that possibility—the literary men were certain that he was fully conscious of his color. As the quoted passages above may already have made apparent, another trait of the black man in relation to his skin color is his self-conscious knowledge of both it and its meaning to the white world around him. The Prince of Morocco's "Mislike me not for my complexion / The shadowed livery of the burnished sun,"[66] is probably the most well-known example of a Moor's expressed consciousness of his color and its likely reception by a white person.

Webster's Zanche, the black servant, pertinently suggests an acquaintance with similar experiences of rejection when she sees Francesco de Medici in his Moorish disguise and is immediately drawn to him.

> I ne'er loved my complexion till now,
> Cause I may boldly say, without a blush,
> I love you.[67]

Until now, evidently, her black skin has inhibited her from freely expressing her feelings to men of another color, for she has not been unconscious of what their reaction would likely be.

One of the major black figures of the period, Eleazer, talks obsessively of his own blackness. He speaks vehemently of tearing "out my tongue / From this black temple for blaspheming thee"[68] and of the delight in having the queen twine her luxurious arms "about my jetty neck."[69] His knowledge of what white society expects in a Moor has fostered in him instinctive defensive poses. Justly accused of adultery with the queen, he vigorously denies his guilt by alluding to a white prejudice against blacks.

> The Queen with me, with me, a Moore, a Devill,
> A slave of Barbary, a dog; for so
> Your silken Courtiers christen me.

The racial image is too noxious for him to refrain from rejecting it in order to assert his basic humanity. "Although my flesh be tawny, in my veines / Runs blood as red, and royal as the best."[70] (His claim to equal human status, of course, inadvertently tends to undercut his plea of innocence.) Because he is so aware of his putative identity as constructed by whites—he hears the tongues of people hissing: "That's the black Prince of Devils"[71] —he attempts to mask his real villainy by accusing others of unwarranted racial prejudice against him and urging them to be more just:

> Look well on Eleazer; value me
> Not by my sun-burnt cheek, but by my birth'
> Nor by my birth, but by my losse of blood,
> Which I have sacrificed in Spain's defense.[72]

His appeal to judge a man by his deeds rather than by his looks constitutes a fundamental irony through which the theme of this play really works. For Eleazer's deeds, once they are brought to light (and, for the audience, his villainy has been evident even before his exposure), do not simply justify the general negative attitude of other characters toward him as a black man but confirm beyond doubt the validity of their conceptions. The creature's own words can be turned against him and, more pointedly, against black men as a race. His own emphasis on race, whether defensively imploring or aggressively proud, becomes a constant reminder of the blackness and hence the racial identity of the villain; consequently it pushes that association between blackness and evil from the shadow of suspicion to the light of certainty.

To fix the point even more firmly in the mind of the viewer, Dekker permits Eleazer to employ more than once the same evasive tactic of accusing his accusers of racial prejudice. When Alvero, his father-in-law, denounces him for having imprisoned Prince Philip and Hortenzo (the audience knows this to be true), Eleazer unabashedly pleads his innocence in words that once more reveal his racial self-consciousness:

> Because my face is in nights colour dy'd,
> Think you my conscience and my soul is so,
> Black faces may have hearts as white as snow;
> And tis a generall rule in morall rowls,
> The whitest faces have the blackest souls.[73]

He speaks in part like Duncan of Scotland who never really knew how true it was "that there is no art to find the mind's construction in the face." Here, however, Dekker's theme is the converse of Shakespeare's. For Dekker's audience, as for the characters in the play including Eleazer himself, the black face advertised exactly what underlay it in reality. The congruity between appearance and reality became an important feature of the black man's image as it was imaginatively constructed in this early work.

Unlike Mrs. Behn, who in her adaption of Dekker's *Lust's Dominion* attempted to reduce the racial overtones, Ravenscroft, in his revision of Shakespeare's *Titus Andronicus*, seemed to emphasize the theme of blackness and race. Shakespeare's Aaron shows little interest in his own racial distinctiveness until his paternal affection is evoked by a threat to his newborn black son. Then and only then does he think of his blackness, eulogizing it and defending the heritage he is passing on. Ravenscroft's Aron, on the other hand, shows more concern over his skin color and its status in a white culture. When he learns that Tamora, his mistress, has firmly entrenched herself as Rome's empress, he repudiates the stigma of his blackness and delights in his plans to match her rise.

> Then Aron, arm thy heart and fit thy thoughts
> To mount aloft with thy Imperial Mistress.
> And rise her pitch; whom thou in Triumph long,
> Has Prisoner held, fetter'd in Amorous chains,
> And faster bound to Arons Charming Eyes
> Then is Prometheus ty'd to Caucasus.
> Hence abject thoughts that I am black and foul,
>
> And all the Taunts of Whites that call me Fiend,
> I still am Lovely in an Empress Eyes,
> Lifted on high in Power, I'le hang above,
> Like a black threatening Cloud o'er all heads
> That dare look up to me with Envious Eyes.[74]

He apparently succeeds in dispelling his belief in the ugliness of blackness, for there are no further passages to indicate he is bothered any longer by his skin color.

The drama largely judged the black-skinned people as totally lacking beauty according to white standards. Even in interracial affairs, as this study will later show, the white partner, consenting or aggressive, is either fully depraved or so uncontrollably erotic as to act *in spite of* the black skin of the partner.

Everywhere black skin is held foul, often by the black characters themselves, more often by whites. In either case, the response measures the tendencies of white psychology and perspective. The nurse in Shakespeare's *Titus Andronicus* (1592) is typical in her revulsion from blackness, which is all the more evident because a newborn black baby repels her. "Here is the babe, as loathsome as a toad / Amongst the fairest breeders of our clime."[75] Ravenscroft, more acutely race conscious than Shakespeare is in his own play, expands the nurse's part to emphasize the racial trait. She refers to "This Black and loathsome child," "this black and dismall issue." Her remarks are followed by Demetrius' epithet, "a thing / So foul and black."[76] In the same play Ravenscroft has changed Shakespeare's description of Aaron's "body's hue" from the indirect "Spotted, detested, and abominable" to the racially blunt "Black, Loathsome, and Detested."[77]

Even Mrs. Behn, although in dramatizing a Moor she softens the cruelty of her model Eleazer, still knows that white women of virtue hold blackness in aversion. Her portrait of Abdelazer includes a sympathetic scene in which the Moor despairs over his skin, in full realization of his condition. Through most of the play, however, Abdelazer has shown very little self-consciousness of his black skin. At least he seldom refers to his own race himself until the woman he loves poses it as an obstacle. Although he does reiterate Eleazer's speech about the reputation of the Moor as a devil, a slave of barbary, he undercuts that image by explaining it as a product of "gay young Courtiers" instead of Eleazer's "silken Courtiers" (cf. p. 100). The change in adjectives here suggests that the damaging image be taken somewhat less seriously. In only one other scene does Abdelazer mention his color, and at first without anger or shame. He is making known his love for the young and beautiful Leonora and acknowledges her natural reluctance to hear his pleas on account of his physical appearance:

> ... had Nature made
> This clouded Face, like to my Heart, all Love,
> It might have spar'd that Language which you dread.[78]

It is only after she rejects him on the grounds of the questionable appeal of his appearance that he becomes painfully aware of his blackness. In spite of his plea to disregard his blackness, she denies him in favor of Alonzo, who, she says, though he may not compete with Abdelazer in pedigree of birth, is a beautiful man. Unlike the replies of the rejected women in the poems of Rainolds and Herbert, Abdelazer's retort is self-derogatory, but like theirs, it at least momentarily provokes compassion.

> Ah! there's your Cause of Hate! Curst be my Birth,
> And curst be Nature that has dy'd my Skin
> With this ungrateful Colour! cou'd the Gods
> Have given me equal Beauty with Alonzo!

Then, following a more vigorous plea to ignore his color, comes a claim to equal human status made on the grounds of his sexual capacities:

> Yet as I am, I've been in vain ador'd,
> And Beauties great as these have languish'd for me.
> The lights put out, thou in thy naked Arms
> Will find me soft and smooth as polish'd Ebony:
> And all my Kisses on thy balmy Lips as sweet,
> As are the Breezes, breath'd amidst the Groves
> Of ripening Spices in the height of Day.[79]

His suggestion to circumvent the unsightliness of blackness by putting out the light is his concession to her privilege of considering her own racial quality superior to his. He makes little effort to modify her attitude: if black skin is repulsive to one nurtured in a white culture, so be it. But he does hope that this obstacle which separates them now will be temporarily removed by a veil of darkness to permit them to enjoy the pleasures of the flesh. The dilemma of his ambivalence toward himself, marked by self-hatred and self-pride, differs considerably from the simplicity of Eleazer's diabolic glee over his blackness and points to Mrs. Behn's increased sensitivity to the black man's plight.

This broader view of the black man, however, was long in coming. For the most part, Leonora's preference for white over black was the dominant choice of most writers in their dealings with black characters. Ben Jonson's *Masque of Blackness* (1605) was typical in its depiction of English taste. Although claims can be made that his interest in black men, following that of his Queen Henrietta, is essentially in their exoticism, the language of his characters and the situation of the masque are weighted with racial ideas and cultural judgments. The Moorish characters indirectly declare the supremacy of whiteness by confessing their hatred of their own blackness. The black women of Aethiopia are introduced as seekers of the land where the sun does not rise or set but where its rays convert all that they touch into forms of beauty. The misery of these women over their blackness has already been described by Niger, the symbol of their race.[80] Now the Moon informs Niger that Britannia is the one place in the world where the sun can "blanch an Aethiop."

> . . . and past mere nature
> Can salve the rude defects of ev'ry creature.
> Call forth thy honour'd daughters then;
> And let the land, with those pure traces
> They flow with, in their native graces.
> Invite them boldly to the shore;
> Their beauties shall be scorch'd no more;
> This sun is temperate, and refines
> All things on which his radiance shines.[81]

After the masquers dance, Niger happily announces to the daughters of Aethipia that no longer will ". . . this veil, the sun hath cast / Above your blood, more summers last." He prescribes a mysterious bathing rite through which their skin color will be restored to its original lustre, that is, to its whiteness.[82]

Seventy years later, John Crowne was still acclaiming the superior beauty of white skin by depicting similar Africans bemoaning their own repulsiveness and pointing an accusatory figure to the same villain, the sun. The African maidens imploringly approach several fair-skinned shepherds, who are about to flee:

Stay gentle swains, be not afraid,
To see our faces hid in shade.
We, but lately were as fair,
As your shepherdesses are,
Did not a frantic youth of late
O'erset the chariot of the sun[83]

In this masque Crowne's intention, unlike Jonson's, is not to eulogize England but to praise love and define beauty. The request of the black women, therefore, to have their original beauty restored is denied. Their blackness is permanent, a knowledgeable African informs them, for the red and white they have lost have been bestowed on the nymphs who accompany Diana in the sky. Heaven itself has now adopted as its standard of beauty red and white. For the unfortuante black women, only the possibility of love remains as compensation.

3rd African   And now instead of what we sought,
              Our black with us must fair be thought

1st African   No losers we shall prove
              By parting with our red and white,
              If black will serve the turn of love;
              For beauty's made for love's delight.[84]

White is beautiful, and provocative of love; if black, too, can move the human heart to love, it also will meet the definition of beauty. The masque, however, ends with no ready lovers appearing on the horizon but only an entry of Africans adding their dark skins to heighten the sparkling qualitites of the white nymphs.

   That blackness is a deterrent to an interracial love affair is evident in many cases. Yet even in an *intraracial* situation, a black woman is made conscious of her own unattractiveness and not permitted an ethnocentric evaluation of herself. Webster's Zanche falls in love with one she takes to be a Moorish gentleman and immediately offers to rob her mistress of money and jewels, hoping to make herself more desirable to him—and that means *whiter*.

          ...It is a dowry
     Methinks, should make that sun-burnt proverb false,
     And wash the Aethiop white.[85]

The view here suggested is that from either perspective, white or black, the preferred complexion, if love is in mind, is the lighter one.

   Anthony Munday,[86] George Peele,[87] and William Rowley[88] all have plays in which appear black characters or characters in black disguises, and each play contains accompanying remarks about their ugliness. A typical remark is made in Peter Hausted's play *Rival Friends* (1632) when Mistress Ursely, "a deformed and foolish" girl with a "crooked back" is told by her father that she cannot hope to win the handsome Anteros because she is "lame . . . mishapen, blacke, [and] besides, ill manner'd."[89]

Throughout the century the Moor's dark skin was the suitable touchstone for ugliness. In a comic scene in Fletcher's *Monsieur Thomas* (1610-1614), Alice and her niece Mary are discussing Mary's lover Thomas, whose wild behavior disturbs Mary. Her aunt, however, takes the young man's side, and in the ensuing banter reveals a distaste for black or tawny skin.

> Alice   . . . for his shape
> If I have eyes, I have not seen his better;
> A handsome brown complexion—
>
> Mary   —Reasonable
> Inclining to a tawny.
>
> Alice   Had I said so
> You would have wish'd my tongue out.[90]

To describe one as tawny, a color ascribed often to the Moor, was obviously to be insulting.

A more explicit debasement of the appearance of the Moor occurs in William D'Avenant's *The Unfortunate Lover* (1643) when Heldebrand compares his wife with the beautiful Amaranta and concludes that Amaranta's fairness makes her look like a Moor.

> . . . the nicest maid
> In Lombardy, strictly compar'd looks like
> A wither'd Lapland Nurse; my teeming wife
> Shewes foule and tawny to her, as sh'ad beene
> The sooty off-spring of a Moore.[91]

The maid Prue in Wycherly's *The Gentleman-Dancing Master* (1672) is just another in a long line of white characters who disdain black skin. Deploring a shortage of suitable lovers for herself, she claims that the only available males are a "couple of ugly little Black-a-more Boys in Bonets."[92] The adjective is not necessary yet revealing.

It was Richard Brome, however, who actually designed a whole comic plot from this cultural pattern of the ugliness of dark skin and the beauty of white. The basic premise of his *The English Moor* (1637) is that black skin repels white members of the opposite sex. Quicksand, an old miser married to the young Millicent, has been persuaded not to consummate the marriage until his bride and he can discourage and dampen the spirits of all the young rakehells of the town who have vowed to cuckold him because of his financial superiority over them. He ingeniously hits on the idea of disguising Millicent in the best way possible to allow her freedom of movement with absolute immunity from sexual assault by the bachelors. She will assume the identity and appearance of a Moor.

> Quick.   That I may fool iniquity and Triumph
>   Over the lustful stallions of our Time;
>   Bed-bounders, and leap-Ladies (as they terme 'em)
>   Mount-Mistresses, diseases shackle 'em,
>   And spittles pick their bones.
>
> Mil.   Come to the point. What's the disguise, I pray you?

The disguise will be black-face, and so ugly is the color that he himself will be prevented from making attempts on her and risking his vow of abstinence.

>   . . . Now this shall both
>   Kill vain attempts in me, and guard you safe
>   From all that seek subversion of your honour.
>   Ile fear no powder'd spirits to haunt my house,
>   Rose-sooted fiends, or fumigated Goblins
>   After this tincture's laid upon thy face,
>   'Twill cool their kidneys and allay their heats.

The beautiful Millicent shrinks from putting on such a loathsome disguise, declaring that beauty (that is, her whiteness) is made in heaven. She asks, ". . . Would you blot out / Heaven's workmanship?" Quicksand's answer is that he is asking her to do nothing unholy, for the Ethiopian, he claims, is as much a product of heaven as is a fair lady.

>   Why think'st thou, fearful Beauty
>   Has Heaven not part in Aegypt. Pray thee tell me,
>   Is not an Ethiope's face his workmanship
>   As well as the fair'st Ladies?[93]

The potentially far-reaching effects of such an idea on the whole racial conflict, however, are certainly far from Brome's mind. Quicksand's argument of God's universality is mainly expressed to persuade his wife to agree to the disguise, not to propagandize in favor of toleration. Convinced that the universality of God does not alter the rigidity of cultural differences, Quicksand commences to paint Millicent black, knowing that her beauty will be completely obscured from the eyes of white men.[94]

Shockingly and ineluctably visible, the black skin of the African strangers was measured in this period of early meetings and found guilty of moral taint and physical unsightliness. In an important literary development these attributes coalesced to form a single major facet of the image of the black man: his conception and treatment as an agent of Satan.

Chapter 4

The Devil and the Moor: "Being Hell's Perfect Character"

In the late nineteenth century, in a short story called "The Lynching of Jube Benson," a white Southern doctor painfully confesses his role in the lynching of a suspected Negro murderer-rapist. Until the crime the Negro had been the doctor's loyal servant, but at the sight of the victim, the doctor joined the lynch mob and now is suffering deep remorse.

> I could only think of him as a monster. It's tradition. At first I was told that the black man would catch me, and when I got over that, they taught me that the devil was black, and when I recovered from the sickness of that belief, here were Jube and his fellows with faces of menacing blackness.[1]

In writing this scene Paul Lawrence Dunbar expressed his own awareness of the tradition (an especially American tradition) of calling the devil the Black Man. This epithet was an obvious continuation of a practice that had its roots in a remote past, but the identification of the black man with the devil developed fully in the drama of the English Renaissance. Somehow in the white world the black man became connected with the devil, and early English playwrights fixed that relationship firmly in the consciousness of the playgoers.

"The Moor's black face supposedly indicates that his soul is especially begrimed, and he is therefore often taken for a devil," says Nemmer.[2] The distinguished Elizabethan scholar E. E. Stoll explains further that the epithet of "devil" was applied to Aaron "because of his color, not his race, for it was an old superstition, not then extinct, that the Devil when he appeared took the form of a Moor."[3] Judging from the Dunbar passage, Stoll is over-stating the tendency of such ideas to die. In the plays there are just too many passages making the assertions, and too many portraits to dramatize its "truth" to permit the idea to die easily.

In the earliest play giving extensive treatment to a Moor, the association between black men and devils begins with the Moor's initial appearance on stage. When Muly Mahamet in Peele's *The Battle of Alcazar* (1588-89) enters in a company of Moors, the Presenter introduces him to the audience with these words:

> Presents himselfe with naked sword in hand,
> Accompanied as now you may behold,
> With devils coted in the shapes of men.[4]

Nemmer suggests that perhaps the black figure was being used as an extension of the devil of the medieval morality plays, who appeared in the midst of smoke and carried a pitchfork. The Moor, as in the Peele scene, could enter waving his scimitar, frightening his audience with his sooty or charcoaled face.[5] Although W. W. Greg felt that one of the Moors was actually provided with "diabolical attributes," as seems implied by the following phrase, "as now you may behold," the simpler and more likely explanation, made by Eldred Jones, is that Muly's henchmen were painted black and "hence to an Elizabethan audience, devilish in their appearance."[6]

The dramatists make the point of hell's color repeatedly. When, for example, the two friars in Dekker's *Lust's Dominion* (1599) see the black Eleazer for the first time, their immediate reaction is to connect him with the underworld. "Oh! no Sir, no but truth to tell; / Seeing your face, we thought of hell."[7] It is likely also that Christopher Marlowe was concurring with this view of the devil's color when he envisioned Mephistopheles apostrophizing himself by coloring black the entire climate of his own appearance and its effect on others. "Monarch of hell, under whose black survey / Great potentates do kneel with awful fear."[8] The impression of his great dread is deepened by the blackness that is generated from his "survey."

In a much lighter but none the less meaningful vein, the devil in *The Witch of Edmonton*, (1621) by Rowley, Dekker, and Ford, appears as a dog. When he nearly drowns a clown who has been involved with him, a chance remark unsurprisingly clarifies just what color the dog-devil bears. "A mangie," cries the clown, "take that black hide of yours."[9]

In another play the widespread belief in the blackness of the devil is implicitly made through its denial. Celanta, in Peele's *The Old Wive's Tale* (1588–1594), hopes that she can get a husband despite her foulness. "Well, though I am black," she says, "I am sure all the world will not forsake me; and as the old proverb is, though I am black, I am not the devil."[10] Significantly enough, her remark points to the process in which the effect of attributing a physical quality to the nature of evil conversely leads to attributing a nature of evil to any who possess that physical trait. Coloring Satan black could easily lead to coloring the black man Satanic. The proverb of Celanta would fail to convince.

Black face was hell's face, as Millicent in Brome's *The English Moor* (1637) insists when she finally sheds her blackface disguise. She decries the insane jealousy of her aged bridegroom, who originally insisted on painting her to look like a Moor in order to discourage the attention of the local rakes. In her relief over removing the black paint, she associates her disguise with the character of hell and identifies her own fair complexion with that of heaven:

> ... This is the face
> On which the Hell of jealousie abus'd
> The hand of Heaven, to fright the world withall.[11]

Although the common practice was to identify the black man more directly with the devil, sometimes, as here, allusions do not literally make of him a satanic figure. But the final effect of linking demonism and blackness, directly or loosely, is to affirm an unholiness about the black man, an unholiness rendered ineluctably visible by his color. In Rowley's *All's Lost by Lust* (1619), a captain of white troops about to engage the Moors in battle utters a boast of superiority in order to encourage his men. The Moor is not openly acclaimed a devil, but there is no doubt about what his blackness signifies. Even the color of his blood is questionable, and that raises the issue of his human status as well.

> They would deter us with their swarty looks:
> Were they the same to their similitude,
> Sooty as the inhabitants of hell,
> Whom they neerest figure; cold feare should flye
> From us as distant as they are from beauty:
> They come to sacrifice their blouds to us,
> If that be red, a mare rubrum.[12]

In similar manner, Bess Bridges, the heroine of Heywood's *The Fair Maid of the West* (1600-1603), and Goodlack, her lieutenant, also condemn the Negro through an insidious juxtaposition of terms. Believing the man she loves to be dead, Bess outfits a ship and orders it to be painted black from stem to stern and equipped only with black gear. Goodlack's concern over its appearance is rooted in a cultural prejudice against black.

> Goodlack   "Twill be ominous
>   And bode disastrous fortune.
>
> Bess   I will ha't so.
>
> Goodlack   Why, then she shall be pitched black as the devil.
>
> Bess   She shall be called the Negro.[13]

It takes little effort to make a minor verbal adjustment to see the Negro "black as the devil" and then to attribute the additional qualities of one to the other.

No such verbal compression is needed in the explicitness of Portia's words in *The Merchant of Venice* (1596), when she hears of the arrival of the Prince of Morocco, who has come to seek her for his wife. "If he have the condition of a saint and the complexion of a devil, I had rather he should shrive me than wive me."[14] Simply viewed, she is voicing the popular association of devil and blackness without actually treating Morocco as anything but a man. Yet it is his blackness of skin—shared by the devil—that instantly predisposes her against him as a suitor. If there is any seriousness in her jest, it is that, for her, inner goodness cannot compensate for external foulness, especially when that foulness has special connotations.

Indisputably, then, the Elizabethans tended to color hell and hell's agents black.[15] Although the vast majority of passages linking the devil and the black man are essentially serious and frequently literal, there are several comic situations involving sexual contacts in which the common epithet that white characters employ for black ones is "devil." In Chapman's *The Blind Beggar of Alexandria* (1598), there appears a scene in which the morally loose Elimene has to choose for a husband between Porus, the king of the Ethiopians, and Bebritius, a white lord. With the surprising words, "In my eyes now the blackest is the fayrest," she chooses Porus, eliciting from Bebritius this retort: "Out on thee foolish woman, / Thou has chose a devill." Porus wittily fends off the allegation by pointing out indirectly that black skin is not the solitary sign of the devil. "Not yet sir," he responds, "till he have hornes."[16]

Another casual and comic reference to the color of devils appears in Fletcher's *The Prophetess*, where Geta, the court jester, has had Delphia, the prophetess and conjuror, arrested on a charge of lewdness. Knowing that she has tame devils under her control, he agrees to release her if she will place at his disposal a she-devil for his sexual gratification. "I would have a handsome, pleasant, and a fine she-devil," he orders. When the devil appears, Geta is delightfully aroused. What is interesting, of course, is the she-devil's color.

Geta	A pretty brown devil, i faith. May I not kiss her?
Delph.	Yes, and embrace her too; she is your servant. Fear not, her lips are cool enough.
Geta	She is marvelous well mounted. What's her name?
Delph.	Lucifera.[17]

Here neatly combined in a single figure are the dark skin, a devil, and a source of sexual pleasure. In a more serious context, but still in a light mood, is

Flamineo's remark about the black servant Zanche in Webster's *The White Devil* (1611). Marcello, Flamineo's brother, is berating Flamineo for his apparent connection with a black woman. He brings up the traditional label for the Moor first, expressing his annoyance that she is lingering in Flamineo's presence. "Why doth this devil haunt you, say." Flamineo picks up the allusion and expands it.[18]

> . . . I know not;
> For, by this light, I know not;
> 'Tis not so great a cunning as men think,
> To raise the devil; for here's one up already;
> The greatest cunning were to lay him down.

The change of pronoun in the last line from feminine to masculine tends to deny her humanity and belie his own sexual use of her. But her open sexual approach to him earlier has already revealed her strong libido, and so his remarks are essentially double-entendres, suggesting not the difficulty but rather the ease of laying a "devil" down.

This tendency to link the black man (or woman) with deviltry and sex is evident in Marston's play *Wonder of Women, Sophonisba* (1606). Syphax, a treacherous seducer, is about to leap into bed to consummate his long pursuit of the chaste Sophonisba. She, however, has arranged a switch, and Syphax finds, instead of Sophonisba, his own black servingman Vangue. The joke is on the lecher, and his remark is appropriate to the times: "Ha! can any woman turne to such a Devill?"[19] That Vangue is a man and has been persuaded to greet Syphax in this situation only adds obscenity to the whole ludicrous scene.

John Fletcher duplicated the mechanics of this episode in *Monsieur Thomas* but gave increased attention to the combination of demonism and sexuality in a longer scene. The lecherous rake Thomas has been trying unsuccessfully to seduce his sweetheart Mary. In encounter after encounter she has wittily outsmarted his attempts. Finally, in an effort to humiliate him while at the same time preserving her own virtue, she tricks him into getting into bed with another woman while thinking that he has at last achieved his goal. The bed partner turns out to be that most undesirable of creatures—a black woman. Disguised as a woman himself, Thomas does not discover the joke until he gets into her bed. Recoiling in disgust more over her blackness than over his disappointment, he reviles the girl in comical, conventional language:

> Holy saints defend me!
> The devil, devil, devil! oh, the devil!
> I am abus'd most damnedly, most beastly!
> Yet, if it be a she-devil—but the house is up,
> And here's no staying longer in this cassock.

> Woman, I here disclaim thee; and in vengeance,
> I'll marry with that devil, but I'll vex thee![20]

Up to this point in the scene, the Moorish woman has been silent, having comically fallen asleep in the soft bed while waiting to serve her mistress' wishes. As she stirs, he commences to beat her, driving her off stage in the typical fashion of riding a devil in a morality play. "Devil, good night! Good night, good devil! / Roar again, devil, roar again."[21] The Moor has been a comic scapegoat to degrade Thomas; her role and his reaction are further illustrations of an important way of looking at the black man of this era. In addition to its comment on the black race, the scene also indicates a popular belief about the kind of white man who could consider an involvement with a black person. Thomas's thought (in line four above) of gratifying himself sexually with the Moor, black devil or not, delineates his powerful sex drive and underlines the characteristic which will be found a central feature of most white characters who contemplate an interracial union.[22] Only a dominating eroticism would permit such a thing.

Far more numerous than the comic treatments of the black man as devil, however, are those vivid scenes in which the putative satanic nature of the black man is verbally asserted in all seriousness. The force of the language as well as the effect of action develops the allegation and firmly establishes the invidious image in the culture. Explicit accusations by white characters and detailed confessions by black ones, both repeatedly and emphatically delivered, hammer out the link between the black man and the devil. From lines in early Shakespeare to passages in late Settle and Mrs. Behn, the language is stocked with allusions to the black man's demonism.

Strangely enough, however, in the earliest dramatization of an evil Moor, Muly Mahamet, there are only a few occasions in which white characters consciously charge the black one with being affiliated with the devil. In Peele's play the black man would make the connection more emphatically himself. There is the famous line of the Presenter introducing Muly's fellow Moors as "devils coted in the shapes of men," but there are no other direct references to Muly as a devil. However, in Shakespeare's *Titus Andronicus* (1589-90) white characters are already facilely equating a black skin with the presence of a devil. Even when it is an innocent baby who bears that skin, the same charge of deviltry is brought against it. Although the period of face-to-face confrontation between the black African and white English worlds had begun just several decades earlier, Shakespeare seems already to have understood what the plight of the black man would be if he stood alone in a dominant white culture. To what extent Shakespeare's own depiction of black characters and white responses would tend to justify the harsh attitudes of white people can only be conjectured. But it need only be said here that Aaron, his first dramatization of a black man and one of the earliest of the period, is effectively demonized by the white world in which he lives, and he plays out the role of demon so fully that his treatment by others seems justified. His child is labeled a devil "loathsome as a toad" and he himself is bitterly denounced as "the incarnate devil" with a "fiendlike face"; "this barbarous Moor / This ravenous tiger, this accursed devil."[23]

Titus relates the Moor with greater detail and precision to the powers of hell when, pretending to be crazed with grief, he locates the natural habitat of Moors in hell. When Tamora seeks out Titus and pretends to be the spirit of revenge in order to uncover his plans, Titus, playing along with her game, notes her similarity to the Empress of Rome. But, he also observes, the Empress is never without a Moor in her company.

> Well are you fitted, had you but a Moor.
> Could not all hell afford you such a devil?
> For well I wot the Empress never wags
> But in her company there is a Moor;
> And would you represent our queen aright
> It were convenient you had such a devil.[24]

In Ravenscroft's adaptation of *Titus Andronicus* (1686) at the end of the seventeenth century, the same white bias appears. Ravenscroft retains Lucius' description of Aron's "fiend-like face" and adds further denunciation as he points to Aron's mannerisms: "Behold the Hellish Dog, see how he Rowls his eyes and grins."[25] In addition Titus calls for the blood of "that dismal Fiend of darkness" and twice describes Aron's black child as "a child of darkness," invoking the ambivalence of a spiritual as well as physical darkness.

Occasionally, the black man's affiliation with the devil is indicated by some means other than immediate identification. In Part II of Heywood's *The Fair Maid of the West* (1630), Clem, in justifiable anger and dismay, curses the Moorish queen whose servants have so casually and indifferently castrated him for service in the king's harem.

> Clem.   Ile see you damn'd as deep as the black
>   father of your generation the devill first.
>
> Toto.   Mistake me not.
>
> Clem.   Nay if you were with childe with a young
>   princelly devill, and had a minde to any
>   thing that's here, Ide make you lose your
>   longing.[26]

If the devil is the progenitor of the black man, then hell is his birthplace, as Prince Philip claims in *Lust's Dominion*. "Villain," he says to Eleazer, "'tis thee, / Thou hel-begotten fiend at thee, I stare."[27] In Mrs. Behn's adaptation of this play, Philip insists in more vivid language on identifying the

Moor's origin with hell: "True-born Soul of Hell, / Not one of thy infernal Kin shall save thee."[28] Regardless of circumstances, white characters tend to think of blacks as affiliates of devils. When Captain Goodlack in *The Fair Maid of the West* realizes that Mullisheg is asking his help to seduce the fair Bess, he thinks instinctively of devils.

> Who but a Moor
> Of all that beares mans shape, likest a devill
> Could have devis'd this horror.[29]

Nathaniel, the "mistress-hopper" in *The English Moor* is another character who cannot escape making the same connection. Even as he plans to seduce the black-skinned Millicent, he thinks of her as "this Devels bird." Syphax, in *Wonder of Women, Sophonisba*, also with seduction on his mind, is seeking a plan to achieve his desire for Sophonisba. As he rummages in his own mind for a device to seduce the girl, he notices that Vangue, his black servant, appears to have hit upon an idea. His comment turns on a thought of hell. "Some light in the depths of hell, Vangue, What hope?"[30]

In Massinger's *The Parliament of Love* (1624), when Clarindore is ordered to marry a Moor as punishment for his lewdness, he invokes the same idea:

> Clarindore   A devil! hang me rather
> . . . .
> This is cruelty
> Beyond expression.[31]

The same punishment is imposed on Mountferrat for his crimes in *The Knight of Malta* (1616). He is condemned to marry his black accomplice Zanthia, and as he leaves into exile, he bears away these words from the blunt Norandine, a vociferous exponent of white culture and its imbedded biases: "Away French stallion! Now you have a barbary mare of your own; go leap her, and engender young devilings!"[32]

This same Zanthia is one of several black characters in the literature whose association with hell is more fully developed. Early in the play she cajoles and encourages Mountferrat to act as a man in plotting to destroy his enemy Gomera and parts from him with the flip remark "be happy." His reply takes her demonism for granted. "No, most unhappy wretch, as thou has made me, / More devil than thyself, I am."[33] But he does not really believe that he is more demonic than she. As she later relates her plans of how she intends to deliver Oriana to him for his sexual pleasure, he shudders as he apostrophizes her:

> Bloody deeds
> Are grateful offerings, pleasing to the devil;
> And thou, in thy black shape, and blacker actions,

> Being hell's perfect character, art delighted
> To do what I, though infinitely wicked
> Tremble to hear.[34]

As she laughs at his fears, he calls her again a devil. And her agreement with him is demoniac, for she offers him an opportunity to copulate with Oriana only once, on condition that once his lust is sated he murder her. When Zanthia disappoints him by failing to produce the drugged Oriana as she had promised, Mountferrat hurls a stream of epithets at her that concisely characterizes her as satanic:

> Thou black swoln pitchy cloud of all my afflictions,
> Thou night hag, gotten when the bright moon suffer'd,
> Thou hell itself confined in flesh, what trick now?

Then he threatens to cut Zanthia into pieces as "a sacrifice to thy black sire, the devil."[35] Under this attack on her demonic geneology, she accepts hell's identity and announces: "If anything, I am the devil, and the devil's heir."[36] Yet the full oratorical summation and condemnation of the black satan comes from the earthy soldier, Norandine, whose valiant, honest and loyal heart would condition an audience to accept the truth and accuracy of his judgment. In Act V, Norandine learns that Zanthia has told the truth about the drugged condition of Oriana. In his blunt manner he characterizes her in a fury of expletives.

> Marry was it, sir; the only truth that ever issued out of hell,
> which her black jaws resemble. A plague on your bacon face! You
> must be giving drinks with a vengeance! Ah, thou branded bitch!—
> Do you stare, goggles?—I hope to make winter-boots o'thy hide
> yet; she fears not damming! Hell-fire cannot parch her blacker than
> she is.—Do you grin, chimney sweeper? We'll call him [Mountferrat]
> Cacademon with his black gib there, his Succuba, his devil's seed,
> his spawn of Phlegethon, that o' my conscience, was bred o' the
> spume of Cocytus.—Do you snarl, you black Gill. She looks like the
> picture of America.[37]

This wild profusion of denigrating invective and accusation so dehumanizing to Zanthia has hardly its parallel in other plays. No other single passage spells out so clearly the supposed origin of the black man with its concomitant disgust that such a belief would produce.

Yet Zanthia hardly matches in her actions and language the consummate evil of Eleazer in *Lust's Dominion*, who is dramatized without such a lengthy and withering verbal attack made against him by white characters. However, the frequency with which he is called "devil" and is described in the imagery of hell amounts to a greater condemnation of his role as Satan's agent. At least forty separate speeches characterize Eleazer as a devil. He is called a "hel-begotten fiend (I,2,123), a "damned Moor, that Devil, that Lucifer" (II,1,742), "this accursed devil" (V,3,5), "Black Devil (II,3,34), "black fiend" (III,2,178), "this Serpent" (V,1,142), "this damn'd hell-hound" (V,1,144), and numerous variations of these epithets.[38]

Several times Philip, from whom comes the strongest statements of the Moor's demonism, talks of "conjuring down the fiend" and "I'le conjure you," language traditionally connected with the supernatural powers of evil and which Philip in all seriousness reserves for Eleazer. As noted before, Eleazer quite early admits his awareness of the white attitude toward him. He knows that when he passes by the people whisper "That's the black Prince of Devils" (I,1,36). Hortenzo, his rival for the hand of the princess Isabella, is one of those who view the Moor as a manifestation of evil. His curses on Eleazer and his black guards are in harmony with the moral perspectives of the play and with the contemporary climate of opinion.

> You damned Ministers of villainy,
> Sworn to damnation by the book of hell;
> You maps of night, you elements of Devills,
> Why do you yoak my neck with Iron chains?[39]

Other enemies at court use similar epithets for him, confirming the accuracy of his early observation. He is referred to as "Moor, Devill, toad, serpent . . . ," all of which appear to be interchangeable, giving to the word "Moor" itself the stigmata of the other three. It also seems obvious that the latter two words have not been chosen at random, for they are traditional forms ascribed to the devil as he walked the earth.[40] The Moor, therefore, was to be considered just another guise of the devil.

Oddly enough, the most condemnatory speech from a white man to identify the black man categorically with the devil comes from a man who, unlike most of the others in the play, is not motivated by a sense of deep personal injury. The King of Portugal has seen his forces defeated by Eleazer's Moors and can explain the disaster only by claiming that his foe has been aided by supernatural forces. And if his own causes are assumed to be those of virtue, the forces of his foe must be those of darkness.

> The Moor's a Devill; never did horrid fiend
> Compel'd by some Magicians mighty charm,
> Break through the prisons of the solid earth,
> With more strange horror, then this Prince of hell,
> This damned Negro Lyon-like doth rush,
> Through all, and spite of all knit opposition.[41]

The black man had little hope of escaping this insidious tradition so long as the drama heightened and perpetuated it in scenes like these. What made matters even worse was that playwrights not only vividly depicted the biased attitude of white characters and their singular conceptions of the black man but in addition frequently showed that the white characters were not mistaken in their condemnation. First, naturally, the villainous behavior of the black character was an obvious justification of white hatred. But almost as important as proof of his demonism was the habit the black man had of admitting his allegiance to the powers of hell, frequently in public as well as in private confession. The language of white characters thus found ready support in the words of black ones. The earliest dramatization of a black man includes just such an admission. In Peele's play *The Battle of Alcazar* (1588–89), the Negro-Moor Muly prepares to enter battle by invoking his allies, the forces of darkness, and thereby defines his own hellish nature.

> You bastards of night and Erybus,
> Fiends, Fairies, hags that fight in beds of steele,
> Range through this armie with iron whips.

And then he addresses himself to Nemesis, goddess and deviser of revenge, and asks her to subject his enemies to "all torments, tortures, plagues and paines of hell."[42]

Eleazer is that far more interesting villain who is so often called a "devil" to his face that by the end of the play he seems to accept the identity proudly. In act five he is named a devil nineteen times (there are a total of forty such epithets in the whole play), and of the ten times he refers to himself as a devil, five occasions occur here at the end of the play. It may not be an exaggeration to suggest that under the steady pressure of such accusations in act five, Eleazer comes to accept its truth himself. The acute awareness of what people think of a man may have no little influence on what he ultimately comes to think of himself.[43]

Although the full impact of Eleazer's explicit acceptance of his kinship with hell's forces is made in act five, culminating in a challenging apostrophe to the devil, throughout the play he has given strong verbal indications of his satanic stature. His first speech is a rejection of the principle of harmony in favor of that of chaos, a traditional attribute of demonic forces. Hearing music, Eleazer scowls: "On me, do's musick spend the sound on me / That hate all unity."[44] Music is only "noise" that "deafs" him. Later as he plots one murder after another to bring chaos to Spain's rule, his metaphors turn naturally to images of hell.

> Spain I will drown thee with thine own proud blood,
> Then make an ark of carcasses; farewell
> Revenge and I will sail in blood to hell.[45]

To him a rapier, the instrument of death, is a "good book . . . deeply written for t'was made in hell." And he urges his two servants to read it well. At one point he gives thanks for his black face, which so well is suited for villainy.[46]

Killing his enemies in battle gives him not so much the pleasure of a victorious strategist, but rather the joy of a successful recruiter of souls for hell's tenements.

> Oh for more work, more souls to post to hell;
> That I might pile up Charons boat so full,
> Untill it topple o're, Oh 'twould be sport
> To see them sprawl through the black slimy lake.[47]

Even the prison he uses to confine his enemies, he names a "hell." However, it is in his final curses that he fully acknowledges his satanism and welcomes its ultimate fulfillment, his journey to the kingdom of hell. Dying from multiple stab wounds inflicted on him by his white foes as he lies manacled and helpless, Eleazer summons up his fading strength and threatens his enemies:

> May thou Hortenzo and thy Isabella,
> Be fetch'd alive by Furies into hell,
> There to be damn'd for ever, oh! I faint;
> Devills come claim your right, and when I am
> Confin'd within your kingdom there shall I
> Out-act you all in perfect villainy.[48]

Although he does not claim hell as his native land—he still talks of "your kingdom"—he adopts it as his rightful dwelling where his citizenship in evil will be certified as he out-devils the devils.

These open declarations of Eleazer are vastly modified by Mrs. Aphra Behn as she rewrote this play over seventy-five years later in 1677. The closest Abdelazer, Eleazer's counterpart, comes to suggesting a connection with the devil is in some rather loose references. For example, the language he uses to warn those who might antagonize him is certainly mild by contrast: "Who spurn the Moor / Were better to set his foot on the Devil."[49] And as he slaughters his enemies in battle, he talks of "more Souls to send to Hell," but the vivid scene of hell's rivers and Charon's boat are not part of his imaginative experience. He obviously has little tendency to see himself as a devil. The white figures in this play, too, are less anxious to identify him as a devil. In only six passages is Abdelazer called "devil" or "hell-begotten fiend"; in addition the epithet is also used against his cohort, the erotic Queen Mother. What Mrs. Behn has done, therefore, is to change the image of the Moor from that of an associate of the devil or the devil himself to that of a human being capable of great evil but no more capable of villainy by virtue of his race than other men or women.

But Mrs. Behn's approach to the Moor is exceptional rather than typical. Her contemporary Elkanah Settle, for instance, could still show a Moorish woman as a manifestation of the devil by having her say,

> Go easie Foole, and dye; and when you Bleed,
> Remember I was author of the Deed.
> T'enlarge Fates black Records, search but my Soul;
> There, ye Infernal Furies, read a scrowl
> Of Deeds, which you want courage to Invent;
> Of which Hells Legends want a President.[50]

The same Moor, when threatened with the punishments of hell a little earlier defies her enemy:

> Hell! No, of that I scorn to be afraid;
> I'll send such throngs to the infernal Shade;
> Betray and kill, and Damn to that degree,
> I'll crowd up Hell, till there's no Room for me.[51]

These are the sentiments of the Queen Mother in *The Empress of Morocco* (1687), who murders her husband, plots to kill her own son and destroy her daughter-in-law, and perpetrates various other crimes.

There is a similar self-conscious sense of diabolism in that early Moor, Shakespeare's Aaron, who is not nearly so seethingly labeled diabolic as are some other characters. Yet he is more fully aware of his essential evil than most. Black he certainly is, and to him is given the most extensive and furious exposition of his own satanism in the whole period. Aaron's final speeches are the clearest, most dynamic expositions by a black man of the basic "truth" of the charge white men would be making. When he has been subdued by his enemies and given the chance to repent his sins, he bitterly proclaims himself not only unrepentant for the crimes he has committed but rather deeply remorseful for those which he did not commit. Furious over the limitations of his evil, he repents in a purely satanic mood only those days void of his villainy. His catalogue of crimes covers the whole range of disaster that can befall some miserable, innocent victim. First, Aaron reminisces over the joy he had in presenting Titus with the heads of his two sons, for whose promised safety Aaron had tricked Titus into cutting off his own hand. Aaron "laugh'd so heartily that both mine eyes were rainy like to his." Then he reviews a calendar of horrors he has committed or would like to have committed:

> ... a thousand more.
> Even now I curse the day (and yet I think
> Few came within the compass of my curse)
> Wherein I did not some notorious ill,

As kill a man, or else devise his death;
Ravish a maid, or plot the way to do it;
Accuse some innocent, and forswear myself;
Set deadly enmity between two friends;
Make poor men's cattle break their necks;
Set fire on barns and haystacks in the night
And bid the owners quench them with their tears.
Oft had I digg'd up dead men from their graves
And set them upright at their dear friends' door
Even when their sorrow almost was forgot,
And on their skins, as on the bark of trees,
Have with my knife carved in Roman letters
'Let not your sorrow die, though I am dead.'
Tut, I have done a thousand dreadful things
As willingly as one would kill a fly;
And nothing grieves me heartily indeed
But that I cannot do ten thousand more.
. . . .

If there be devils, would I were a devil,
To live and burn in everlasting fire,
So might I have your company in hell
But to torment you with my bitter tongue.[52]

That conditional sentence, "If there be devils, would I were a devil," is patently superfluous in a speech which itemizes actions for which the devil is notoriously recognized. As a product of Aaron's experience and imagination, his words read like a black mass, a curse on man, a pledge to Satan. He finally implores the powers of evil to grant him the gift of language that will equal the fury in his heart.

Some devil whisper curses in my ear
And prompt me that my tongue may utter forth
The venomous malice of my swelling heart.[53]

If Aaron had a doubt about his true nature, the audience watching him did not.

Moor after Moor paraded on stage, and of the large majority who were dramatized manifestations of a supernal evil, so many were self-proclaimed as well as alleged agents of hell that their image as devils must be considered to have been a fairly fixed one and thus an important force in shaping the negative attitudes of Englishmen toward black men generally.

Chapter 5

The Rites of Satan

The idea that the devil was black probably had its origins in the deep psychological recesses of the minds of men for whom "white" symbolized the normal standard of goodness and beauty. But when and why black skin in human beings came to signal the presence of evil are more difficult questions. Somehow English dramatists, knowingly or unknowingly, did their best to engender in their spectators the notion that black men were of the devil's party and could be expected to act as devotees of evil in all of its multifarious forms. The whole verbal assault that imposed on the black man an identity with the demonic powers of a dark underworld was not to exist alone as the oratorical claptrap analysed in the preceding chapter. Black characters were not to be designated devils in name only. In the hands of the playwrights they turn out to be a collection of some of the worst villains on the stage, stereotyped as cruel murderers, quite prepared to express, like Satan, a deep joy in their cruelty. As they perform their heinous deeds, bursts of demonic laughter can be heard issuing from their dark throats.

Why these white writers imagined only certain narrow prescribed courses of behavior for their black characters can probably never be fully understood. Certainly the pressures of knowing that their nation had become instrumental in the subjugation and enslavement of black people had an effect on their assessment of what blacks must be like. But there were probably equal pressures from within to shape their views, pressures from psychological needs to transfer to a scapegoat figure the very forces of inhuman behavior they must have sensed in the slave trade. Could the writers have been projecting their own or their countrymen's buried impulses toward cruelty and sadism onto the black? Could the "cruel Moor" really represent the return of the repressed, that is, the emerged form of an irrepressible national guilt? When black after black, man and woman, are seen perpetrating crime upon crime, it seems more than possible that the writers are not holding a mirror up to historical reality, nor are they simply swallowing lies and rumors defaming the black. More likely they are responding to something deeper, more complex. Ralph Ellison, sharply aware of the problem, pointed out a root of prejudice. "Color prejudice springs not from stereotype alone, but from an internal psychological state; not from misinformation alone, but from an inner need to believe."[1] If this thought has any validity today, it also can apply to human prejudice three hundred years ago.

One of the needs then was to believe that the villainy of a whole race of people could be explained by the effect of planetary influence. The villainous behavior of the black man could therefore be understood as a direct result of his relationship with Saturn. The black man was saturnine in disposition, for black skin indicated the influence of Saturn, which "was the most malign of planets in pseudoscientific astrology" of the day.[2] That Saturn was so associated with the black man probably derives from the accepted belief of that time that Saturn was the governing planet of the melancholy humor, and that humor as found in conjunction with blackness. In Thomas Newton's translation of *The Touchstone of Complexion* (1581), for example, the author states with confidence: "Last of all, if you tourne up the whole masse or lumpe, you shall finde Melancholy, altogether of a colour black."[3]

Strong evidence of this relationship between black men and Saturn is found in Shakespeare himself. In *Titus Andronicus* Aaron states plainly that his physical characteristics are proof of his falling under the influence of Saturn, whose power affects "my silence, and my cloudy melancholy." Furthermore, the saturnine effect carries deeper into his being so that "Vengeance is in my heart, death in my hand, / Blood and revenge are hammering in my head."[4] "Saturn is dominator over" his desires, he proclaims. Such a disposition, ruled by Saturn, is one that moves in an orbit of evil, frequently leading the human agent into acts of evil for their own sake.[5] Phineas Fletcher, in language simple and unequivocal, makes the connection between blackness, evil, and Saturn in his description of the creature Perindus:

> All blacke and foule, most strange and ugly fram'd.
> Begot by Saturne, on a sea-borne witch,
> Resembling both, his haires like threads of pitch
> Distorted teete; and eyes sunke in his head.[6]

Much earlier Chaucer had clearly characterized the baleful force of Saturn: its planetary influence, he says, leads man to "the stranglyng and hangyng by the throte . . . the groynynge, and the pryvee empoysonynge," to "vengeance" and "derke tresons."[7] Although he does not attribute any racial color to the Saturnine sphere of influence, the deadly villainy of those who feel its effect is undeniable, and their treacherous mode of operation is insidiously unique.

In keeping with these notions, the playwrights seldom favored a Moor by granting him the moral capacity to kill his enemy in a fair and honorable battle. The stage black man seldom dispatches his white foe with a bold sword thrust in a frontal attack, allowing him a clean, heroic death.[8] More often the Moors stab their victims with a sneaky unexpected dagger thrust, or they resort to the strangler's cord, or to poison, mutilation, smothering and even to the late fiendish innovation, the firearm, against which victims had little defense.[9] Of course white characters who commit the same kinds of unpardonably brutal crimes and unspeakable acts also abound. But their presence in the drama as a whole and within individual plays is usually counterbalanced by their moral opposites, men of nobility and decency of the same race and nationality. The corruption of the Caucasian villain, therefore, tends to remain particularly his own and does not indicate an inherent judgment on his race or the nationality to which he happens to belong. Even in plays or in clusters of plays which dramatize villains predominantly of one nationality—the Italians, let us say—there are also enough noble Italian figures to prevent an impugning of the whole Italian nation as Machiavellian. That is, for every Mendoza, Flamineo and Deflores, who contrive to bring death and chaos to their worlds, there is also an Altofronte, a Giovanni, an Alsemero, who maneuver to reestablish a sane order.[10] Similarly, for every Richard III, there is a Henry IV or V; for every Macbeth there is a Macduff; for every D'Amville, a Charlemont.[11] Among the portraits of Europeans, then, radiated virtue enough to offset the disparaging effects of typed villains. The same cannot be said for the treatment of black men.

Of approximately thirty speaking characters, excluding Othello, who are black-skinned or who use black skin as an appropriate disguise, at least fourteen commit or assist in brutal murders or rapes, four others boast of having killed, presumably in open battle (but none are shown to do so), three others are unscrupulous and cruel, five are singularly exotic and are used only to heighten the idea of white supremacy, several disguise themselves as Moors for innocuous purposes, two for villainous ones, and the remaining few, to varying degrees, could be classified by white standards as decent human beings.[12] Only one black man exhibits a high sense of morality, an admirable integrity, and a capacity for human compassion. Indeed, Nemmer concludes that the Moor is often depicted as a destructive agent, a natural force of evil who would be expected to perpetrate heinous acts when he appeared on stage.[13]

The image of this cruel and implacable Moor may have had its origin—at least as it grew in English consciousness—in John Poleman's translation of Frey Luis Nieto's *Relacion de las Guenas de Berbera*, which Poleman called *The Second booke of Battailes* and published in 1587. The book is a vivid account of the Battle of Alcazar that took place in 1578 in which the Christian army of Sebastian, the flowering young ruler of Portugal, aided by the well-known Irish adventurer Thomas Stukely and his cohorts, was annihilated by Abd-el-Malek, the rightful claimant to the throne of Barbary, and his army of Moors. Sebastian had somehow unwisely been persuaded to champion the cause of Mulai Mohamed, the preceding ruler of Barbary, who was trying to drive his uncle from power.

In his dramatization of this historical situation, George Peele followed Poleman quite closely for details and characterization, including the condemnation of Mulai Mohamed, the usurper (the Muly Mahamet of Peele's play) and Poleman's admiration for Mulai's confederates, Sebastian and Stukely. Poleman describes Mulai as a villain who "set three cut throat villains for to dispatch him [his uncle] out of ye way, no auctor of the trecherie and villainous fact being known."[14] Poleman explained that Mulai's father, Abdallas, the ruler of Fez, was supposed to permit his throne to pass to one of his own brothers. Instead, he ordered all of his brothers murdered to preserve the kingship for his own son. Two brothers, one of whom was Abd-el-Malek, escaped, but later Mulai was able to locate and assassinate one of them. Abd-el-Malek lived to return to Barbary with assistance from the Turkish emperor, and drove Mulai out. Mulai fled to Portugal and pleaded with the youthful Sebastian for help, offering him as an incentive a license to proselytize the Christian faith in his land.

Throughout this account Mulai is depicted as the dastardly usurping villain, a judgment that Peele adopted fully. On the other hand, Peele heightened the character of Sebastian to contrast sharply with Muly. Sebastian becomes "an honorable and courageous king," a "sweet Sebastian," a "brave boy," and Muly remains a "barbarous Moore," a "tyrant king."[15] Muly's villainy grows theatrically vivid in his bloodthirsty speeches, but not in his acts. His historical battleground behavior evidently gave Peele little opportunity to dramatize him as a butcher except through the device of pompous oratory that works to show him bloody minded but perhaps cowardly.

> Sith they begin to bath in bloud,
> Bloud be the theame whereon our time shall tread,
> Such slaughter with my weapon shall I make
>
> As through the streame and bloudie chanels deepe,
> Our Moores shall saile in ships and pinnaces,
> From Tanger shore unto the gates of Fesse.[16]

Knitted into this pattern of Muly's empty threats, impotent gestures, and cowardly behavior is the blackness of his skin. Again and again there appears a Presenter, who acts like a chorus in narrating the coming action and commenting on its moral aspects, to remind the audience that Muly is black: "Black in his looke, and bloudie in his deeds / And his shirt stained with a cloud of gore."[17] On Muly's entrances he is repeatedly identified as the "Negro Moor," "this foule ambitious Moore," "this unbelieving Moore." The combination of villainy, cruelty and blackness (Negroness) is strongly forged in this the first full scale portrait of a black man. That the historical Mulai did have a Negro mother—according to Poleman's book—can explain why Peele portrays him emphatically as a black man. But historical accuracy does not account for the concentrated effort to make the point. Nor is there a valid explanation why Sebastian, who fought and died for Muly's unholy cause of usurpation (and, in addition, was an intervening power with little justice supporting his efforts), comes through without blemish on his memory. The play's action does not justify his glorification at all, unless what is really being judged is Sebastian's goal—the propagation of the Christian faith. Muly's only concern is personal power. Whatever the reason, by the same acts of killing and attempted usurpation, the Christian is ennobled and the Moor degraded.[18]

What remains unsaid in this play also contributes to the denigration of the black man. By failing to identify positively the racial qualities of the good Moor in the play, the dramatist loses the opportunity to offer a portrait balancing Muly's evil. Abdelmelec is treated as a considerate, humane, generous person who tries to persuade Sebastian to give up a hopeless and dangerous cause and spare himself and his young troops. The picture is certainly a favorable one, but Abdelmelec is not racially distinguished in any way. Peele's omission of any reference to his skin color led Eldred Jones to believe that Abdelmelec was portrayed as a *white* Moor. However, there is no other basis for considering Abdelmelec as anything but a nonwhite. He is called a "Moor," and the word was becoming synonymous with Negro and Black-a-more, as Chapter 3 has made clear. Whatever the case might have been, the more significant point is that while the black Moor is vilified, his white confederates are ennobled, and his racially undifferentiated enemy is dignified and respected. What could likely evolve from such a pattern of judgments is the conclusion that there is something particularly evil in a black skin. In a short time the man wearing a black skin could be expected to act treacherously because he had to.

Jones, however, does not accept the analysis of the stage black man as a natural, predetermined force of evil. He argues, for example, that Aaron, one of the most insidious villains of implacable evil, is not depicted without free will. He points out that Shakespeare sought to avoid the stereotype of the Moor of innate evil by allowing Aaron to choose between grace and evil.[19] "Although he looks like the stereotype [of the devilish Moor], yet there is also a tacit suggestion in the rhymed couplet, 'Let fools do good, and fair men call for grace, / Aaron will have his soul black like his face,' that his choice of evil is deliberate."[20] Perhaps this is one possible interpretation. Yet Aaron's preference for evil instead of grace need not be a matter of free choice. Nowhere, except in his defense of his black son, one of his own kind, does he choose anything else but the baleful route of evil, and often he is moved by no deeper purpose than to quench his thirst for a revenge that seems unclearly motivated. The passage Jones quotes does, however, prove that Aaron recognizes an alternative course of action. But simple recognition that there is a choice is not proof of a capacity to exercise it. He steadfastly remains demonic in all situations except the scene in which he staunchly defends his child against those who would kill it.

In the manner of the pure Machiavellian, Aaron beams over his plans to destroy Titus's sons by accusing them of the murder of Bassianus. He plants a bag of gold near the murder scene and then offers it as evidence that Titus's sons have been paid to kill Bassianus. The whole plot gives him a keen pleasure that he must express. As he conceals the gold, he exclaims:

> Know that this gold must coin a stratagem,
> Which, cunningly effected, will beget
> A very excellent piece of villainy.[21]

Satan-like, he can either use others as his tools of evil or perform a sadistic act himself. He manipulates Demetrius and Chiron, whom he finds arguing over the right to seduce Bassianus's wife, Lavinia. He simply advises them to share her together in a violent rape and explains how easily the deed can be accomplished.

> The forest walks are wide and spacious,
> And many unfrequented plots there are,
> Fitted by kind for rape and villainy.[22]

The two unscrupulous lechers agree to follow his instructions, murder Bassianus, commit the double rape on Lavinia and then mutilate her body so that she can not expose her attackers. When Aaron finds dormant evil in these two young butchers, he awakens it and shapes its force into a criminal action which gives him joy. With a deep gusto for cruelty beyond imagination, Aaron is the paradigmatic figure of the sadistic villain. Even when he does not personally participate in inflicting pain, he takes vicarious pleasure in it. The rape of Lavinia, the brutal amputating of her hands and the cutting out of her tongue are to him great sport. Although others had the immediate pleasure from the act, he has had the satisfaction of planning it. Publicly he admits that the sons of Tamora may have learned their lechery from their mother—their "codding spirit" was her gift to them. But their "bloody minds," he boasts, are owed to him, for he had instructed them in the "washing" and "cutting" and "trimming" of Lavinia's limbs and tongue: "Twas / trim sport for them which had the doing of it."[23] Even this speech is less a confession than a joyful declaration.

Just as readily as he can structure a villainy, Aaron can perform the deed himself. He is not merely the guiding force for others. The joy of actual participation is too great. Therefore, by announcing that Titus can save his two sons by making some personal sacrifice, he lures the old man into surrendering his own hand for amputation under Aaron's blade. The fiendish brutality of such a bargain bears heavily against Aaron and gives weight to the concept of his satanism. Yet this act seems almost humane when set against its aftermath. For Aaron cold-bloodedly and unhesitatingly chops off Titus's hand and shortly thereafter sends him the heads of his sons, who were supposed to be spared. All the while he has enjoyed himself immensely. "O how this villainy / Doth fat me with the very thought of it."[24] Being finally caught by his enemies and facing death does not daunt him at all. On the contrary he expounds on the glee the entire diabolic plot has brought him.

> I play'd the cheater for thy father's hand,
> And when I had it, drew myself apart
> And almost broke my heart with extreme laughter.
> I pried me through the crevice of a wall
> When for his hand he had his two sons' heads
> Beheld his tears, and laugh'd so heartily
> That both mine eyes were rainy like to his.[25]

The sadistic pleasure Aaron has gotten extends beyond the act, for like a reminiscing lover, he has joyed also in describing to Tamora the details of his "sport" and received from her twenty kisses for a reward. Even now in his final speeches, as he retells the story, he appears to be relishing the whole scene again in his mind. His cruelty and the delight he takes in it are too sustained in the play to consider him much less than an active force of evil moving toward its own inevitable fulfillment.

Ravenscroft has maintained much of Aaron's cruelty in his adaptation of the play. In plotting the death of Bassianus and the framing of Titus's sons, Aron explains more fully what he desires. Addressing himself to the bag of gold which will convict the sons of murder, he happily expounds its nefarious power.

> Know that this Gold must Coin a Stratagem
> Which cunningly Effected will beget,
> A very Excellent piece of Villainy.
> Lye there Sweet Gold, thou poys'ner of Virtue,
> Thou powerful destroyer of all good,
> And glittering Seed of Mischief—
> When e'er thou dost appear to Eyes again,
> Sprout up a plentifull harvest of Ills,
> With Blood thou shalt be water'd, Human blood
> Shall fatten the soil, and men shall reap the crop
> In Penitence and Sorrow.[26]

Aron gloats over his accomplishments after his plans have been put into operation: Bassianus has been murdered, Lavinia raped and mutilated, and Titus's sons lured into a trap by a promise of sexual entertainment (Aron had deceived them into believing that some willing women were waiting for them in the woods):

> Ha, ha, ha, Poor early loving fools,
> How is their Amorous Expectations cross'd,
> Death wayted for their coming here, not Love,
> Woman's a sure bait to draw to ruint.
> How Easily men are to confusion hurl'd,
> 'Tis gold and women that undo the world.[27]

The obvious didactic purpose of such a speech notwithstanding, the knowledge it contains—a knowledge of man's base weaknesses—is the Moor's, and as such it puts him in a position to manipulate people for his own evil purpose.

One dramatic change that Ravenscroft does make can be thought either to extend or reduce the degree of Aron's cruelty. Instead of cutting off Titus's hand himself, Aron stands by and watches Titus cut off his own hand. In one sense, Aron is spared the savagery of executing the act himself; yet in another sense, the ultimate mental anguish that will fill Titus when he realizes he has sacrificed his hand for nothing can be ascribed to a higher sense of cruelty in Aron. When, in Shakespeare, Aaron delivers the blow, Titus's emotions can be externally objective, but when, in Ravenscroft, Titus delivers the blow himself, his final misery has to include his own partial responsibility and must be more severe. Either way, of course, the Moor's infamy is the dominant force in the play.

With other important black characters there is just as little doubt that villainy is the essence of their being. The evil that pervades the lives of black characters like Eleazer, Mulymumen, Zanthia, or Abdelazer cannot be easily offset by some positive gesture of decency, and although some of these people do faintly exhibit some capacity for human feeling—Aaron's sense of paternal loyalty, for example—it hardly mitigates the judgment against them.

Eleazer, for instance, makes a brief noble gesture on a battlefield when he declines to fight an enemy who has the marked disadvantage of being armed with a broken sword. Yet even in a climate of evil and corruption that is the world of *Lust's Dominion*, filled with lechery, deception, venality, treason, and murder, it is Eleazer's cruelty and treachery that dominate all else in the play. His opening scene shows him "boiling with fire or rage," rejecting the sexual advances of his royal paramour, the Queen Mother. Her eroticism does not blind her to the fact that her black lover is using his sexual promise as a means of tantalizing and controlling her for his own ends. When he turns from her embrace, she expostulates with him:

> I'le wage all Spain
> To one sweet kisse, this is some new device
> To make me fond and long. Oh! you men
> Have tricks to make poor women die for you.[28]

She does fail to realize, however, that "all Spain" is exactly the price he wants for that "one sweet kisse." He secretly hopes that

> ... her amorous flames
> Shall blow up the old King, consume his sons
> And make all Spain a bonfire.[29]

Although he needs the Queen Mother to advance his plans, he cannot always control his disgust, and in such moments he resorts to cruelty that appears more instinctive than deliberate. And so turning from her embrace, he callously accuses her of an insatiable lust and ridicules her appearance as "Ugly as hell." When she complains that he loved her once, he coldly replies: "That can thy bastards tell." He ends by calling her a strumpet, and defends himself against her charge that he first seduced her by declaring that her own lust has nearly destroyed him.

This void in feeling toward her indicates a deeper need to revenge himself against his enemies, the Spaniards, who have killed his father and reduced his empire. Thought of the unfulfilled desire rankles deep within him, smothering other passions before they can rise. Satan-like he dedicates himself to the spirit of vengeance:

> Sweet opportunity I'le bind my self
> To thee in base apprentice—how so long
> Till on thy naked scalp grow hair as thick
> As mine, and all hands shal lay hold on thee
> If thou wilt lend me but thy rusty sithe,
> To cut down all that stands within my wrongs,
> And my revenge.[30]

As a revenge figure of Renaissance drama, however, Eleazer is not typical. His destructive force reaches out in all directions at once to strike down the innocent as well as the guilty. He is willing to sacrifice his own wife to the lust of King Ferdinand so long as it suits his aims. The king's young sister and her suitor would also fall prey to his cruelty if he had his way. The Queen Mother herself, his all too willing mistress and partner in crime, will not escape his secret plots. The list grows longer. Two friars, whom he employs as instruments to undermine the reputation of his arch enemy Prince Philip, will die at his command. The king himself will fall beneath Eleazer's dagger thrust in a scene contrived to make the murder seem an act of just revenge. Furthermore his own faithful servants can not escape his brutalizing energy and suffer both physical abuse and verbal disparagement at his will.

Like Aaron and Eleazer the white Elizabethan revenge hero is also implacable in the pursuit of his enemy, but unlike the black spectres, he directs his wrath against specific people and maintains a core of nobility within himself. Hieronimo, Hamlet, Charlemont, and even Vindici are men highly motivated by a desire for revenge, but none grows so bloodthirsty and destructive as the black revenger. When these white avengers act, the guilty die by design; the innocent may suffer, but only by chance. The black man's revenge, on the other hand, tends to be directed not so much against individuals as against whole social orders, including both the innocent and the guilty.

> O! Saint revenge: to thee
> I consecrate my Murders, all my stabs,
> My bloody labours, torture, stratagems.
> The volume of all wounds, that wound from me,
> Mine is the stage, thine is the Tragedy.[31]

In this apostrophe to revenge, and especially in the theatrical metaphor of the last line, Eleazer declares himself an embodiment of a force external to himself. Revenge, as an independent force, provides the will; he provides the physical means to its fulfillment. In Thomas Kyd's prototype of the revenge play, *The Spanish Tragedy* (1584-89?), the figure of Revenge appears in the induction and in the chorus sections, but in the action itself, its presence is only inferred from the acts of revenge taken by the characters. In *Lust's Dominion*, however, Eleazer's words and deeds indicate that he is more of a natural force or instrument of revenge, filled with cruel destructive power, than he is a human being choosing to annihilate specific enemies who have injured him. Unwaveringly, he moves across the stage like a dark shadow in a white world, blighting all those who enter the sphere of his being. Ironically, it is only through a betrayal by one of his own black henchmen that Eleazer's power is stopped.

In his preface to the play, Dekker informed his audience that Eleazer was intended to represent cruelty and the Queen Mother to signify lust. Mrs. Aphra Behn modified the cruelty of Eleazer in the character of Abdelazer but still sustained the central driving forces within him. Revenge is still his dominant thrust, but in his invocation to its spirit there is a marked absence of bloodiness. Like Lady Macbeth's prayers to the "murdering ministers," his plea is that whatever goodness resides in him be transformed into evil so that he can carry out his vengeance.[32] To emphasize this central concern of her play, Mrs. Behn has changed the earlier title with its stress on lust (*Lust's Dominion*, 1599) to one with an emphasis on revenge (*The Moor's Revenge*, 1677). Thus even in the hands of a more moderate writer—one who, in her novel *Oroonoko* (1688), would shortly initiate a whole movement to elevate the black man to the position of noble savage—the black man still suffers the imputation of cruelty and a heathenish dedication to revenge. With attributes like these the image of the black man developed steadily and surely. Whenever he appeared on stage he could generally be counted on to act it out with gusto and glee.[33]

Jacinto in Rowley's *All's Lost for Lust* (1619), responding to Mulymumen's threat of bitter revenge for her rejection of his love, characterizes all Moors as inwardly blacker than they are externally. Cruelty is what is expected from such a creature. Mulymumen first raises the idea of the Moor's spiritual blackness himself when he says:

> If thou repell a proferred arme of love
> There will rebound a hate blacker in act
> Then in similitude.[34]

That his acts will be blacker than himself ("Then in similitude") is a promise that she will find his inner blackness deeper than his outer. Like Aaron, he has had his soul as black as (or really blacker than) his face. Typically, Jacinta recognizes his boast as a statement of truth on the moral nature of the black man. Therefore, as Mulymumen leaves with a final warning to look for his vengeance, she stigmatizes not the individual villain but his whole nation.

> Yes, some barbarous one,
> 'Tis naturall to thee, base African
> Thine inside's blacker than they sooty skin.[35]

Her experience has forced the moral equivalence between inner and outer darkness out of balance, and the ensuing action of the play in which Mulymumen mutilates and then butchers both Jacinto and her helpless father bears out this judgment.

Linking a black man with a white hero of nobility still fails to alter the basic lines of the black's character. In D'Avenant's *The History of Sir Francis Drake* (1659), for example, the renowned Drake is in Central America on a campaign against the Spaniards. His allies are a Negro people called Symerons, who escaped from Spanish slavery years before and have been living freely in the forests. Acting as guides for the English, they have proven brave and trustworthy. But the traditional savagery of the race is not easily overlooked. In a short vignette that has little to do with the overall structure of the play, the Negroes' taste for cruelty and revenge against the innocent as well as guilty is exploited. The scene depicts the English party with their black allies moving through a wood, when they suddenly break in upon a Spanish wedding in progress. D'Avenant fails to imagine any other possible reaction of the Negroes than immediate demand for the blood of the bride and groom, innocent though they may be of any crime against the blacks. The Negroes immediately seize the hapless couple.

> the Sym'rons now
> Much more than fury show;

> For they have all the cruelties exprest
> The Spanish pride could e'er provoke from them
> Or Moorish malice can revenge esteem.[36]

The savagery of these black men, then, can be understood not simply as a response to "Spanish pride" but as a reflection of their natural malice that brings them to blind revenge.

Perhaps one or two other examples of the Moor's cruelty would be sufficient proof of its place as an inherent quality of racial significance. In Rowley's *All's Lost by Lust*, Mulymumen matches point for point the inhuman cruelty of Aaron and Eleazer. As an unrelenting figure of treachery and lust, he delights in a cruelty no less sadistic than that of either of his predecessors. Like them he plots for revenge and power and takes an obvious joy in his bloody acts for their own sake. He treacherously turns against those who have helped him and destroys them with the same gusto he wars against his enemies. A simple destruction of those who antagonize him is not sufficient revenge; he devises, instead, fiendish methods to crush them. His treatment of Julianus and his daughter fully dramatizes his savagery. Julianus, the Spanish general, has assisted Mulymumen in gaining his liberty from a Spanish prison and achieving great power in Spain. In return, Mulymumen attempts to seduce his daughter Jacinto. Because the reluctant girl rejects his advances, denouncing his inner blackness, Mulymumen seizes her father and orders him to be blinded. He then has Jacinto's tongue cut out so that she ". . . shall in silent sorrow then lead him, / Her eyes shall be his starres."[37]

When he finally achieves total power as ruler of Spain, Mulymumen's force of evil is implacable. As he watches the two women Margaretta and Donysia commit suicide over the dead body of their beloved Antonia, his wry comment is "Excellent pastime." At this very moment the mutilated Jacinto enters, leading Julianus, his dignity and glory now gone like his eyesight. At the sight of the pathetic old Julianus, Mulymumen laughs demoniacally. Then, by promising the fallen hero an opportunity to earn a soldier's noble death, he diabolically tricks him into killing his own daughter. He offers Julianus the chance to die in combat by permitting the old general to strike at him with a sword and receive a sword blow in return. Julianus expresses his gratitude to Mulymumen for granting him a soldier's death. But when, in his blindness, he makes his thrust, the cunning Moor pushes Jacinto in front of him to die impaled on the sword of her miserable father. The sight tickles the Moor's fancy, and his laughter rings across the stage.[38] As the play closes, the picture of the deadly Moor expands in Mulymumen's last speech into a kind of verbalized prototype of Moors in western culture. Mulymumen proudly calls on the historians of the future to take special measure of his ascension to the Spanish throne. "Let Chroniclers write, here we begin our reigne, / The first of Moores that ere was King of Spaine."

Having defined himself as a symbol of evil, he proudly suggests the possible successors of others like himself.

These Moors have shown little compunction in their actions. Unhesitatingly they stalk from one deadly act to another. They "never think of conscience;/ there is none to a man resolved." The resolution they embrace seems always to serve an ungodly cause. The barbaric quality of their acts of cruelty, treachery, and pitilessness is not limited to any one act but extends into some peripheral details of the black man's cultural practices, as white authors purported they were. Acts of cannibalism and castration, for example, are ascribed to the black man in such a way as to seem common or natural behavior. In the second part of *The Fair Maid of the West*, the black Mullisheg suggests that young Clem would be a suitable servant in the court harem and offers the position to him. The doltish Clem does not understnad Mullisheg's allusions to a "taste of the razor" that is a condition of eligibility, and he lightly accepts. With just as little fuss as though they were taking him to a barber shop, the Moors lead him off stage and return him a short while later, a qualified eunuch. But now he curses them for what has so casually happened. The whole episode serves little more than to round out a view of the Moor's barbarous character.

In the earlier play by Peele, *The Battle of Alcazar*, other atrocious practices of the black man are put on show to create a more vivid picture of the savagery of black men. Muly's ambassadors to Portugal, for instance, offer proof to Sebastian of their master's sincerity by thrusting their naked hands into a fire to scorch their flesh.

> We offer heere our hands into this flame,
> And as this flame doth fasten on this flesh,
> So from our soules we wish it may consume
> The heart of our great Lord and soveraigne
> Muly Mahamet king of Barbarie
> If his intent agree not with his words.[39]

In the same play, Muly's crude nature is exposed when he and his family are fleeing from defeat. To supply food for his family he somehow has managed to seize raw meat from a lionness who has made a kill. He enters on stage carrying the bloody raw meat spitted on his sword and offers it to his wife for her dinner. His manner is not apologetic but rather boastful as though the rough fare he is providing is consistent with their daily diet. To her credit, though, Calipolis, his wife, genteely prefers not to eat and offers as an excuse her "quasie stomach." As barbaric as he appears, she seems civilized and sensible and becomes one of the few Moors in the whole body of the drama to exhibit such qualitites.

In other plays the black man, with his reputation as a barbarian, was frequently linked with medieval notions of the monstrous creatures supposedly inhabiting the African continent. In *Orlando Furioso*, Orlando talks of "the savage Moors and anthropagei" (1,1,111) and refers to these peoples as "cannibals" (1,1,117) lumping them together in the same class. Ravenscroft also raises the subject of cannibalism when he depicts Aron, on seeing Tamora stab their black infant, calling out angrily for the corpse in order to eat it. Unlike Shakespeare's Tamora, who does little more than provide the Moor with a safe base for his evil machinations, in the later version, Tamora, as she lies dying, calls for the black child Aron has fathered on her and then stabs it in vengeance. Aron's shock is over being surpassed in evil. The thought that he might be outdone moves him to go one step further in his bestiality:

> She has out-done me in my own Art—
> Out-done me in Murder—Kill'd her own child.
> Give it to me—I'le eat it.[40]

If Tamara has the cruelty to commit infanticide, he can outdo her through cannibalism.

Not only in name, then, was the Moor believed to be a devil. His actions, his tastes, his language—all proclaimed him a creature of villainy, a being whose basic humanity was certainly to be questioned. When the travelers and cosmographers, the ethnologists and cartographers made their "scientifically objective" report to the white European, they declared the black man to be animalistic, brutal, corrupt, and inferior. Much of the reporting was based on hearsay and imagination, although some concrete sociological evidence was offered. But because there was no sufficient attempt to understand what they saw or to allow for variety and differences among the people they described, the writers tended to develop a single perspective of the black man that emphasized those traits which, when measured against white criteria, could only be debasing and even dehumanizing. To worsen matters considerably, the dramatists of the sixteenth and seventeenth centuries, with but few exceptions, failed to transcend imaginatively the stock responses of the reporters. Their portraits of the black man largely corresponded to the disparaging views they found in their sources, whether those were written or hearsay; thus almost all black stage characters wore the face of villainy.

Dekker, in concluding his treatment of the black man in *Lust's Dominion*, unwittingly expressed this syndrome that leads men to be inclusive in their judgments of aliens. The young Philip, representative of white Christian Spain, announces imperiously: "And for this Barbarous Moor, and his black train, / Let all the Moors be banished from Spain."[41] Thus did the black man of the stage, growing out of the stories and legends of the travelers, develop early into portraits of villains like Mulymumen, Aaron and Eleazer, into stereotypes that doubtlessly satisfied some psychological need of the white writers and their audiences. Thus, too, do almost all Moors, with Eleazer, seem to have been banished from the realms of goodness and humanity.

Chapter 6

The Erotic Moor

> For Southward, Men are cruell moody, madd,
> Hot, blacke, leane, leapers, lustful.

When John Davies of Hereford wrote these lines, he was poetically tracing what he felt was the influence of geography upon the human temperament.[1] Like many others of his time, he accepted as fact the belief that torrid climates produced men of melancholy nature who were as cruel as they were black, as moody as they were hot, and, more importantly, as libidinous as they were depraved. Actually of all the traits that were discovered in or attributed to the black man, none was more intriguing to the white European than his sexual power. Another versifying commentator in seventeenth-century ethnography gave his view on complexion and character in the form of friendly advice:

> To a red man, reade thy reed;
> With a brown man breake thy bread;
> At a pale man draw thy knife;
> From a black man keep thy wife.[2]

The sex drive of the black man, it was generally supposed, was unhampered by a Christian conscience and freed from any self-imposed moral restraint; such licence could make him a dangerous threat to the white man's female, and undoubtedly to the white man's own ego. His capacious sexual hunger, served by the formidable combination of cruelty and diabolic cunning, could not be ignored. Writers would exploit it, not for its sensationalism alone but out of a response to cultural pressures to view the black man as depraved.[3] That there appeared to be such little sexual restraint among black people only deepened the belief in their affinity with creatures of a lower order and furthermore justified their subjugation into slavery. The creative literature of the period seems to follow the same fairly sharp pattern of cultural beliefs and taboos concerning the sex life of the black man, especially when it involved white people, as it usually did in the plays. The sexual nature of black women, their relationship with white men and black, the prowess of black men and their danger to white women, the nature of white people who could submit to miscegenation—all these sexual ramifications raised by racial confrontation are consistently manipulated by the writers: they leave little doubt as to the current definition of sexual "normality" and "depravity."

Shakespeare himself provides one of the earliest references to the reputed moral looseness of black people, especially of black women, who were generally considered to be easy. Although no black woman actually appears in *The Merchant of Venice*, a Negro is mentioned by Lorenzo as he engages in a duel of wits with the clown Launcelot. Launcelot teases Lorenzo with the thought that his marriage to a Jew and her conversion to Christianity have raised the price of pork. The young lord's reply unexpectedly alludes to an affair Launcelot seems to have had with a Negro woman. Lorenzo claims that he could more readily justify his marriage to a Jew than Launcelot could his copulation with a black woman.

> Lorenzo   I shall answer that better to the commonwealth
> than you can the getting up of the Negro's belly.
> The Moor is with child by you, Launcelot.

In a tricky play on words Launcelot answers saucily that the Moorish woman is no better than she should be; that is, he implies that she is little better than a prostitute and that is a suitable role for her.

> Launcelot   It is much that the Moor should be than
> reason; but if she be less than an honest
> woman, she is indeed more than I took her
> for.[4]

This reputation of the availability of black women as prostitutes—some were known as the "black prostitutes of London"—has been cited by G. B. Harrison, who calls attention to several little-known volumes of poetry that contain references to them. In 1598 Edward Guilpin published a collection of epigrams called *Skealethia*, four of which (57, 61, 62, and 65) satirize a loose woman named Nigrina. To protect her "painted face," she frequently wears a black mask indicating that she is a prostitute. In number sixty-one the poet calls her a "light wench" who cares "not for light." In number sixty-five he ridicules her use of a mask.

> Because Nigrina hath a painted face,
> Many suspect her to be light and base;
> I see no reason to repute her such,
> For out of doubt she will abide the tuch.[5]

G. B. Harrison concludes that Guilpin's use of the name "Nigrina" was intended to relate this woman who "abides the tuch," with the black prostitutes of London. Harrison also tentatively identifies the "Lucy Negro" who appears in *Gray's Inns Revels* with the "courtesan" dark lady of Shakespeare's sonnets.[6] He quotes a letter from Denis Edwards to Thomas Lankford, secretary to the Earl of Hertford: "Pray enquire after and secure my negress; she is certainly at the Swan, a Dane's beershop, Turnbull Street, Clerkenwell." To Harrison this reference substantiates the presence of black prostitutes in London and hence the use of names like "Lucy Negro" to refer to courtesans. Furthermore, he singles out another epigram in John Weever's *Epigrams* (1599) to note the association of moral laxity (indicated by the use of the mask) with black women.

> Is Byrrha browne? who doth the question aske?
> Her face is pure as Ebonie jeate blacke,
> It's hard to know her face from her fair maske,
> Beautie in her seems beautie still to lacke.
> Nay, shee's snow-white, but for that russet skin,
> Which like a vaile doth keep her whiteness in.[7]

Although the black prostitute was evidently well known in London, black women on the stage were more often portrayed as bawds, serving the lusts of white men by acting as procurors of white women, than as sexual partners themselves. Like Francis Bacon's "Spirit of Fornication," who, when called upon to appear, turned out to be an Ethiope,[8] so the personification of bawdiness was also an Ethiope.

> . . . hale me from my sleep like forked Devils,
> Midnight, thou Aethiope, Empresse of Black
> Souls, Thou general
> Bawde to the whole world.[9]

The bawdy Moorish woman is usually depicted relishing her role as procuror, for she is highly sexed herself, and her motive is one of lust rather than a greed for gold. What she hopes to get for her services is some sexual gratification herself from the very man she assists. Thus black women are shown lusting after white men in a manner totally self-debasing. The earliest dramatized example of such a black libertine is the Zanthia of Marston's *Wonder of Women, Sophonisba* (1606), who is ever ready to betray her mistress to the villain and would-be seducer Syphax. Her sense of loyalty to Sophonisba is a flimsy defense against a direct attack on her sexual susceptibilities. Syphax flatters her with a few words, supports his promises with a kiss, and then offers her gold if she will help him rape Sophonisba. But that last offer of gold is superfluous. For the sake of his promised love alone, Zanthia is eager to help him to her mistress's body.

> Syphax Zanthia, Zanthia!
> Thou are not foul, go to; some lords are oft
> So much in love with their known ladies' bodies,
> That they often love their—Vails [Maids];
>   hold, hold, thou'st find
> To faithful care kings' bounty hath no shore.

His cry "hold, hold" evidently is to ward off the embraces she has thrust on him.

> Zanthia You may do much.
>
> Syphax But let my gold do more.[10]

Contrary to his promises and despite his own depravity, Syphax, it seems, would still prefer to pay the Moor with gold than with kisses. Villains were no different from other men in this way: they were just as reluctant to involve themselves sexually with black women.

Sophonisba, however, has knowledge of the general untrustworthiness of all servants, and her speech denouncing this weakness, interestingly enough, does not focus on black servants only but rather on the whole class of servants.

> But above all, O fear a servant's tongue
> Like such as only for their gain do serve.
> Within the vast capacity of space,
> I know no vileness so most truly base.
> Their lord's their gain; and he that most will give,
> With him (they will not die, but) they will live.[11]

Perhaps to Marston's credit, the easy opportunity here to further debase the woman for her blackness was not taken. Perhaps Marston was illuminating a broadmindness in his "wonder of women" and deliberately avoided giving her the tunnel vision of racial prejudice. Although Sophonisba does stereotype the servant, her perspective is not formed by racial bias, and so Zanthia, though she does not escape an impugning of her moral character on the dramatic level, does escape from a direct verbal attack on her racial identity. Of course, in the final analysis she still appears as "a type of the light waiting-woman who is easily corrupted because of her lustful inclinations."[12]

John Webster's *The White Devil* (1611) provides a fuller treatment of the Moorish woman servant, but the greater attention permits only greater attack on her character. The play is heavily laden with characters of corruption and vice who generate an environment of overwhelming evil. Those who plot and those who are instruments for plots almost deny the possible existence of goodness. The Moorish woman seems well suited to this world of active evil, and her connection with the adventurous self-seeker Flamineo is natural.

Each is a tool for others to use. The hireling of the wealthy Duke Brachiano, Flamineo, has bribed the Moor Zanche to arrange a convenient time and place for a liaison to develop between his master and his own sister Vittorio, the white devil herself. Flamineo comments on the delight Zanche takes in playing a part in an erotic affair.

> I have dealt already with her chambermaid,
> Zanche the Moor; and she is wondrous proud
> To be the agent for so high a spirit.[13]

When Zanche first appears, she is carrying the accoutrements for sexual activity: a carpet and two fair cushions. Her only words concerning Brachiano's opening sexual gesture to the receptive Vittoria are voyeuristically approving: "See," she gloats, "now they close."[14]

Later, at Vittoria's trial for adultery, Zanche is accurately designated by the prosecutor Monticelso as Vittoria's "bawd."[15] But like Zanthia of Marston's play, she appears to have acted not for the sake of money but for the promise of Flamineo's love. When these two meet again in act five, she berates him for his coolness, and he admits to his friend Hortenso that he had offered her marriage once and now fears to deny her because of her threat to destroy him. But Zanche will not let his disdain discourage her. Her unsightliness, she hopes, can be mitigated by cosmetics and dress. She coaxes him: "Believe it, a little painting and gay clothes make you love me."[16] At that moment Flamineo's distraught mother Cornelia enters and ironically orders the Moor to a whorehouse, knowing quite well that her own daughter Vittoria is as much a whore as her black servant. Zanche lewdly replies that Cornelia is "good for nothing, but to make her maids / Catch cold a nights; they dare not use a bed-staff / For fear of her light fingers."[17]

Marcello, Cornelia's other son, then steps in, calls Zanche a strumpet and kicks her. Their condemnation of Zanche's sexual morals or lack of them is justified by the text. As soon as she resigns herself to the hopelessness of securing Flamineo for a lover or husband, she brashly offers her love to the disguised Francisco de Medici, masquerading as a Moor. Her approach is blunt and public. "I ne'er loved my complexion till now, 'cause I / may boldly say, without a blush, I love."[18] Francisco puts her off, complaining of his advanced years and his vow to celibacy. But Zanche stubbornly thinks that it is her poverty that inhibits him and therefore she promises that she can acquire a dowry for which he might love her. Virtue, she feels, need be of little consequence in provoking a love. She would as soon "be better loved for my dowry than my virtue."[19] She feels no misgiving over aggressively bribing him for his love, and simply admits that she is burning with desire for him. "Nor blame me that this passion I reveal; / Lovers die inward that their flames conceal."[20] When she meets Francisco again, she unabashedly describes a dream she has had of him as a sexual partner. "Methought, sir, you came stealing to my bed." Whether the dream was actual or only contrived to lure him to an affair, the disguised duke pretends to be interested in the implicit offer and plays along with her story of a dream.

Fran. de Med	Wilt thou believe me, sweeting? by this light
	I was a-dreamt on thee too; for methought
	I saw thee naked.
Zanche	Fie, sir! As I told you,
	Methought you lay down by me.
Fran. de Med.	So dreamt I;
	And lest thou shouldst take cold, I covered thee
	With this Irish mantle.
Zanche	Verily I did dream
	You were somewhat bold with me; but to come
	to it . . .[21]

At this point she is evidently so aroused by the thoughts of copulation that she moves unashamedly to embrace him in the presence of his attendants. Her behavior brings a startled retort from Lodovico, one of de Medici's attendants. "How, how! I hope you will not go to't here."[22]

The image of the black woman in heat is fully outlined in these scenes; in future decades this same image would become the means to mitigate the guilt of those men who would make the black woman an outlet for sex and blame her aggressiveness for their own lusts.[23]

In Webster's play, however, the white men want no part of what Zanche is offering. Lodovico is finally provoked by the titillated Zanche to degrade her by comparing her appearance to dirty bath water: "Mark her, I prithee; she simpers like the suds / A collier hath been washed in."[24] But the only bath Zanche hopes to wash in is a dowry of a hundred thousand crowns which she has stolen from Vittoria. She thinks that when she offers it to her "black" lover (we recall that Francisco is disguised as a Moor) the gold will bleach her skin white and make her more desirable.

> . . . It is a dowry,
> Methinks, should make that sun-burnt proverb false,
> And wash the Aethiop white.[25]

Her hope that riches will lighten the color of her skin significantly supports the belief that black men themselves were considered to prefer white women to those of their own race.

A similar but more villainous black bawd is the treacherous Zanthia of Fletcher's *The Knight of Malta*. For the sake of the embraces of the white Lord Mountferrat, she connives to arrange for him to rape her mistress

Oriana, depicted as a paradigm of virtue. Earlier, Mountferrat, by proclaiming his love to Oriano, abrogated his vow of chastity sworn by his order of knighthood. The fire in his blood has burned hotter than the flame of his honor.[26] When Oriana flatly refused to accept his proposal, he turns to Zanthia whom he finds willing to assist him to Oriana's body in exchange for his love.

Like her counterparts in the plays of Marston and Webster, Zanthia lacks any conscience in the fulfillment of her own lust, and like her earlier namesake, she is bothered not at all over the thought of helping her lover to enjoy the body of another woman. Her open sexuality is freely professed in the looseness of her language as she talks with Oriana, who has in the meanwhile been married to the knight Gomera. Zanthia argues that a soldier is the best kind of husband a woman could have. A military man, she explains, wants nothing more from his wife than what she can easily and pleasurably grant him: sexual gratification. The soldier brings his booty home to lay at his wife's feet.

> . . . and seeks no further
> For his reward than what she may give freely
> And with delight too, from her own exchequer
> Which he finds ever open.[27]

When Oriana, who is visibly pregnant, scolds her for her immodesty, Zanthia bluntly protests what she takes to be stark reality:

Zanthia	Why, we may speak of that we are glad to taste of, Among ourselves I mean.
Oriana	Thou talk'st of nothing.
Zanthia	Of nothing, madam? You have it something; Or, with raising up this pretty mount here My lord hath dealt with spirits.[28]

It is this reputation of a dominant libido in black people that first leads Mountferrat to tempt Zanthia to help him in his pursuit of Oriana. Knowing that as a black woman she must be sexually viable, he appeals to her through a declaration of love:

> Oh, my Zanthia,
> My pearl that scorns a stain! I much repent
> All my neglects; let me, Ixion-like,
> Embrace my black cloud, since my Juno is
> So wrathful and averse. Thou art more soft
> And full of dalliance than the fairest flesh,
> And far more loving.[29]

Always conscious that Zanthia is aware of her color, Mountferrat does not naively ignore it but brings to it a loving attention just as he flatters her sexuality. "Oh, my black swan, silkier than cygnet's plush, / Sweeter than is the sweet of pomander."[30] Listening to these persuasive words of a man of distinctive social rank, Zanthia is immediately ready to admit her love. She confesses that her black skin prevents her from playing the coquette. Unlike the white woman who can blush "yes" while mouthing "no," she must be open and unashamed.

> My tongue, sir, cannot lisp to meet you so,
> Nor my black cheek put on a feigned blush,
> To make me seem more modest than I am.
> The groundwork will not bear adulterate red,
> Nor artificial white to cozen love.[31]

She is compelled to emphasize the naturalness of her appearance and the frankness of her love. She continues her confession by promising him that, black though she is, she can offer him sexual pleasure beyond the scope and capacity of a white woman to give. She needs no cosmetics to beautify herself; her natural looks are matched by her natural and unrestrained sexuality.

> These dark looks are not purchased, nor these teeth,
> For every night they are my bed-fellows;
> No bath, no blanching water, smoothing oils,
> Doth mend me up; and yet Mountferrat, know,
> I am as full of pleasure in the touch
> As e'er a white-faced puppet of 'em all,
> Juicy and firm; unfledge them of their tires,
> Their wires, their partlets, sins, and perriwigs,
> And they appear like bald-coates, in the nest;
> I can blithly work in my love's bed,
> And deck they fair neck with these jetty chains,
> Sing thee asleep, being wearied; and refresh'd
> With the same organ, steal sleep off again.[32]

The speech is not only a devastating expose of current practices in cosmetics but a glowing assessment of the rich sensuality of the black woman, bold and aggressive in her pursuits, seductive in her temptation.

The relationship between Zanthia's blackness and the sexual fire it contains is restated in the next act when she offers him compensatory love after he has failed to enjoy Oriana.

> Am I not here?
> As lovely in my black to entertain thee,
> As high and full of heat to meet thy pleasures?[33]

Zanthia's charms, however, are not so palatable to Mountferrat's taste as he has led her to believe. In an early speech he privately reveals his emotional responses to the thought of an interracial liaison. Without denying Zanthia a basic humanity (which will ultimately be superseded by a spirit of demonism rising through her own actions and the treatment of others), he limits the extent of a physical union with a black-skinned person and indicates the white man's distaste for blackness. He understands full well that it is only the stirrings of a libidinous drive not to be denied that makes Zanthia acceptable as a sexual mate. But, he adds, her blackness is too much of an obstacle in the eye, and therefore must be obliterated in darkness. The white libido can serve itself freely and unbiasedly only in the dark where all women are alike.

> It is not love, but strong libidinous will
> That triumphs o'er me; and to satiate that,
> What difference 'twixt this Moor, and her fair dame.
> Night makes their hues alike, their use is so,
> Whose hand's so subtle he can colours name,
> If he do wink, and touch 'em? Lust, being blind,
> Never in women did distinction find.[34]

A different aspect of the black woman's sexual notoriety is suggested in another play when a white lecher determines to seduce a Moor even at some jeopardy to himself. Richard Brome's *The English Moor* (1637) presents a rakehell whose reaction to a woman he supposes to be black adds another degrading detail to the popular conception of the black woman and her sexual nature: intimacy with a Moor could be injurious to one's health. Nathaniel, a confirmed fornicator, catches sight of Millicent, who has been disguised as a Moor for the explicit purpose of keeping her out of the hands of the likes of Nathaniel. But what Millicent and her husband have not reckoned with is the possibility that some men are governed by such extraordinary lust that a black skin is no barrier to their desire. Nathaniel, furthermore, recognizes that black skin is not the only possible obstacle he must overcome. He also remarks that the Moor might very well be diseased. Yet neither thought is enough to prevent him. That a man needs a "good stomack" to "clap your Barbary buttock" is recognition of the revulsion Brome supposed white people feel at the thought of interracial copulation. That there is something unwholesome and even dangerous about intercourse with a Moor is an additional slur on her nature as a normal human being.

> He keeps this Rie-loaf for his own white tooth
> With confidence none will cheat him of a bit;
> Ile have a sliver though I lose my whittle.[35]

The extent of the belief in the oversexed black female can be inferred from references to her in the casual conversations of white characters. For example, Jonson's elderly lecher Volpone entices the young Celia with promises of sexual variety that he can promote to sustain their sex life at an intensity limited only by his rich imagination. He will have her dressed in different costumes from a variety of countries to make her seem a different woman each time she comes to him. His description of the roles he envisions for her reads like a list of current national stereotypes. She will be the "Sprightly dame of France," or a "Brave Tuscan lady," then a "proud Spanish beauty," or an "artful courtesan," now a "cold Russian." But she will also entice him as a "quick Negro," the word "quick" connoting a burning, vibrant vitality, which in Volpone's mood can only mean a sexual one.[36]

The reputed lack of restraint among black people was thought to lead not only to sexual intensity and promiscuity but to premature sexual experiences as well. At least one playwright, Philip Massinger, alluded to the unusually early sexual fulfillment of black people that white culture would find crudely animalistic. In his play *A Very Woman* (1634), Massinger imagines a slave market in Sicily where, among other slaves, are two Moorish children for sale. The slave trader gives his honest appraisal of their worth:

> . . . they'll do little
> That shall offend you, for their chief desire
> Is to do nothing at all, sir.[37]

A citizen finally purchases the young Moors as amusing playthings, subhuman and unfeeling. But then he raises the questions of their sexual potential.

Cit.   I'll have them, if it be to sing in cages.

Merch.   Give them hard eggs, you never had such black birds.

Cit.   Is she a maid, dost think?

Merch.   I dare not swear, sir:
        She is nine year old, at ten you shall find few here.[38]

Lines like these in the early literary response to the black race prove that there were strong and persistent tendencies to dehumanize the black female, sometimes by emphasizing her animal-like sexuality, sometimes by describing her as unworthy of producing from white men anything more than a conditional sexual interest void of any deeper or more tender feelings. What the writers were doing, in effect, was to create a demeaning image of the black woman and to define the normal and expected behavior of white men toward her.

In the whole literature of the period no writer seems to have imagined the possibility of a love deeper than physical lust existing between a white man and a black woman. The fact that black women could love white men is illustrated in Zanthia's attachment to Mountferrat. She says that if she

>   ... thought
>   There was a hell hereafter, or a Heaven
>   But in enjoying him, I should stick here,
>   And move no further. Bid him yet take comfort;
>   For something I will do the devil will quake at.[39]

She is willing to die for him, but not he for her. As a matter of fact, in the final view, the harshest punishment the white society can inflict on Mountferrat is a forced marriage with Zanthia.

It was not thought likely, then, that a white male could return to a black woman such devotion as she might offer him. The poems of Herbert, Rainolds, and King make that point quite clear. Philip Massinger's *The Parliament of Love* (1624), also contains passages that illuminate the improbability of such a relationship between a white male and black female. Clarindore, a lustful rakehell, is trying to seduce Bellisant, who firmly rebuffs him. He turns his attentions, therefore, to the Moor Calisto, who is really the white Beaupre in disguise. She voices her surprise that her dark complexion has not inhibited him from making the sexual approach. "Like me Sir! / One of my dark complexion!"[40] The response is a simple, matter-of-fact statement of her culture's tendency to view members of the black race as repulsive. Clarindore implicitly accepts that attitude, but he is one of those erotic men whose sexual drives override cultural inhibition. He hardly flatters her by pleading on the same grounds that enabled Mountferrat to consider copulating with Zanthia. What light can vivify, darkness can conceal. At night, he argues, or in the shadows of a curtained room, her dark skin will be no hindrance at all.

>   I am serious:
>   The curtain drawn, and envious light shut out,
>   The soft touch heightens appetite, and takes more
>   Thou colour, Venus' dressing, in the day time
>   But never thought on in her midnight revels.[41]

The scholarly Ben Jonson, who was just as sensitive to the warp and woof of contemporary London life as to the form and structure of classical literature, was still another writer who expressed his awareness of the disdain white men would hold toward black women. The *Mask of Blackness* asserts that black skin is patently inferior to white skin and proclaims the superiority of the English over the African. Lines from *Volpone* go somewhat further by characterizing Moors as sexually base and revolting. Mosca, Volpone's servant, is attempting to persuade the greedy old Corvina, who hopes to inherit Volpone's wealth, that Volpone has no legitimate heirs, but only bastards he has fathered on low and repugnant women. Volpone, Mosca claims, has gotten "Some dozen or more on beggars, Gypsies, and Jews and blackmoors "[42] This allusion to four groups of undesirables at first seems more a slur on Volpone's lechery than on them; however, it turns out to be more a derogation of the women themselves when, at the close of his speech, Mosca adds an exonerating afterthought that the old man copulated with these creatures only when he was drunk. Although he needed to exaggerate Volpone's carnality, Mosca still could not go so far as to attribute to him a sober sexual interest in such women, who were obviously considered the very dregs of a social order.

This same expectation that a white man could not love a black woman except under the strongest erotic impulses is nearly upset by the little-known play *The Thracian Wonder* (1599). Now considered of uncertain authorship, the play was once attributed to John Webster. It contains a subplot that shows a white Thracian youth falling romantically in love with the daughter of the King of Africa. It is quite clear that King Alcade is dark-skinned, for he contrasts his own appearance with the "pale skins" of the Europeans. His daughter, however, turns out in act 5 to be white, thus justifying the love affair between her and the Caucasian youth. What is odd, however, is that a reading of the first four acts of the play leaves her color in doubt. Although her name is Lillia Guida, perhaps suggestive of a light skin, and although there is a passage in which her ". . . beauty shines / Like a star amongst so many clouds / Of her own nature,"[43] it is still not certain, according to the text, that she is meant to be white, especially because it is definite that her father is dark. But in the last act the author seems to grow conscious of the ambiguity, as it may confuse the casting or costuming of the part. He therefore rather clumsily takes steps to clarify his conception of the princess. When she appears in earlier scenes, the stage directions note her entrance by her name "Lillia." Now in act 5 two separate stage directions use another phrase to mark her entrance with her father: "Enter Alcade and a white Moor." Since she is the only other Moor present, the term designates her, and the reader of the play can finally realize what was immediately apparent to a theater audience on Lillia's first appearance: daughter of Africa notwithstanding, she is white. Her Thracian paramour, therefore, has been romantically in love with a white woman, and in clear conscience. The implicit demands of the culture have been met all along.

A woman, then, Moorish or not, must be white to qualify for a white man's love. A Caucasian male who seeks to break this cultural pattern separating the races—that is, by seeking a serious attachment with a black woman— can only debase himself and his race. No doubt the total absence of any such relationship between white man and black woman in the literature of the period is further proof of how cultural pressures affect the imaginations of writers. On a level of animal sexuality, a white man could be thought capable of engaging a black woman; but even then, the man was portrayed as corrupt, and his behavior and language made it quite clear that he realized the woman was a base creature, deserving only his lust and often his scorn. In this way the creative writers were wittingly or unwittingly sustaining the belief in the inferiority and animality of a race that had already been harshly enslaved by a white society.

It hardly matters whether the mood of the plays is serious or not; the inevitable result of the interracial episodes is to place the black character in a subordinate place in the world of men. Even in a flimsy scene like the one in Berkeley's *The Lost Lady* (1637), two rakes make the Moorish woman appear thoroughly distasteful. Phormio sees the woman Arcanthe, who is disguised as a Moorish fortune teller. He is suddenly seized by a whim to seduce her; yet he recognizes that his feelings are abnormal. "I have a strange capricio of love entered me; I must court that shad."[44] Arcanthe turns him away, but his friend Cleon, seeing the fun in the situation, urges him to pursue the matter with a kiss. The language he chooses dehumanizes the Moor and adheres to the traditional idea of her deep sensuality.

> Cleon   Dost thou not see that all the fire is out of the coal?
>   If thou wouldst have it burn lay thy lips to the spark
>   that's left, and blow it into flames.
>
> Phormio   What wouldst thou have me do?
>
> Cleon   Kiss her.
>
> Phormio   Not for five hundred crowns.
>
> Cleon   Wouldst lie with her and not kiss her?
>
> Phormio   Yes, and can give reasons for't besides experience;
>   and when this act is known—this resolute encounter,
>   rich widows of threescore will not doubt my prowess [45]

A kiss is a declaration of affection for the receiver, an acknowledgement of the humanity and equality of the partners. Copulation, on the other hand, may be necessary and gratifying, but it can remain on the animal level without the kiss and still be satisfying. With a black woman, the kiss is too much to give; if the white disposition against blackness did not extend to the intimacy of the body, it did to that of the lips. And the body is Phormio's interest. His last line in the scene above obviously implies a common belief: mating with a black woman, in the light of her reputed sexual drives, requires not affection but great stamina. The news of such a feat, Phormio feels, can only enhance his reputation for sexual virility.

With the same racial handicap that excludes black women from the interests or affections of men other than low fornicators like Phormio, black men, excepting one, find "decent" white women deaf to their overtures of love and sex.[46] Actually, the extent of a white woman's decency appears often to be measured by her appraisal of and reaction to proposed miscegenation.

In *Two Gentlemen of Verona* (1594), Shakespeare cites the proverbial attraction the black man has for white women.

> Proteus   . . . and the old saying is
>   'Black men are pearls in beauteous ladies' eyes.'[47]

This male response to the black man's attractive sexuality is a corollary to the white belief that black men are always in pursuit of white women The threat in that combination gives rise to a remark such as Proteus's. Writers who dramatize interracial courtships in their works, however, are more likely to deny the possibility that a virtuous white woman could love a black man. Shakespeare, again, in the same scene defines the traditional attitude that a white man could expect from a morally good white woman. Julia, the charming heroine, answers Proteus's quote of the old proverb: " 'Tis true! such pearls as put out ladies' eyes, / For I had rather wink than look on them."[48] Shakespeare would later develop the power to imagine the possibility of a deep, devoted love evoked by a black man in the heart of a good white woman although the real nature of that man is still highly disputable. But most writers, including the early Shakespeare, allowed only the oversexed, corrupted white female to give herself willingly to a black man. The simple state of her willingness to enter such a relationship would mark a tendency toward evil.

The Moor's Revenge (1687), contains a definitive scene with respect to this cultural judgment and confirms Mrs. Behn's thorough familiarity with the ramifications of the black man's dilemma in a white society that was profiting so heavily from his enslavement. In act 5 Alonzo, who was once a friend of the Moor's, now exposes his deeply ingrained prejudices when he measures the Queen Mother's capacity for evil by the touchstone of her union with the black Abdelazer. Speaking emotionally to the Moor, he blurts out: "And she that cou'd love you, might after that / Do any other sin." Abdelazer angrily demands to know what is so inherently wrong about loving a black man. He proclaims his human qualities and demands the right to be loved like any other man. "How, Sir! that cou'd love me! What is there here, / Or in my Soul, or Person, may not be belov'd?" Somewhat dismayed by the accusation of racial bigotry, Alonzo recovers quickly and denies he has intended a racial slur. What he means, he protests, is that a woman who will commit adultery can be expected to do even worse. "I spoke without Reflection on your Person, / But of dishonest Love."[49] His denial, however, is weak and ineffective. Mrs. Behn knew that in white society loving a black man would signify a moral deformity.

Whenever such a relationship does develop, the deformity that creates it is clearly one of a voracious sexual appetite seeking satisfaction where tradition already determined it could be found—in the embraces of a black man. An early but minor exploitation of the black man's reputed sexual prowess and its attraction for the immoral white woman is in Chapman's *The Blind Beggar of Alexandria* (1596). In a tale of the philandering Cleanthe, who deceives two sisters into false marriages with him and keeps them in separate homes, Elimine, one of the young women with the same libido as her "husband," seeks and secures another lover shortly after she "marries." She has complained that her husband is absent from home every other night (fulfilling his obligations as "husband" to her sister) and now determines to put her freedom to good use, which actually means increasing her sexual activity:

> My husband makes as if each other night he had occasion,
> To ride from home at home serves not his turne,
> To my good turne it, Cupid I beseech you.[50]

Immediately following this request, she accepts a lover and, though he happens to be her own Cleanthe in disguise, the basic nature of her character has been clearly marked by lechery. The significance of this development becomes clearer when, later in the play, Elimine, in an advanced state of pregnancy, loses her "husband." Through a fanciful manipulation of plot, however, she finds herself with an opportunity to choose a husband from among four petty kings recently captured in battle. With her pregnant condition a visible symbol of her sexual promiscuity, it is not surprising that she chooses the black-skinned king of Aethiopia, Porus. Her judgment that he is more suitable to her needs is implicit.

> In my eye now the blackest is the fayrest,
> For every woman chooseth white and red,
> Come martiall Porus thou shalt have my love.[51]

Being singled out by a bawdy woman is, of course, a dubious honor, but the ridicule of Porus has already been anticipated by the earlier ludicriousness of Porus' instantaneous obsession with the swollen-bellied white woman. It was love at first sight, he proclaims:

> For neare did eye behold a fayrer face
> . . . .
> As Sodynely as lightning beautie woundes
> . . . .
> Loves dartes are swift as is the lightning fier.[52]

The white strumpet would become the suitable partner of the black man, and together they would form the perfect counterpart of that other mixed couple of the white lecher and the black bawd. Mountferrat and Zanthia, Syphax and Zanthia, Flamineo and Zanche have their opposite numbers in the unions between Aaron and Tamara, Eleazer and the Queen Mother, Porus and Elimine.

Where there is voluntary miscegenation, it seemed necessary to underscore a basic condition; the black cohort is valued first and mostly for sexual gratification. Aaron's opening speech in *Titus Andronicus* establishes such a relationship with Tamora. Though she has become Empress of Rome, she remains enslaved to his will under the pressure of her love. Tamora, he announces, has climbed high in Roman life, and he hopes to "mount aloft" with her:

> ... whom thou in triumph long
> Hast prisoner held, fett'red in amorous chains,
> And faster bound to Aaron's charming eyes
> Than is Prometheus tied to Caucasus.[53]

His first impulse "to wait upon this new-made empress" smacks too much of "servile thought," for he thinks more of her own sexually inspired subservience to him.

> To wait, said I? To wanton with this queen,
> This goddess, this Semiramis, this nymphe,
> This siren that will charm Rome's Saturne
> And see his shipwracke and his commonweal's.[54]

The sexual origin of his power over her is emphasized in their first encounter alone while on a hunt in the forest. Tamora takes the opportunity to profess her love for the Moor in rapturous language and proposes they enjoy sexual intercourse under the trees. That they may be apprehended there by others in the royal hunting party does not inhibit her. Of them she says:

> Let us sit down and mark their yellowing noise;
> And—after conflict such as was suppos'd
> The wand'ring prince and Dido once enjoy'd,
> When with a happy storm they were surpris'd,
> And curtained with a counsel-keeping cave—
> We may, each wreathed in the other's arms
> (Our pastimes done), possess a golden slumber,
> Whiles hounds and horns and sweet melodious birds
> Be unto us as is a nurse's song
> Of lullaby to bring her babe asleep.[55]

But the peaceful sleep—and she makes this point twice—must come after a sexual "conflict" which she romantically models on Aeneas and Dido's copulative escapade in the woods. The beauty of her language is an embroidery of a direct and persuasive proposition to make love.

As noted earlier, Aaron's control is greater than hers, and though she tries to provoke him to passion, his concerns are elsewhere. Revenge, rather than love, is what he puts his mind to. Ravenscroft altered this conception of the union by making Tamora even more susceptible to the Moor's charms and hence more racially deplorable in her white culture. In the later play she repeatedly refers to him as her "lovely Moor." And whereas in Shakespeare's play other characters scornfully object to Tamora's behavior because it is adulterous and dishonors both her and her husband, in Ravenscroft's version the characters who reflect on the affair despise her for her trespass across racial boundaries. For example, the sight of Tamora in the arms of Aron reminds Bassianus that white is lost in conjunction with black. He employs what had by then become a traditional metaphor drawn from astronomy to describe miscegenation, an image that expresses an inherent psychological fear of the black man's sexuality:

> By Heavens I saw you in Ecclipse,
> The bright Imperial Sun of Rome Eclips'd
> With a black Cloud, ne'er to shine forth again.[56]

Later in the play, when the Gothic soldier captures Aron and his black infant son, instead of reporting simply what he has heard Aron saying—as Shakespeare pictured the scene—he includes his own feelings about the mixing of the races by describing them in an animal image reminiscent of Iago's obscenities. Denouncing Tamora as guilty of bestiality, he denies Aron his human status.

> Behold the Moor the Sire of this squab toad.
> For this he and Tamara club'd together,
> The Queen of Goths Tup'd by a Goat.[57]

Dekker's Queen Mother of Spain, like Tamora, is another aggressively lascivious woman and is clearly marked as the dramatization in the female of the corrupting power of lust, which is the central subject of the play *Lust's Dominion*. It is the black lover that she needs. Ferdinand, her son, who lusts after the Moor's wife, and Mendoza, the Cardinal, who just as heatedly pursues the Queen Mother, are the masculine counterparts of her lust. For Eleazer, sexually powerful as he is, physical love is only an instrument for achieving revenge; the source of his power is in the Queen Mother's lust.

The development of this dominant trait of her character begins immediately. Dekker, as a well-trained Elizabethan dramatist, does not fail to make the character's opening speech expose the mainspring of her inner being. To establish the Queen Mother's sexual drive as the core of her selfhood, defining her interests and motivating her behavior, Dekker opens the play with a scene in which the Queen Mother appears in all her lewdness, stirring her reluctant black paramour to physical love. She tries to soothe his distraught mind by purring into his ear her wishes that

> ... delicious Musicks silken wings
> Send ravishing delight to my loves ears
> That he may be enamoured of your tunes.
> Come let's kisse.

When he refuses her request, she insists, gently but firmly, and will not be denied.

> No, no, saies I; and twice away saies stay:
> Come, come, I'le have a kiss, but if you strive,
> For one denial you shall forfeit five.[58]

She makes an effort to embrace him, and when he still appears reluctant she teases him boldly with a lewd thought:

> Eleazer   Nay prithee good Queen leave me,
>   I am now sick, heavie, and dull as lead.
>
> Qu. Mo.   I'le make thee lighter by taking something
>   from thee.[59]

With this proposal to relieve him of his heaviness by helping him to an orgasm, she underscores the basic voluptuousness of her nature. In a later scene her appetite for carnal love inspires her to apostrophize night in her prayer that Eleazer return before daylight

> Fair eldest child of love, thou spotlesse night,
> Empresse of silence, and the Queen of sleep;
> Who with thy black cheeks pure complexion,
> Mak'st lovers eyes enamour'd of thy beauty:
> Thou art like my Moor, therefore will I adore thee,
> For lending me this opportunity,
> Oh with the softskin'd Negro! heavens keep back
> The saucy staring from the worlds eye,
> Until my Eleazer make return.[60]

The source of Eleazer's attracting power can only be inferred from the Queen Mother's habit of behaving like a rutting animal over the thought of him. Her poetry cannot conceal the reality of her lust. Mrs. Behn, in adapting this play for another age, takes some measures to offer explicit reasons for the Queen Mother's fascination with the Moor. In separate scenes, for example, both the Moor and the lustful Queen elucidate his sexual stamina, each boasting of his great capacity to please. In one instance the Queen is expecting Abdelazer (the Moor) in her bedchamber and has ordered all things to be arranged properly for a night of lovemaking. Her maid jestingly suggests that the Queen is acting as though this were her first night with Abdelazer.

The Queen quite bluntly, but happily, exclaims: "My first! Oh Elvira, his Powers, like his Charms, / His Wit, or Bravery, every hour renews."[61]

Abdelazer recognizes his superior virility and openly vaunts his sexual strength in a vain attempt to gain the princess Leonora for his wife. He expostulates first on his worth as a human being, but acknowledges that some natural antipathy toward blackness could inhibit a person of the opposite sex and color from embracing it in the full consciousness that broad daylight must create. He suggests, therefore, that darkness will remove her understandable reluctance to couple with a black man. With self-derogating impact, this proposal parallels the pleas of white rakes to their black women. He assures her of his gentleness and the exotic sensation she will experience in his embrace. Finally, he boasts of his capacity to satisfy her each time they make love as though it were their first union—just as, although he omits to mention it, he has been able to do with her mother.

> Yet as I am, I've been in vain ador'd,
> And Beauties great as thine have languish'd for me.
> The lights put out, thou in thy naked Arms
> Will find me soft and smooth as polish'd Ebony;
> And all my Kisses on thy balmy Lips as sweet,
> As are Breezes, breath'd amidst the Groves
> Of ripening Spices in the height of Day:
> As vigorous too,
> As if each Night were the first happy Moment
> I laid thy panting Body to my Bosom.
> Oh that transporting thought—[62]

Leonora, however, who is the object of his words, has been depicted as innocent and decent; a symbol of virtuous white womanhood; his pleas are fruitless. Abdelazer's only recourse, then, is to violence and revenge, which he is finally prevented from achieving. Like Abdelazer, the other black men of this entire period may find success with white women of corrupt nature, but with women of reputed purity, they meet firm and often degrading rejection. With Desdemona as the one exception, women who are not immoral are portrayed as unmoved by the tempting charms of the black man. Yet black men are almost always shown in pursuit of white women.

It could be concluded that these early dramatists not only may have prophesied the development of a phase of the white psyche (especially as it was to manifest itself in the deep South of the United States) but may also have added to that fear of the black ravisher ever threatening his white victim.[63] The plays present a fairly consistent picture of this preference of black men to copulate with white women. Since white was the standard of beauty, few men could imagine even black men preferring any other color. From *The Merchant of Venice* (1596) to *The Moor's Revenge* (1687), black characters were generally shown seeking unions with white females. Some black men demonstrated a willingness—unrealizable, of course—to give up their blackness for the sake of triumph. It was simply another way for white writers to stress the relative values of white and black. "I would not change this hue," says the Prince of Morocco, "except to steal your thoughts, my gentle queen."[64] Sincere perhaps for the moment, Eleazer conveys the same idea to Isabella, whom he desires in marriage, but because of his own pride, he adds a wish that she were black. Either color would suit him so long as both were of the same hue. Eleazer's words contain the critical idea of the anathema of miscegenation.

> . . . why did this color
> Dart in my flesh so far? Oh! would my face,
> Were of Hortenzo's fashion, else would yours
> Were as black as mine is.
>
> Isabella   More like yours, why?
>
> Eleazer   Hark!
> I love you, yes faith, I said this; I love you,
> I do, leave him.[65]

The response of the white women in these situations are somewhat different. Portia casually repudiates black skin after Morocco has chosen the wrong casket and left in grief: "A gentle riddance. Draw the curtains, go. / Let all of his complexion choose me so."[66] Isabella's refusal is more profusely stated, but she avoids racial condemnation. She simply loves another and urges Eleazer to be loyal to his own wife. Mrs. Behn's adaptation of this scene once again reveals a greater consciousness of the traditional judgment of black as ugly. In rejecting Abdelazer's offer, Leonora does not excuse herself only by claiming a love for Alonzo, but protests Alonzo's superior beauty as well. Unlike the women in Herbert's and Rainold's poems and more like the young black man in Cleveland's (see Chapter II), Abdelazer reacts in self-hatred and expresses a desire to be white.

> Ay! There's your Cause of Hate! Curst be my Birth,
> And curst be Nature that has dy'd my Skin
> With this ungrateful Colour! Cou'd the Gods
> Have given me equal Beauty with Alonzo![67]

Regardless of how a black suitor reacts to a refusal, it is important to remember that it is his reputation for sexual aggression that grows more notorious, his proclivity for white women that makes the notoriety more insidious. As the lecherous Antonio remarks enviously in *All's Lost by Lust* (1619), the Moors have the advantage of "the lustfull lawes of Mahomet," whereby "I may have three wives more." His companion Lazarello adds another attractive thought: "And concubines besides."[68] Such Moorish values permitting the free exercise of a man's need for variety in his sex partners are precisely manifested in the character of Mully Mullisheg, the black Fezian king of Heywood's *The Fair Maid of the West,* parts I and II. He demonstrates a strong promiscuous nature and reveals a penchant for white sex partners. In his initial appearance late in part I, he enters with his court officials, issuing directives about taxation and other state matters, and impresses us as a prudent statesman interested in the welfare of his country. After settling these practical matters, he turns his attention toward the state of his own comforts and pleasures. What comfort and pleasure mean to a Moor is not long left in doubt: he orders his subordinates to replenish his harem with a wide variety of women. What is particularly critical in his description of his sexual tastes is that among the variety of women he desires, it is the white woman who takes precedence. His command is first for "the fairest Christian damsels you can hire or buy for gold."[69] His appetite is voracious, his desire catholic. After honoring white women as most desirable, he next names women of his own race:

> . . . the loveliest of the Moors
> We can command, and negroes everywhere;
> Italians, French, and Dutch, choice Turkish girls,
> Must fill our Alkedavy, the great palace
> Where Mullisheg now deigns to keep his court.[70]

The availability of women in such numbers and variety constitutes for Mullisheg a "terrestrial Heaven."[71] His god, he informs us, is his pleasure, "for so our Mecan Prophet warrants us." And since his pleasure is copulation, it is natural to conclude that he worships his own erotic impulses as divinely originated.

When word is brought to the king that a beautiful English woman has landed on his shores in a ship called the *Negro,* Mullisheg is immediately inflamed; in his imagination he is already coupling with the white Christian.

> Alcade I never saw a braver vessel sail.
> And she is called the Negro.
>
> Mull. Ominous
> Perhaps, to our good fate; she in a Negro
> Hath sailed thus far to bosom with a Moor.[72]

He pursues his interest in Bess openly at the court. As a reward for an act of mercy in sparing a Christian missionary at Bess's request, he demands and receives from her a kiss. Her acquiescence apparently reflects her acceptance of Mullisheg as a human being; she acts respectfully awed by his claims to royalty. She explains her attitude: " 'Tis no immodest thing / You ask, nor shame for Bess to kiss a king."[73] Mullisheg thrills over the kiss from the fair Bess. He is set afire. "This kiss hath all my vitals ecstasied."[74] Nevertheless he restrains his impulses and makes no further move toward her. Part I of this two-part play pictures Mullisheg well in control of his libido. He respects the love between Bess and her fair Englishman Spencer; he grants her requests, bestows generous hospitality on her party, and deports himself honorably. He arranges for a lavish wedding of Bess and Spencer and acknowledges their worthiness by giving them expensive gifts. With the exception, perhaps, of his private sexual promiscuity, he could by white standards be judged a good man.

Yet there is another opinion of Mullisheg and it is expressed by the dolt Clym when he sees Bess and Mullisheg kissing. In earthy, racist language the naive but honest sailor bursts forth with a remark that was surely more typical of white reaction to such a display between the races than Bess's casual and probably prudent acceptance:

> Must your black face be smouching
> My mistress' white lips with a moorian!
> I would you had kissed her a—[75]

His instinctive revulsion at the sight of black and white in intimate conjunction intimates a deeper psychological distrust of the black man's intentions.

When Heywood returned to this play years later to write a sequel it was not totally inconsistent that he adopted another point of view—Clym's view, as a matter of fact—and drastically changed the image of Mullisheg.[76] In part I Heywood treated Mullisheg as a man responsive to virtue and capable of sexual restraint, a fairly remarkable departure from common belief. What happened to change Heywood's perspective over the next two or three decades will probably never be known. But his second portrait of Mullisheg is in greater harmony with the cultural environment in which he was working. Although there is no passage of dramatic time between parts I and II, Heywood, in the latter play, conceived of a black figure more easily recognized by his stereotypical qualities—especially his sexual urge which now drives him to "satisfie my appetite with fulnesse" on the person of Bess. He no longer can keep his lust in check, and by trying to subvert one of Bess's companions, Captain Goodlock, he hopes to enjoy her. He rationalizes his behavior by declaring that frustration of the king is harmful to the whole nation.

> I should commit high treason gainst my self
> Not to do that might give my soule content
> And satisfie my appetite with fulness.[77]

Again he has identified his spiritual well-being (soul) with the fulfillment of animal lust (appetite).

To complement the figure of the lustful black man, Heywood has given Mullisheg a suitable wife, not mentioned at all in part I. Eldred Jones, in discussing this play, emphasizes her uniqueness by comparing her with the historical wife in a polygamous society, who would be expected to accept the fact of her husband's interest in other women. Mullisheg's wife, Tota, however, resents his fascination for Bess and vows to give him tit for tat by seducing Bess's husband, Spencer. Jones mistakenly finds her insistence on a single moral standard more interesting than the method she chooses to achieve it. Jones does mention Heywood's probable debt to the stereotyped black woman of the plays by Marston, Fletcher, and Webster, but he minimizes its significance: when Heywood decided to give the Moor a wife, he found the most suitable woman would be lascivious like the Moor himself. The result, of course, was to be a ludicrous scene in which the two black lechers try to bed their opposite member of the white couple and are easily outwitted by Goodlack and Clem into bedding only each other.

> Goodlack   Could a man propose
> A stratagem to gull this lustful Moor,
> To supply him, and then to satiate her?[78]

After Goodlack's weak stratagem of switching partners in the darkness has been put into operation, he curses the black seducers soundly: "One fury claspe another, and there beget / Young devills between you."[79] The black couple get no more than they deserve, and that is, each other.

In summary, then, black skin came quite early to be an indicator of a powerful libido, related in its manifestations to an animal bestiality. Revenge, therefore, is not the singular mainspring propelling the black man to his evil; the irrepressible impulse rising from the loins is just as often what drives stage Moors to their plots and machinations. When Mullisheg has his final change of heart under the influence of Bess's and Spencer's virtue, he describes rather definitively what the reputation of Moors has been:

> Shall lust in me have chief predominance?
> And vertuous deeds, for which in Fesse
> I have been long renoun'd, be quite exilde?
> Shall Christians have the honour
> To be sole heirs of goodness, and we Moors
> Barbarous and bloody?[80]

The answer that most playwrights gave to this question was often an unqualified "yes." A white woman raped by her king cries out that she has been defiled of her "white lawne of chastity with ugly blacks of lust."[81] That her rapist is white still fails to change her inbred beliefs in the meaning of white and black. Lust, revenge, cruelty, demonism, ugliness—these are the major qualities that compose the image of the black man as he was fashioned by the playwrights. But then these were not the only derogating features that cut him off from the compassion and understanding that other characters could invoke in a theater audience. Other ideas about his beliefs and practices would complete the process of isolating him from the family of man (as conceived by Europeans) and retard any appreciable growth of sympathy for his cause.

Chapter 7

Other Sources of Denigration—Paganism and Failure

> I being a Moor, then, in opinion's lightness
> As far from sanctity as my face from whiteness.

Out of the formidable complex of forces that lay beneath the widespread maltreatment of the black man—an abuse first perpetrated in his enslavement and then reflected in a body of creative literature that tended to justify that slavery—one portentous bias that surfaced with notable regularity was the concern over his religion, or rather the lack of it. Although modern anthropology recognizes that there were great differences between the Moorish peoples of North Africa and the black tribes of the sub-Sahara, the writers of this period made no such distinctions. Negroes or Moors, sub-Sahara tribes or Ethiopians—all were viewed as belonging to the single category of a black people. Through a process of synecdoche the Moor was usually made to stand for the African. When a writer, therefore, used the word, he meant any person whose central identifying characteristic was his black skin. Other physical or cultural traits were generally minimized or not considered at all. Religious differences, too, were ignored. Islam may have been recognized as the basic religion of the Moors and differed radically from the animism of other African peoples, but the creative writers viewed them all simply as infidels or pagans (see Chapter III, pp. 82-87).

Like other people who refused to acknowledge Christianity, the black man was condemned as a heathen threat to the Christian world; if tolerated at all, he was tolerated with great suspicion.[1] The black man's seemingly deliberate rejection of the white man's faith could easily be contorted into his preference for an anti-Christ, the devil himself, perhaps. Their common black skin made such an interpretation plausible and even probable. As chapter 4 has argued, faulty religion and devil worship appeared as bedfellows.

Were the black man to adopt Christianity in recanting his own beliefs, he could make himself more acceptable to a white world so certain of its inherent superiority. However, Winthrop Jordan has called notice to the fact that in the early stages of the exploitation of Africa and the establishment of slavery, white colonialists and merchants made little attempt to convert what they considered to be black heathens as they had been doing with New World Indians. Because the black man was intended for slavery, it was first thought unwise to bring him into the church, where his servitude would be more difficult to rationalize. However, some blacks evidently did convert to Christianity and found, at least on the theatrical stage, some preferential treatment. The conversion, it must be noted, always implied the higher truth and greater beauty of the white man's faith and culture.

Ben Jonson and Richard Crashaw both testify to this belief in different ways through the same image. When Jonson eulogized England in his *Masque of Blackness* (1605) by describing its climate as perfect, a place where the sun shone temperately and transformed everybody it touched into beautiful people, he was invoking geography as the explanation for the Aethiopians' blackness, wittily claiming that ugliness such as their blackness could be cured on British soil. Brittania could readily "blanch an Aethiop" and no longer would "this veil the sun hath cast / Above your blood, more summers last."[2] Assuming the role of chauvinist when he wrote the scene, Jonson may or may not have believed in the theory that black men would turn white when brought to a northern climate.

Richard Crashaw, on the other hand, with much greater certainty had a better idea of how black men could be washed clean of their stigmatic blackness. To him the black skin represented a paganistic being. The real blackness, therefore, was an inner darkness rather than a surface skin pigment, and that kind of darkness had a cure: conversion to Christianity. Crashaw's short Latin verse "Aethiops lotus" bears this point as its spiritual message.

Ille niger sacris exit (quam lautus!) ab undis.
Nec frustra Aethiopem nempe lavare fuit.
Mentem quam niveam piceae cutis umbra fovebit
Tam volet et nigros sancta Columba lares.[3]

Crashaw provided his own English translation:

On the baptized Aethiopean

Let no longer be a forlorne hope
    To wash an Aethiope:
He's washt, His gloomy skin a peacefull shade
    For his white soul is made:
And now, I doubt not, the Eternall Dove,
    A black-fac'd house will love.[4]

With the smug assurance of one who has God's confidence, the poet pronounces the unconverted pagan as unloved by God, who was acknowledged as the Father of all. Under the transforming magic of conversion, the "gloomy" look of the black heathen becomes a "peaceful" shade for a white soul. The poem cannot fail to call to mind William Blake's "The Little Black Boy" and its own subtle expression of the superiority of white: "My mother bore me in the southern wild / And I am black, but O! my soul is white."[5] Blake, so unorthodox himself, is not promulgating the Christian faith, but he does echo the cultural tones that for hundreds of years resounded in the West.

The certainty of the higher nature of whiteness and the superior turn of white English faith is sharply dramatized in an episode of a masque involving the conversion of a Moor. The masque, Thomas Middleton's *Triumph of Truth* (1613), honored the installation of a new mayor of London. The Spirit of London, who is also the Mother of Englishmen, welcomes the new mayor and presents the Angel of Truth, who offers the mayor his services. Accompanying Truth is Zeal, whose force will also assist the mayor to a successful and productive term of office. Obviously, the mayor is expected to accept two such forthright aides. But another figure looms competitively on the scene to woo the mayor into a program of self-aggrandizement. This is the seductive figure of Error, who warns him that he has only one year in which to fatten his own purse from the bribes and payments he now has the power to exact. His lure is attractive. But the power of Truth and the spirit of Christianity are a combination too powerful for Error. To demonstrate just how persuasive these forces are, Middleton chooses a candidate most unlikely to be susceptible to their arguments: the black Moor! In the midst of the splendid procession of Truth and her adherents appears a ship carrying a Moorish king, his queen, and a troop of Moors.

The Moorish king observes that his arrival with black companions has produced

> many wild thoughts . . .
> Opinions, common murmurs, and fix'd eyes,
> At my so strange arrival in a land
> Where true religion and her temple stand.[6]

He goes on to repudiate his past errors and acknowledges the superiority of the Christian God; by so doing he purchases his status as a human being. He also knows what the popular attitude toward black men is: "I being a Moor, then, in opinion's lightness, / As far from sanctity as my face from whiteness."[7] But in true Christian spirit he forgives those whose censure is based only on what they see superficially and not on what they can reason. Those who believe that the black man's paganism is irredeemable, he announces, are wrong.

> However darknesse dwells upon my face
> Truth in my soul sets up the light of grace;

And though, in days of error, I did run
To give all adoration to the sun,
The moon, and stars, nay creatures base and poor,
Now only their Creator I adore.[8]

The Moor is thus made to inadvertantly debase his own brethren by being the spokesman for the ethnocentric doctrines of white Christianity. He, himself, however, because he has adopted the values of white culture, has achieved acceptance.

But what of the black men who have not? The spirit of Error, in a voice of hurt betrayal, informs us of where they stand. "What, have my sweet-fac'd devils forsook me too?"[9] The unconverted black man remains an outsider, a devil's advocate. He lives in the shadow of error, and though not absolutely circumscribed from salvation, must bring himself to accept Christianity and acknowledge the superiority of its cultural milieu. The whole passage is additionally significant because it so explicitly equates the Moor's faith with the paganism of sun worship and reveals no indication of the Moslem faith.

Conversely, when a black man is shown as capable of admirable emotions and noble actions, he turns out to be either a de facto Christian or a willing proselyte to Christianity. Webster's *The White Devil* (1611), provides a detailed analysis of this point. Flamineo exudes praise of a Moor recently come to the court; his enthusiasm, however, is built on his belief that the Moor is a Christian. The fact makes the Moor's good qualities visible. Having identified the "sunburnt gentleman" as a Christian, Flamineo feels a eulogy of the man is proper:

I have not seen a goodlier personage,
Nor ever talked with man better experienced
In state affairs or rudiments of war
He hath, by report, served the Venetian
In Candy these twice seven years, and been chief
In many a bold design.
. . . .
I never saw one in a stern bold look
Wear more command, nor in a lofty phrase
Express more knowing or more deep contempt
Of our slight airy courtiers. He talks
As if he had travelled all the princes' courts
Of Christendom: in all things strives to express,
That all that should dispute with him may know.
Glories like glow worms, afar off shine bright,
But looked to near, have neither heat nor light.[10]

The Moor, to be sure, is really the white Francisco de Medici, disguised. All this praise, as the audience knows, is really not for a black man, but the fact that it is addressed to a putative black man is possible only because Flamineo is conscious of the Moor's Christianity. On the two levels of putative reality on the stage and objective reality in the audience, therefore, the Moor's goodness is either the result of his being Christian or his not being a Moor at all.

Similarly, the solitary figure of a virtuous Moor, Basha Joffer, a captain of the king's guard in the second part of Heywood's *Fair Maid of the West* (1630), indicates the source of his goodness by finally apprehending the superiority of English virtue over that of his own people. He concedes this fact despite his own generous behavior that ennobles him above all the other Moors of the period. Capable of deep compassion for others, trusting and brave, Basha Joffer achieves great stature when he risks his own life to enable two English lovers who have been separated seemingly forever to meet once more. Spencer has been ordered imprisoned by the king, and in order to arrange for the two English foreigners to have their last reunion, the Moorish captain offers his own person as security for Spencer's temporary parole; he is willing to die for the Englishman in whom he recognizes great goodness. When Spencer refuses to seize this opportunity to flee the country with his wife and returns to redeem Joffer and face his punishment, the black Moor declares his love for Christian virtue and converts to the Western religion. That he himself embodies a virtue as great as Spencer's is never viewed as sufficient evidence of the basic worth of his own faith. Instead Joffer enunciates the doctrine of white ethnocentrism. Referring to Spencer's return, he says:

> Such honour is not found in Barbarie.
> The virtue in these Christians have converted me,
> Which to the world I can no longer smother,
> Accept me then a Christian and a brother.[11]

Only with a formal declaration of intention to convert can Joffer advance his offer of brotherhood. Earlier, the conniving leader Mullisheg also admitted indirectly the supremacy of Christianity, and although he did not offer to convert, he did promise to imitate its virtues.

Very few black men were considered by the writers to be ready to accept Christianity. More preferred their own spiritual conditions and were happy to admit it. Aaron, for instance, professes atheism and scornfully mocks those who believe in a God. Yet he knows how foolishly the pious will fulfill a pledge sworn on their oath to their God. He therefore accepts the word of the Christians that they will not harm his child if he confesses his crimes. Lucius is surprised that a pagan would even request such an oath in the first place.

Lucius   . . . Thou believest no God.

Aaron   What if I do not? As indeed I do not.
          Yet, for I know thou art religious
          And hast a thing within thee called conscience,
          With twenty popish tricks and ceremonies
          Which I have seen thee careful to observe,
          Therefore I urge thy oath. For that I know
          An idiot holds his bauble for a God
          And keeps the oath which by that God he swears.[12]

What the black character is frequently denied, it seems safe to conclude, is the Christian conscience. The passage here evokes the thought of Zanthia's comment to Mountferrat that "to a man resolved there is no conscience." That same Zanthia is not so willing as Aaron to trust the hold a conscience has on a Christian. She prefers to rely on the efficacy of an oath made in the manner of her own people. She demands from Mountferrat a more primitive, more physical bond than words uttered to an invisible being, a contract that is

          Cemented with blood, as this of ours is,
          Is a more holy sanction, and much surer
          Than all the superstitious ceremonies
          You Christians use.[13]

Her perspective is just as ethnocentrically determined as that of the majority of white commentators. To her the physical mingling of blood is a more binding agreement between the parties than are the "superstitious ceremonies" of swearing oaths that she finds in Christendom—and especially so, since their agreement will ultimately lead to the shedding of a victim's blood.

Generally, however, it is the white point of view that is expressed more directly and in that context it is pagan superstition that is put on display. The heathen practice that captured the highest attention of white society was the worship of the sun, a ceremonial rite believed to be common among black peoples. *Sejanus* (1603), Jonson's tragedy, contains a passage succinctly alluding to this belief while at the same time mocking it. Lepidus comments on the former glory that Sejanus once radiated.

          He that this morn rose proudly as the sun,
          And breaking through a mist of clients' breath,
          Came on as gazed at and admired as he
          When superstitious Moors saluted his light.[14]

The awesome feeling of the Moor in the presence of the rising sun—manipulated in Jonson's metaphor to characterize the stature of a Roman dictator—is expansively detailed in a speech by the arch villain Mulymumen. In the crisis of a military defeat he apostrophizes the sun as the deity of the

Moors and angrily deplores the shame he must now suffer in its presence. He bids his god not to look upon his disgrace, which is all the greater because he has borne it at the hands of white Christians.

> Descend thy spheare, thou burning deity,
> Haste from our shame, go blushing to thy bed;
> Thy sonnes we are, thou everlasting ball,
> Yet never shamde these our impressive brows
> Till now; we that are stampt with thine owne seale,
> Which the whole ocean cannot wash away:
> Shall those cold ague cheeks that nature moulds
> Within her winter shop, those smoothe white skins,
> That with a palsey hand she paints the limbes,
> Make us recoyle.[15]

The moon as well as the sun was thought to be an object of pagan worship attributed to the Moors. Jonson made this idea of moon-worship explicit when he portrayed the spirit of Aethiopia, Niger, addressing the moon in reverential tones:

> Great Aethiopia goddess of our shore,
> Since with particular worship we adore
> Thy general brightness, let particular grace
> Shine on my zealous daughters . . .
> . . . .
> Beautify them, which long have deify'd thee.[16]

This paganism, it should be noted, though seemingly innocuous in a romantic masque that uses its exotic quality to great advantage, often functions more injuriously as an abrasive between the cultures. Whatever made their religious differences more noticeable further separated the races and made compatibility less likely. When the Spanish King Rodericke, in Rowley's *All's Lost for Lust* (1619), leads his troop against the Moors, he sounds the cry of a religious war—the Christian world in a life and death struggle with a pagan one.

> Scourge back again those half-nak't Infidels
> Into their sun-burnt clymate; in thy heart
> Be loyaltie and courage, strength in thine arme:
> With Christian valour strike the heathens dead,
> And for thy triumph, bring the Mulyes head.[17]

In the same play when Mulymumen bargains with the betrayed Spanish general Julianus to help him to vengeance against their common enemy Rodericke, his price is marriage to Julianus's daughter, Jacinto. Julianus agrees because of his blinding need for revenge, but Jacinto's response is quite different. Mulymumen's black skin is not singularly what produces her absolute refusal. Rather it is the thought of his unregenerate condition, anathema to Christianity, that repels her. "O my second hell, / A Christian's arms embrace an infidell!" Jacinto's first hell was her betrayal by her own Christian king, who cruelly raped her when her father was off fighting the king's war. It is certainly indicative of the dramatist's religious convictions that this brutal attack that destroys Jacinto's virginity does not diminish her Christian faith and adherence. But marriage to a pagan would be an abomination. She therefore refuses marriage to the Moor, preferring the cruelty he has promised her and which his paganism assures. His stance as a conscious anti-Christ becomes unmistakable when, for example, he hears of the death of some Spaniards and chortles in a mood of religious animosity: "More fruits of Christians."[18]

This spiritual antagonism between Christian and pagan worlds so apparently irreconcilable was certainly a major source of the contemptuous superiority white men felt toward black men.[19] Whether the playwrights were reflecting the beliefs of their audience or expressing attitudes they harbored themselves, their words were increasing the likelihood that the white English world would apprehend these people—rapidly becoming the richest source of slaves—only as inferior beings whose enslavement could thus be justified. If either race were to modify its sense of infallibility to achieve some kind of mutual respect, it would have to be the black man, the non-Christian, who had to concede.

John Fletcher's *The Island Princess* (1619) makes this inevitability as clear as possible. Armusio, the Portuguese hero, has succeeded in championing the cause of the princess Quisaria against the evil governor who has been posing as a Moor. Armusio's reward is Quisaria herself. But she is a pagan and proud of her beliefs, while he is a Christian. Before she accepts him as a husband, therefore, she asks him to purify himself spiritually: she requests that he renounce his Christianity and adopt her gods: "The sun and moon we worship." The vehemence of his reply and its ominous tone are the barometers of his religious fervor. He denounces her paganism and proudly eulogizes the truth of Christianity, affirming his unshakable devotion. It is she, he remonstrates, who should be converting to his faith for the health of her total being.

> I look'd you should have said, "Make me a Christian!
> Work that great cure"; for 'tis a great one, woman;
> That labor truly to perform, that venture,
> The crown of all great trial, and the fairest;
> I look'd you should have wept and kneel'd to begg it,
> Washed off your mist of ignorance . . . I look'd
> You should have brought me your chief god ye worship,
> He that you offer human blood and life to,

> And made a sacrifice of him to Memory,
> Beat down his altars, ruined his false temples.[20]

The belief that blood sacrifice was part of paganistic ceremony fits well into a broader pattern of ideas that had been woven by white society. Similarly, the power to read the future and the possession of black magic to contact the spirits of the dead are easily accepted as natural skills of the disguised Moor Arcanthe, of Berkeley's *The Lost Lady* (1637). People unquestioningly accept her claim that she is a black magician, one of "those that sell themselves to hell."[21] Her pretense to these powers nearly results in her murder. Arcanthe is never explicitly despised for her assumed race or color. When the truth of her identity is revealed she is simply called that "cur'd magician,"[22] suggesting that her blackness was to be considered a kind of disease.

So long as they remained infidels, black people were imagined to engage in nefarious practices such as ritual murder and black magic. They were counted as something quite different from normal humanity and valued as less. In the great chain of being that measured the relative worth of all things, the place of the black man became highly questionable. In the seventeenth century, and certainly by the middle of the eighteenth century, theories arose to classify the black man below the species man but above the species ape.[23]

On the stage, too, he often was given roles that left little doubt about his subhuman condition. The late-sixteenth-century scene in Marlowe, one of the earliest portrayers of black men, shows "two Moors drawing Bajazeth in his cage" as though they are two beasts of burden.[24] A century later the same dehumanizing effect is partially effected by the refusal to give a black person a name, and hence an identity. In Wycherly's *The Gentleman Dancing-Master* (1672), a black boyservant, who has a considerable speaking part, is never called by a name. Instead, his master Don Diego simply calls him "Black" or "Sirrah Black" and in the dramatis personae he appears simply as "a little Black-a-More."[25]

George Peele follows his historical source quite closely by including Negroes among groups of people who were obviously ranked as inferior. Of the Portuguese army, he writes:

> He found he had two thousand armed horse,
> And fourteene thousand men that serve on foot,
> Three thousand pioners, and a thousand cochmen,
> Besides a number almost numberlesse
> Of drudges, Negroes, slaves and Muleters,
> Horse-boies, landresses and curtizens,
> And fifteene hundred waggons full of stuff
> For noble men, brought up in delicate.[26]

All of the types listed from the fifth line are clearly in the category of impedi-
menta, each, with the exception of the Negroes, identified with some demeaning and lowly task. Only the Negro seems to be included for an assumed
debased racial condition. The low value placed on the black person by white
culture is evident everywhere. Zanthia's painful awareness of the natural
place she holds in Mountferrat's esteem is another case in point.

> But, like a property, when I have served
> Your turns, you'll cast me off, or hang me up
> For a sign somewhere.[27]

That she is only so much baggage in his eyes she is sure of. But she knows
also that she is baggage he needs, at least temporarily. "And since I know / I
am used only for a property," she requires from him that strong pledge,
signed in blood, that he will not abandon her.

There are many other expressions in the theater to make the same evaluation. The fair Bess, epitome of English womanhood, doubts that a Moor can
ever learn virtue by imitation. She raises the question:

> Could my Spencer
> Think that a barbarous Moor could be so train'd
> In human vertues?[28]

It is her opinion that Moors are either debased humans beyond salvation or
subhumans incapable of nobility. More worldly and liberal and far less closed
to the idea of human potentiality, Spencer also questions the essential humanity of the Barbary people. Appealing to his guard Joffer to allow him to see
Bess, he questions Joffer's capacity for compassion and words his statement
in a way that is racially divisive, suggesting white superiority. Instead of
using a harmless phrase such as "If your heart isn't made of stone, it would
melt," his words become culturally noxious:

> . . . Or if you had a heart,
> Made of that metall that we white men have,
> How would it melt in you?[29]

Surprisingly enough to Spencer, Joffer's heart, black though his skin is,
does melt, and he grants Spencer leave to visit Bess. He has shown that in its
capacity for humaneness his heart is not unlike a white man's. But as we
have already seen, this revelation of Joffer's goodness will be rationalized
by his later rejection of the barbarism of his own society and his conversion to Christianity. Inner goodness and paganism had to remain relatively
incompatible.

Clem, of the same play, expresses a judgment more blunt and vulgar, but
more widely representative of class feeling toward the black man. He does
not allude directly to the religious differences between the English and

Moorish worlds but is more conscious of an "uncleanliness" in the black man, suggestive of an inner dirtiness as well. To a request that he compare the English with Moors, Clem details mechanical similarities:

> Our countrymen eate and drinke as yours doe for all
> the world, open their eyes when they would see, and shut
> them again when they would sleepe; when they goe they
> set one let before another, and gape when their mouths
> open, as yours eate when they have stomackes, scratch
> when it itcheth.[30]

Up to this point Clem has granted the Moors nothing that makes them any more like the English than, say, a dog or an ape. On the animal level there are similarities. When he turns to civilization's attribute of hygiene, however, he finds the Moors sorely wanting.

> . . . only I hold our nation to be the cleanlier.

Toto   Cleanlier, wherein?

Clem   Because they never sit downe to meat with such
            foule hands and faces.[31]

Despite its quality as a low joke, the line suggests a deep psychological condition that made the white man incapable of accepting the black man in a positive framework. The black infidel had this additional stain to his spiritual being: his skin bore a sign of uncleanliness.[32] Clem is also the source of other derogatory stories passed off as typical of the low mentality of the black man. He tells of visiting a chief Bashaw who was sitting close to a huge fire. When the fire got too warm, and he was advised to move back, he ordered several masons to remove the fire from him. The same Moor, Clem relates, requested that they put out the candle and sleep in the dark so that "the fleas may not know where to find us."[33]

Stories like these tend to "document" the alleged stupidity of the Moor and further debase an image already characterized by demonism, treachery, lechery, and bestiality. It is little wonder, then, that when Spencer, once safely aboard the English vessel, states his intention to save Joffer's life by honoring his oath to return to Mullisheg's court, Captain Goodlack protests in typical fashion. "But what's the lives of twenty thousand Moors, / To one that is a Christian."[34] The ethnocentric force of his remark is not diminished in the least by the extravagance of the hyperbole.

Late into the seventeenth century the situation showed little sign of improving, except perhaps, for the works of Mrs. Behn. John Crowne's masque *Calisto* (1675), for instance, reflects the extent to which the English economy had become enmeshed in the slave trade. Four nymphs representing four parts of the world stand before the spirit of England and vow that they

will continue to supply her with their most precious gifts. What each offers is
actually a significant comment on the central worth of the four continents,
at least as Crowne understood them. The superior place of Europe is quite
obvious:

Europe	Thou shalt in all my noblest arts be skill'd,
Asia	My jewels shall adorn no brow but thine,
America	Thy lovers in my Gold shall shine,
Africa	Thou for thy slaves, shalt have these
	Scorched sons of mine.[35]

The improbability of replacing ethnocentric pride with a moderating sense of
imaginative possibilities would long block the black man's emergence into the
human family. According to Crowne's pithy summary of Africa's worth, the
most black men could hope for was service under the English.

Further confirmation of the white man's failure to imagine the black
infidel as anything but a low creature comes from an examination of the
denouements of the plays involving this group of black characters. What
ultimately happens to blacks in the hands of white dramatists indicates
the role society has created for them. Whether the characters finally live or
die, whether they succeed in their aims or not, whether they are happy or
unhappy says much about the ways they were conceived in relation to white
culture.

Of the approximately thirty black charcters only five can be said to
triumph in some way. Abdelmelec (*The Battle of Alcazar*, 1588-89) is victorious defending his throne, although he dies of illness following the battle
(in accordance with historical fact); Joffer's faith in Spencer (*The Fair
Maid of the West*, part II, 1630) is upheld, his life is saved, and he converts
to Christianity, certainly considered the highest reward possible for a black
man; Mulymumen (*All's Lost by Lust*, 1619), evil and triumphant, accedes
to the throne of Spain (in accordance with historical fact); the King of
the Moors (*The Triumph of Truth*, 1613) is accepted as a Christian by the
English, and the Daughters of Niger (*The Masque of Blackness*, 1605) are
hopeful of regaining their beauty on English soil—not a very flattering conclusion. Of these characters, it must be noted, only two—Abdelmelec and
Mulymumen—are uncompromising in their adherence to their own culture,
and both are historical figures whom the dramatists could not readily alter.
Joffer, the King of the Moors, and the Daughters of Niger, on the other
hand, all admit the inferiority of their own origins and so do little to enhance
the worth of their race except to show that some of its members have the
sense to recognize the superiority of the English.

Of the remaining characters twelve meet violent and often ignominious
deaths. Because they are villainous, only one is allowed some redemptive

stature by displaying physical bravery. Only from the pen of Mrs. Behn does a scene develop in which a Moor grows admirable as he dies. Her sensibility enabled her to conceive of a black man achieving some dignity by dying violently against insurmountable odds. The other black antagonists are not given this opportunity.

The cowardly Muly Mahamet (*The Battle of Alcazar*) flees from a military defeat, falls from his horse, and drowns basely in a stream. His body is to be stuffed with straw for display (his confederate Sebastian, on the other hand, is to be given a hero's burial). Eleazer (*Lust's Dominion*, 1599) is manacled and stabbed repeatedly by a mob of his enemies. His vassals in evil, Balthazar and Zarack, are both stabbed to death in ambush. Vangue and Zanthia (*Wonder of Women, Sophonisba,* 1606) are both slaughtered by a wrathful white master. Zanche (*The White Devil,* 1611) is knifed to death by masked assassins. Aaron (*Titus Andronicus,* 1589-1590) is starved to death while buried in the ground up to his neck. Osmin (*The Moor's Revenge,* 1677) is slain by Abdelzaer for betraying him, and Aron (Ravencroft's *Titus Andronicus,* 1686) is burned alive at the stake.

The other black characters either fail to attain their ends or earn only a derisive kind of success. The Prince of Morocco (*The Merchant of Venice,* 1596) chooses the wrong casket and is condemned to a life of celibacy. Portia privately jeers at him as he departs. Mullisheg and his wife Toto (*The Fair Maid of the West,* part II, 1630?) win only each other and fail to enjoy their white counterparts. Porus (*The Blind Beggar of Alexandria,* 1596), defeated in battle, happily accepts as a wife a strumpet already pregnant with another man's child. The African women of *Calisto* (1673), resign themselves to their blackness, hopeful that love will somehow not pass them by.

The black men constructed by the language and action of the plays confirm the negative reports by travelers and commentators who believed they were recording objective truth. Without doubt the public was further persuaded that a general condemnation of the black man as an inferior being, an infidel, and a slave by nature was legitimate. What people could read about in travel books and cosmographies, they could now experience more immediately through the dynamics of theater performances.

Insofar as the creative writers, especially the dramatists, expressed a public mood, they can be studied objectively for what they reveal about the way ethnological information—and misinformation—contributes to shaping human disposition towards a foreign people and their culture.[36] And since playwrights failed, on the whole, to imagine the possibility of a more human disposition in the black man than they did, they are to be held partially responsibile for supporting and legitimizing an unfavorable and seldom justifiable verdict against the black man. It should be possible for a writer in a single work to reflect the current popular opinions of a society, and at the same time to suggest that that opinion could be faulty. Through the enveloping action of a play, the acts and words of the characters surrounding the black man, writers often did mirror the current public attitude toward aliens. Yet at the same time they could—and sometimes did—dramatize in the figure of the black man himself quite different possibilities of human conduct. A black man could be reviled by the white society as an infidel and devil, a lecher and villain, and still exhibit in his own behavior a capacity for human feeling to confute his reputation.

Therefore it would be a serious omission to ignore any favorable comments that might mitigate against the seemingly persistent attack against the black man. There are in the plays studied above certain scenes and actions that do intimate that white writers could, if only infrequently, conceive of the black man acting in ways that were not only acceptable by white standards but even admirable in a case or two. His potential for goodness, however, was severely limited and heavily overshadowed by the concentration of his capacity for evil. As a matter of fact, a positive gesture or admirable quality of a black man is often so deeply obscured among the details of his depravity that only a careful examination of the text can bring it to light.

Chapter 8

Some Asides on Positive Aspects of the Image of the Black Man

Like their contemporaries in the fields of geography and ethnology, who were by and large in agreement about the "scientific truth" of the black man's lowly status, creative writers also shared a "poetic truth" concerning him. That "truth" too was overwhelmingly damning. Condemned by his external blackness and by an imagined inner darkness, the black man stood before his white jury with little to defend himself from the revulsion and fear these attributes provoked. As either an uncivilized man of undeveloped potential, a savage and a barbarian, or as a creature of a different species altogether, higher than animal but lower than man, he was denounced with monotonous repetition. Yet, even as some "scientific" commentators were capable of citing some worthy quality of the black man, so in the creative literature there gleam here and there signs of black virtue (measured, of course, by white standards), some moments in which white characters are made to express respect for the black man, or some scenes in which a black man appears admirable. There may even be a completely noble black man or two in the cast of characters.

In the face of the ponderous weight of material unfavorable to the black man, these scattered scenes showing higher potential in his character raise the same general question already applied to the main body of negative treatment. If the general opinion was that the black man was essentially base and villainous, why did there appear in the midst of the clamor an occasionally favorable portrait or scene? To be sure, the favorable view appears more often in dramatic asides than mainstream action, but even the worst black villains are sometimes shown to have a jot of potential goodness, of humanness in them. (Strangely enough, the same cannot be said of the worst white villains like Iago and Deflores.) The primitivist conception of the New World man as a "noble savage" would not expand to include the black man until the end of the seventeenth century, so it cannot account for some of the scenes and characters that will be discussed in this chapter. Playwrights like Shakespeare, Dekker, Rowley, and Heywood may have unconsciously harbored ambivalence toward their black subjects. Perhaps they occasionally experienced a sense of guilt over their narrowed vision of the black man and consequently felt an urge to expand it through a scene or two of positive presentation.

A more satisfactory explanation for these glimpses of the black man's potential is that their inclusion in the plays frequently heightens the realism of the characters, giving them another dimension and a greater truth, making a stronger impact on the spectator. The black villain who has a soft spot for something or somebody is more like life than he might have been as an unadulterated criminal without feeling or heart. It is more convincing, then, to attribute the greater realism of these scenes to the authors' purposes than to theorize that they wrote from a psychological ambivalence toward the black man.

One might argue that it is sometimes too startling to find positive human values exhibited by a man who has already displayed a huge capacity for cruelty and murder. However, from what we have learned of the unspeakable bestiality of twentieth-century tyrants who have shown the possibility of being good fathers and husbands, kind to children and dogs, we have come to realize that the will to great evil and the potential for humaneness can reside in the same individual. Therefore, there is not much shock in seeing someone like Aaron fondling his son and defending him with the devotion of an ideal father. The strange mingling of capacities for brutality and tenderness within one man is not fanciful or preposterous. A contemporary psychologist has actually felt the necessity to authenticate Aaron's behavior by comparing it to clinically evaluated similarities in case studies.[1]

The surfacing of humanity in a being otherwise inhuman occurs several times in the plays discussed in this study. Aaron has shown himself the cruelest of men, yet he protects his newborn son against Chiron and Demetrius. Because their mother has born the child, they want to kill it to escape the inevitable disgrace to their family. Drawing his sword, Aaron vows:

> Stay, murtherous villains! Will you kill your brother?
> Now by the tapers of the sky,
> That's shone so brightly when this boy was got,
> He dies upon my scimitar's sharp point
> That touches this my first-born son and heir![2]

In answer to Demetrius' charge that the Queen's adultery will be betrayed if the child is revealed, Aaron states his priorities unhesitatingly:

> My mistress is my mistress; this myself,
> The vigour and the picture of my youth.
> This before all the world do I prefer;
> This maugre all the world will I keep safe,
> Or some of you shall smoke for it in Rome.[3]

When Aaron is finally captured by his enemies, he sacrifices his own chances for life to save that of his son. "Lucius, save the child / And bear it from me to the Empress," he pleads. In exchange for his son's life, he makes a defiant public confession of his whole criminal career.[4] The episode tends to strengthen the psychological truth of his character.

In the hands of Ravenscroft, who claimed he had "heighten'd" the principal characters of Shakespeare's play, Aron's villainy is perhaps altered for the worse. Yet his paternalism gains emphasis. Including Shakespeare's scenes of Aron defending his son from the threats of Demetrius and Chiron, Ravenscroft adds the objective observation from a nurse who has already voiced her disgust over the whole affair: "O Sir he loves this black Imp above the World."[5] Furthermore, Ravenscroft creates a torture scene to dramatize Aron's endurance to bear pain and his will to remain silent. Aron is put to the rack in a brutal but vain attempt to make him confess his crimes. Physical pain and the threat of death do not loosen his tongue. He bears both, stubbornly refusing to talk. In sharp contrast, however, when Marcus moves to kill the black child, Aron quickly exchanges his confession for the life of his child. The entire scene, with its juxtaposition of Aron's responses, has served the singular purpose of sharpening the relationship between him and his son.

Naturally, paternal affection was not attributed to black men generally. But physical bravery was certainly attributed to them as a dominant trait. With the exception of Muly Mahamet (*The Battle of Alcazar*), the black man was always granted at least this one important virtue. The Crusades had already proved the Moor a fierce and bold fighter, and the defeat of the Portuguese army at Alcazar in 1578 reinforced European fears of Moorish daring and bravery. Furthermore, conceding this quality to the Moor did not necessarily mean that his humanity was enlarged, for courage is so easily defined as a trait shared with animals and is not limited to or definitive of human beings of a civilized society. In addition, treachery and cruelty could be carried to extreme ends when buttressed by a daring spirit. Eleazer's unquestionable courage, for example, receives special praise from the dying King Ferdinand, who recommends Eleazer as one useful to the throne. When his army has been routed, Eleazer's servants bid him flee to escape capture. They cry:

> Oh flye my Lord! flye; for the day is lost.

> Eleazer   There are three hundred and odd days in a year,
> And cannot we lose one of them, come fight.[6]

Admirable though it is here, it is this same fearlessness that aids him in his machinations and destructive plots.

Dekker surprisingly goes a bit further to complicate Eleazer's character by creating several strange scenes that unexpectedly reveal in the arch villain a tenderness and a sense of honor. In the critical battle, Eleazer is raging in the throes of a blood lust for his foes when he spies a fallen Moor. Suddenly sobered, he is moved to express his feelings of respect for a dead comrade:

> But thou didst well, thou knew'st I was thy Lord:
> And out of love and duty to me here,
> Where I fell weary, thou laidst down thyself
> To bear me up thus: God a-mercy slave,
> A king for this shall give thee a rich grave.[7]

His sense of gratitude and his pledge of remembrance are indicative of some hitherto unseen side of Eleazer. The incongruity of this view with the image of evil already developed is expanded in the following scene also on the field of battle where Eleazer is allowed a noble gesture. Weary after intense fighting, Eleazer comes face to face with his sworn enemy Philip, who challenges him to single combat. The hotheaded young prince, however, is armed only with a broken sword, a piece of a weapon. Eleazer refuses to fight because his foe has this disadvantage. He urges Philip to equip himself with better weapons, but Philip issues the challenge again. He prefers the odds against himself. Eleazer then insists that they exchange swords to reverse the advantage. "Fling me thy sword, there's mine I scorn to strike a man disarm'd." Philip again refuses to even the match and Eleazer breaks off the confrontation: "I'le run way / Unlesse thou change that weapon, or take mine."[8] There could appear to be something deceptive in Eleazer's behavior here, but there is no textual evidence of treachery in his proposals and actions; his warriorlike dignity, contrasting so sharply with his fiendish plottings, must be taken as genuine. These two scenes may make him slightly more believable, but they do not attenuate his guilt as a demonic villain. The dramatic impact of the total play is too overwhelmingly against him.[9]

Mrs. Behn achieved a similar deepening of the Moor's character through developing a different human quality. Whereas Dekker seems to have heightened the Moor's portrait by bringing out his sense of military honor, Mrs. Behn endowed her Moor with a genuine capacity for love. Both Eleazer and Abdelazer exhibit some affection for their wives, but Eleazer is more easily prepared to sacrifice his wife to another's bed than is Abdelazer. Abdelazer's feelings towards his wife, a mixture of affection and jealousy, prevent him from making her a political tool. Furthermore, in another situation Eleazer's courtship of the Princess Isabella is motivated less by affection than by sexual desire and political ambition. He has little tenderness within him. Abdelazer, on the other hand, is drawn with more human qualities. Mrs. Behn portrays his love for Leonora as genuine. He seriously offers her the throne he has won in battle and pleads in tears that she accept his love. His outraged reply to her refusal is more an emotional product of his jealousy over her fidelity to a white man (who, she insultingly suggests, is handsomer than the Moor) than it is a sudden exposure of his pretense of a love never really felt.

> See—I can bend as low, and sigh as often,
> And sue for Blessings only you can grant;
> As any fair and soft Alonzo can.[10]

A few moments later he kneels again and tearfully pleads with her to kill him, for her denial, he claims, is the end of his life anyway. The sincerity of his tears perhaps can be intimated from his earlier explanation to his henchman Roderigo as to why he has given the crown to Leonora. Spoken in a situation that demands no pretense, his words are an honest confession of love. When Roderigo demands to know why he has thrown the crown away, he retorts:

> What every Man that loves like me should do;
> Undone myself for ever to beget
> One Moment's thought in her, that I adore her;
> That she may know none ever lov'd like me,
> I've thrown away the Diadem of Spain.

And a few lines later, he continues rhapsodically: "Ah, she's a Goddess! a Creature made by Heaven / To make my prosperous Toils all sweet and charming!"[11]

The overdone scene is typical of the exaggerated passions displayed on the Restoration stage. Yet here the passions are attributed to a black man and establish his potential as an equal of a white courter. However, Abdelazer is still a black moor and is shaped to reflect some qualitites deemed typical of black people. Therefore, when Leonora repudiates him, his initial disappointment grows into a furious response filled with threats of force and rape. Here again are two seemingly antagonistic strains of behavior within the same being; the first, a tenderness and capacity for love, surfaces briefly only to be finally obscured by the savagery brought on by frustration.

There are but few other positive acts by black characters to mitigate their villainy—or, perhaps more accurately, their creators' view of the black man as villainous. *All's Lost by Lust* (1619) offers the example of the loyal Moor in the character Fydella. As her allegorical name suggests, she is absolutely loyal to her white mistress Margaretta. Fydella will kill for her and is prepared to die with her; and since Margaretta herself is not basically villainous, Fydella's devotion is not unworthy of respect. However, because of Fydella's willingness to assist in a strangling simply at the request of her mistress, she approaches the stereotyped role of the murderous Moor. In the same play there is also the arch villain Mulymumen, who exhibits on the battlefield both bravery in action and devotion to honor. As King of the Moors in battle against the Spanish, he learns that his brother has been surrounded by the enemy and is doomed to death or capture if he is not immediately reinforced. Rather than permit either, Mulymumen resolves to die or suffer captivity with him.

> They are both noble; but to basely flie
> Is to preserve life, and let honour die,
> Fall then my flesh, so there survive my name,
> Who flies from honour, follows after shame.[12]

His proclamation of honor, however, has the reverse effect of obscuring any feelings he may have for his brother. Mulymumen seems more concerned about reputation than saving the life of his own brother. The motive for his decision is hardly selfless and, in view of the circumstances, could be judged less than admirable.

Fletcher was another writer who included a scene in which Moors are shown possessing some softer human feelings. In *The Island Princess* (1611), the villainous Governor has employed two Moors to guard and torment his prisoner, the King of Tidore. The presence of the Moors doubtlessly was intended to contribute to the aura of the Governor's evil. But the author manages to humanize the black guards by making them capable of respecting their prisoner's courage and endurance and even feeling some pity for him.

> 2nd Moor   His eyes not sunk, and his complexion firm still,
> No wildness, no distemper'd touch upon him:
> How constantly he smiles, and how undaunted!
> With what a majesty he heaves his head up![13]

After the Governor has ordered the king's hardships increased so that he suffers a living death, the Moors commiserate with their prisoner.

> 2nd Moor   I wish him better,
> But much I fear he has found his tomb already.
> We must observe our guards.
>
> 1st Moor   He cannot last long;
> And when he's dead he's free.[14]

Although their hearts seem to be in the right place in this scene, the Moors still carry out their orders to intensify the torture ("We must observe our guards") and therefore retain their reputation for cruelty.

There were some playwrights, then, like Fletcher in the scene above, who complicated the nature of the villainous Moor by exposing here and there a soft spot in an otherwise flinty core of evil features. Although such displays expand the image of the black man somewhat, the noble gesture or the expression of a decent feeling does too little to alter the predominantly negative characterization. The potential to act humanely is so little developed that it hardly appears likely that the stage black man was greeted with any expectation other than that he would violate the moral code of white Christian culture and that in almost any circumstances he would act diabolically. An audience would hardly anticipate being moved to sympathy for such a figure.

Though he might occasionally be thought capable of a worthy deed, in the long run it did the black man little good. On the other hand, there was some understanding that the preference for oneself and one's own culture could also be felt by those on the other side of a racial boundary. Racial pride was not expected to be unique to the white race. Blackness might be considered beautiful—by a black man. But the sight of a black man praising himself might prove quite ludicrous to a seventeenth-century audience. This was the same audience that might have answered Shylock's questions protesting his humanity with a riotous "no."[15]

To the modern sensibility racial pride must appear as a positive attribute of the abused black man, but three centuries ago it probably seemed more like a ridiculous and stubborn blindness to the "truth." And so perhaps to the amusement of an audience, black characters were often given the chance to declare their pride in blackness.

One of the earliest examples of an ethnocentric pride in black beauty comes in the anonymous play *Captain Thomas Stukley* (1596), illustrating the probable ludicrous effect such a posture could have. The plot of the play is similar to that of Peele's *The Battle of Alcazar* (1589-90) but focuses on the Irishman Thomas Stukley as its central dramatic interest. When Muly Mahamet greets Stukley and the Portuguese King Sebastian, who have offered him assistance in regaining his throne, the black ruler offers Sebastian the seat of honor at a banquet. The place has been so designated because it places its occupant at the side of Muly's black wife Calipolis, whom he eulogizes as "faire Calipolis," and whose beauty he boasts would challenge Juno's.

> Jove would exchange his Scepter for thy seat,
> And would abandon Junos godlike bedd
> Might he enjoy my faire Calipolis
> Beauty a Phenix burneth in her eie,
> Which there still liveth as it still doth die.[16]

What effect these lines could have on an Elizabethan audience is a moot point, but Stukley's comment could hardly be one of sincere praise.

> Why heers a gallant, heers a king indeed,
> . . . This is pure fire.
> Every look he casts flasheth like lightning.
> There's mettle in this Boy.[17]

If there is an ambivalence in these lines, it is faint indeed. The sarcasm of his tone is almost too clear to miss.

There is no question of tone, of course, in Aaron's defense of blackness with which he buttresses his relationship to his son. Chiron and Demetrius hate the infant for its blackness, and Aaron conversely reviles them for their whiteness.

> . . . is black so base a hue?
> Sweet blowse, you are a beauteous blossom sure;
> . . . .
>
> What, what ye sanguine, shallow-hearted boys!
> Ye white lim'd walls! Ye alehouse pointed signs!
> Coal-black is better than another hue
>
> In that it scorns to bear another hue
> For all the water in the ocean
> Can never turn the swain's black legs to white,
> Although she lave them hourly in the flood.[18]

Ravenscroft, who generally tended to sharpen the differences between black and white people in his treatment of Shakespeare's play, again chose to extend this speech, thereby deepening Aron's contempt for white skin. Hearing the son of his own flesh and color denounced as ugly and threatened with death, Aron bursts forth with some racially vituperative epithets of his own:

> What, what ye sanguine hollow-hearted Boys,
> Ye gaudy blossoms, checquer'd white and red,
> See, here is a glass that will not sully
> Like your water colour'd complexions,
> Which Chance does fade and Sickness washes out.
> I say that black is better then another hue,
> In that it scorns to bear another hue.

White men can blush and betray their hearts, but

> Here's a Young Lad form'd of another Leer,
> Look how the Black Slave smiles upon the Father,
> As who would say, Old Dad I am thine own.
> . . . my Seal be stamped on his face.[19]

Shakespeare more than once faced the problem of the black man's attitude toward himself. Through Aaron he acknowledged the black man's possible acceptance of himself for what he was. Aaron has little self-hatred that reveals itself in any self-derogating act or speech. The Prince of Morocco, however, is highly sensitive to the disadvantage his skin color places him under as he attempts to win Portia. His opening speech to her pleads—not humbly, to be sure—that she ignore his color. He asserts, first, his common brotherhood with all men regardless of skin color; the color of the inner man, that is, the color of his blood, his ultimate reality, is the same everywhere.

> Mislike me not for my complexion,
> The shadowed livery of the burnish'd sun,
> To whom I am a neighbor and near bred.
> Bring me the fairest creature northward born,
> Where Phoebus' fire scarce thaws the icicles,
> And let us make incision for your love
> To prove whose blood is reddest, his or mine.[20]

Morocco, however, does not openly voice pride in his own complexion except, perhaps, for its intimidating aspect. He recalls the terror his black face has produced in the grave hearts of his foes, and he implies that his blackness is the source of that terror. Nor does he intimate that women of his own race are beautiful when he boasts to Portia that many have loved him.

> I tell thee, lady, this aspect of mine
> Hath fear'd the valiant. By my love I swear,
> The best regarded virgins of our clime
> Have lov'd it too.[21]

He admits a willingness to change his color, if he could, were it to win her favor. It is only to prove the extremity of his love that he says all this, but though the speech is hardly exemplary of ethnocentrism, it does hint at some degree of self-respect Morocco possesses.

Webster's Zanche alludes to an argument similar to Morocco's when she claims her fundamental humanity on the grounds of the universality of red blood. She goes further to proclaim the superiority of blackness over whiteness. The circumstances of her defiant remarks increase its force, for she is talking of her approaching death and is addressing her killer, urging him to strike.

> . . . I have blood
> As red as either of theirs: wilt drink some?
> 'Tis good for the falling-sickness. I am proud
> Death cannot alter my complexion,
> For I shall ne'er look pale.[22]

Zanche's brave and willing confrontation with death turns her last thoughts to her blackness and endows her racial pride with a dignity found missing elsewhere.

In a droll mood, Ben Jonson employs similar trains of thought to describe blackness defending itself in a white society. *The Masque of Blackness* (1605) contains all the arguments: the permanence of blackness, its esteem even by white people when it appears in the hair of fair ladies, its origin in the power of the sun. The river Niger, representing Aethiopia, says that his purpose is the sustenance and nurture of the daughters of his country. He calls attention to an old belief that the people of the south "were the first begotten of the earth" and that the beauty of the women there takes its nourishment generously from the sun, the source of feminine beauty everywhere:

> Tho' he [the sun] (the best judg and most formal cause
> Of all dames beauties) in their firm hews, draws
> Signs of his fervent'st love; and thereby shews
> That in their black, the perfect'st beauty grows;
> Since the fixt colour of their curled hair,
> (Which is the highest grace of dames most fair)
> No cares, no age can change; or there display
> The fearful tincture of abhorred grey;
> Since death herself (her self being pale and blue)
> Can never alter their most faithful hue:
> All which are arguments, to prove how far
> Their beauties conquer in great beauty's war.[23]

Thus Niger has a logical justification for his ethnocentric pronouncements. If the sun is the ultimate cause of all feminine beauty, how much more generous has he been with the Aethiopian women whom he has indelibly marked with gifts offered to no other women![24]

Hindered by the same cultural disability that limited the degree of decency and self-respect they were willing to grant to black characters, white authors also wrote with restraint of the possibility that black men could earn the expressed respect of white men. The manly virtue of courage was most frequently the quality that evoked respect, although occasionally there were other virtues singled out. Eleazer, for example, one of the consummate black villains of the stage, has earned from his Spanish king the epithets "wise" and "warlike." He has also managed to gain the favor of his father-in-law, Alvero, who has come to accept him openly and warmly as his "son," and who even defends Eleazer early in the play by pointing out to those who would condemn him that "he underwent much injurie."[25] In *Captain Thomas Stukley*, the Portuguese lieutenant Antonio praises black soldiers for their bravery at the same time that he disparages the Negroes, in whom bravery, he says, is unexpected.

Our very slaves, our Negros, Muleteers,
Able to give you Battaile in the field,
Even think of those that you must cope withall,
The Portingall and his approved power,
Muly-Mahamet and his valliant Moors,
The Irish Marques, Stukley and his troup
Of warlike Germans and Italians.[26]

The black allies of Sir Francis Drake in Davenant's *The History of Sir Francis Drake* (1659) are described as "trusty Symerons," and their king as "monarch of much and still deserving more." These Symerons are the escaped Negro slaves who were originally brought to Peru by the Spaniards "to dig in mines; and having lately revolted from them, did live under the government of a King of their own election."[27] Here are black men in love with freedom who are brave enough to battle to achieve it. D'Avenant has written one of the earliest imaginative accounts of black revolutionaries, and he has shown that the English nobility could recognize their accomplishments and treat them with respect and friendship.[28]

Sometimes the respect shown a black man is only intimated, as in King Ferdinand's plea of love for Florella, Abdelazer's wife (*The Moor's Revenge*, 1677). Florella reminds him that she already has a husband, and his answer gives some recognition of the Moor's selfhood. Instead of trying to undermine Abdelazer's humanity (as the earlier Ferdinand in Dekker's play did), he dwells on the "sacriligious theft" that made her the Moor's wife before he had a chance to court her. Finally he vows to seize her from the Moor, without deceiving himself that it is his kingly right to do so or her duty to obey him. His attitude and speech are an implicit acceptance of the legality of the marriage, and therein an acknowledgement of the Moor's human status.[29]

One of the most interesting treatments of a black figure who elicits a positive response from white characters appears in Berkeley's *The Lost Lady* (1637). Here the Moor Arcanthe is really a white lady in disguise, and in a sense whatever favorable views are expressed about her as a black woman could be considered annulled at the moment her true identity is exposed. Her disguise, however, which she adopted to escape from imprisonment in her uncle's house, is not dropped until the fifth act. Since no one is aware of her real identity, her behavior up to that point must be accepted at face value, both by the stage characters and the audience, as possible for a Moor. The denouement is not likely to dispel all the good impressions made by the "Moor" during the first four acts. Throughout the play she suffers no racially motivated attacks. She is treated simply as a woman, one with some special powers in black magic, to be sure, but not one singled out by racial prejudice. Even when she is rejected by other characters, the cause is personal rather than racial. Philomeda, one of the court ladies, resents her presence "near the court," not because she is black but because she, like so many other serving women, is probably "too inquisitive" and may ferret out the secrets of lovers. Philomeda, therefore, considers Arcanthe just a part of the human race, susceptible to the human weaknesses of curiosity and gossip. Her negative reaction to the Moor is really a positive judgment of Arcanthe's humanity. Irene, on the other hand, who is a friend of Arcanthe, extols the very opposite quality. She is secret as the night she resembles."[30] Herminoe, too, for whom Arcanthe has expressed compassion, has been convinced of the Moor's sincerity and sympathy. She describes Arcanthe's basic worth to the king:

> When you her know, you will believe
> That virtue chose that dark inhabitation
> To hide her treasure from the envious world.[31]

At the same time, however, praise for a black person is often given condescendingly, and its ultimate effect is more malign than benign. Hermione has implied that virtue is more naturally visible; that is, more characteristic of white people. In a black person it "hides" and is infrequently discovered. The impact of the line is the same as in the common expression, "He's different from the rest of them." Arcanthe, as an individual, does not suffer from this twist of language. As a matter of fact she seems to be the voice of virtue in the play, preaching the need for faith and constancy in love, predicting divine punishment if Hermione breaks her vows of fidelity to her lover Eugenio. Hermione's reply to this warning once again transforms an intentional praise of an individual (Arcanthe) into a condemnation of a class (black people):

> Where cannot virtue dwell! What a still shade
> Hath she found out to live securely in,
> From the attempts of men?[32]

Inner virtue shielded by an outer ugliness of black can rest easy, secure in its inviolable position. This is hardly a compliment to the black world. Nevertheless, the total portrait of Arcanthe, before she drops her mask, is not unflattering. The fact that she turns out to have been white all along does not change the effect she has had on others concerning the potentiality of a Moor's ethics. Within the play itself the shock of recognition is not accompanied by a reversal of attitudes to deny earlier positive assessments. A Moor of high character has been dramatized and accepted for what she is. This is what matters.

These moments showing a black character earning the respect of white characters, moments of affirmation of racial pride, and gestures expressive of human decency and even nobility, have occurred in characters who are not necessarily noble in the full scope of their natures. Some of these characters are neutral in their moral lives and some are consummate villains. But there are a very few characters who are fundamentally noble people of the best sort, whose genuine goodness is not marred by lapses into cruelty or evil.

In the same play that gave us the first vilification of a Moor, *The Battle of Alcazar* (1588–89), Peele also created the first noble Moor. The problem of his color has already been discussed, but it would not be amiss to repeat here that because the villain Muly is called the Negro Moor it need not follow that Abdelmelec, the good Moor, is white. As chapter 3 has stressed, the fusion of racial concepts and the interchangeability of names argue that Abdelmelec, in the absence of concrete textual evidence to the contrary (such as that provided in the fifth act of *The Thracian Wonder*; see p. 93), is also intended to be nonwhite, although he may have been presented as lighter than Muly. He is undeniably a Moor, and Peele draws him as a leader possessing admirable proportions of mercy and a sense of justice, a man who wishes to avoid useless bloodshed. Abdelmelec has a strong feeling of the justness of his own cause, and puts that feeling to the test only when he finds he has no alternative. He appeals to the foolish Sebastian to reconsider the moral right of the Portuguese forces to be in Africa.

> For seeing that he goeth about to take the kingdom from
> him, to whome it doth of right appertaine, and to give it
> to the Negro, and that with no profit nor commoditie to
> the Christians, that will almightie God, who is a just
> Judge, never suffer.[33]

Abdelmelec is apostrophized as the "courteous and honorable Abdelmelec,"[34] who has "in pittie" sent messengers to the "Portugall" to persuade him to recall his troops. Abdelmelec knows only too well that his own seasoned Moorish troops will massacre the Christian forces. Sebastian, however, obstinately informs him that "we scorne his curtesie" and leads his armies to their doom.[35] In the final battle all the leading figures die, including the worthy Moor Abdelmelec, who dies of a fever he suffered before the engagement. His appearances in the play have been shaped to contribute to the essential worth of his character, so much in contrast with the treacherous Muly.

The Prince of Morocco is another black figure who, in the few short scenes allotted him, manages to reach a level of dignity which, although the white ladies in his company fail to take notice of it, cannot be ignored by an audience. As he ponders his choice among the caskets, which have been devised by Portia's father as an instrument to win her the right kind of husband, Morocco philosophizes about the vagaries of fortune. If he chooses wrong, he knows that he is sworn to lead a celibate life, a dismal existence for one who has already won the hearts of "the best-regarded virgins" of the dark race. Without pomposity, he describes his own great prowess, his skill in battle, his bravery in outfacing bears and lions. But he reminds us that such qualities are of little consequence in a game of chance such as the one he now faces. He displays a touch of humility in his initial willingness to recognize that, much as he esteems himself, he may not "deserve" so much as the person of Portia. On second consideration he does persuade himself that he is deserving of her but he still shies away from the silver box with its inscription: "Who chooseth me shall get as much as he deserves." Silver, he concludes, is baser metal than gold, which he now chooses in the belief that Portia is what all men want. In the face of failure that condemns him to a life of frost, his dignity remains unruffled. He accepts his punishment without despair or anger but rather with a genuine sadness over losing Portia. "Portia, adieu. I have too griev'd a heart / To take a tedious leave. Thus losers part."[36] In contrast to the French suitor Aragon, who in defeat loses his head and angrily curses his fate, Morocco presents a picture of control and reserve amounting to a nobility rare among black men on the stage.

Morocco's stature and demeanor derive from a background of noble birth and military experience. Consequently, his level of speech and his self-awareness are beyond those of the common man. He is the extraordinary man. His image could not be said to typify his race. In addition his role in the play is limited to two short scenes involving little interaction with other people; his character hardly develops into more than a broad sketch, although the measurements are large. By contrast, the figure of Basha Joffer in Heywood's *The Fair Maid of the West*, part II (1630?), lacks the noble proportions of Morocco but is more appealing in its basic humanity, for Joffer contains an emotional life nearer to a common core of experience. In Joffer, Heywood has created a man possessing a sensibility developed to a degree that makes him responsive to the emotional needs of other human beings, a quality white Christianity would find common among its own adherents but one that could be imagined only as a rarity among black pagans.

But the unlikely compassion becomes a reality when Joffer, who has Spencer in his custody, is moved by the Englishman's appeal to see his beloved Bess once again before their separation becomes permanent. Speaking of the great love the fair maid Bess and he have shared, Spencer pledges his word to return to Joffer if he is given a brief parole to say goodbye to his wife. Joffer is deeply touched, and at the risk of his own life, which must be forfeited if Spencer fails him, grants the request.

> You have deeply touch't me: and to let you know
> All morrall vertues are not solely grounded
> In th' hearts of Christians, go and passe free.[37]

The theme of rivalry between the two races over which is morally superior is never out of Joffer's mind and is evidently a major concern of Heywood. Spencer's incredulousness upon discovering such compassion and trust beneath a black skin is typically ethnocentric. In recognizing Joffer's goodness he cannot refrain from asserting that the locus of such virtue is in Christendom.

> Is honour fled Christians unto Moors,
> That I may say in Barbarie I found
> This rare black Swan.[38]

This nearly total paralysis of imagination that blinded white writers to the possible existence of a decent moral code among blacks is one of the remarkable failures of the times—or one of the remarkable consequences of cultural and psychological pressures operating within a society. The black cannot be allowed to surpass the white. Spencer matches the Moor's generous act by honoring his promise to return himself to Joffer's custody to face imprisonment and possibly even death at the order of the angry King Mullisheg. His decision is difficult, for once he is free and aboard Bess's ship, nothing but his word to the black soldier stands between him and an escape with Bess to Europe. His own sense of honor, however, and the honor of the white race compel him to return to Joffer. His arrival at the court comes just in time to save Joffer, who has been condemned to death for releasing the white prisoner.

Spencer eulogizes Joffer for his kindheartedness and open trust in permitting him his brief reunion with Bess, who, he claims, was on the verge of suicide over his own fate. In this scene it is clear that both Moor and Christian possess virtue and faith; each is noble in his own way and acknowledges the worth of the other. Spencer praises Joffer highly.

> Great Mullisheg, cherish this noble Moor,
> Whom all thy confines cannot parallell
> For vertue and true nobleness.[39]

Thereupon Mullisheg pardons Joffer, and in amazement over the virtue of an Englishman—a parody of Spencer's earlier remark about Joffer's goodness—the king releases Spencer to join his Bess. "Is't possible? can England so farre distant / Harbour such noble vertues?"[40] The answer to the question of the source of virtue comes from both racial views. Each believes his own culture and its moral fibre to be supreme, and each admits, somewhat grudgingly, the possible manifestation of virtue in other peoples.

To argue that Heywood's intention was less the glorification and humanization of the black man than the idealization of the love between Bess and Spencer, with its power to move the pity of the traditionally pitiless, does not minimize the significance of this black figure. Joffer appears as a sensitive human being with noble values and a will to act by their dictates. Heywood, however, could not resist that last surrender of Joffer's claim to equality: the black man will finally have to admit Spencer's higher honor, the supremacy of Christianity, and a desire to convert to the white man's blessed faith.

As we have seen from this chapter, the time had not yet come for the white European to accept unreservedly a possibly indigenous virtue in such an unusual and different culture as that of the black man of Africa. Whenever a black character exhibits a sign of decent behavior, either it is so buried among acts of evil that it fails to leave any lasting impression, or it appears conditioned by a recognition of the higher virtue of white culture. The fine gesture and even the honorable mind, when they appeared in a black skin, are both treated as patently inferior to those of white characters. A black man could on rare occasions turn out to be a decent human being, but only if he reached a consciousness and an acceptance of Christian ethics and white manners.

Epilogue

To summarize the study of these materials, we can note the following tendencies: First, the dramatists were likely to express without much modification the popular ideas and attitudes toward black men generally held by the dominant white culture. The ethnologists and travelers claimed that blacks lacked reason, were governed by superstition, were given to lying and deception, and exhibited savage and cruel behavior. The black characters who parade across the English stage, like those described in journals and in rumor, also lie, cheat, kill, worship the sun and moon, and act in passionate disorder. The lack of feeling the travelers claimed to have noted among the African peoples they visited became a central characteristic of stage figures like Muly Mahamet, Aaron, Eleazer, and Mulymumen. Of course, this is not to say that the creative writers simply and naively followed the materials provided by cosmographers and travelers. The greater probability is that like the nonliterary writers, they, too, were responding to similar cultural pressures, personal prejudices, and mistaken beliefs. The complexity of forces exerted on both groups of writers makes any final resolution of cause difficult.

A major facet of the iconography of the black man shaped by this complex of pressures is his demonic persuasions. He is pictured not only as being cruel but as enjoying his cruelty. The black man is a living devil; sadism and treachery are his popular trademarks. Again and again the belief that he is an agent of Satan, a devil in man's shape, is hammered home. White characters are frequently obsessed with their own concept of the black man's demonism. The color of his skin and the way he is made to accept the identity confirm in the white mentality that black men are devils. The consistency with which white men make this identification is sustained by the frequent open confessions of the black man that the accusations are true. When the white man says "black devil," the black man scowls in agreement.

Another crucial feature of his image, one that has probably survived to this day to plague the black man, is his reputed sexual prowess. Although blackness was considered repulsive, the black man was thought to be a serious sexual threat to white women, either as a cunning and libidinous seducer or as a violent and conscienceless rapist. His sexual goals and capacities were the objects of much attention in the plays and frequently became focal points of interest. In general, his sexual appetite usually showed him to be little better than an animal.

What reinforced these concepts of the black man is another facet of his image: his heathenism. In England little attempt was made by Christians in this early period to understand the black man's religious beliefs, whether Islamic or animistic. That he worshipped God through the prophet Mohamed or prayed to the sun and the moon made little difference to men who recognized Christianity as the only possible truth. Black men were purely and simply pagans, and as such were considered to be perversely rejecting that truth. As pagans, therefore, they were easily removed from the circle of the human family and readily accused of living in league with the devil, the anti-Christ.

Finally, as a consequence of all of these tendencies, white characters habitually express unfavorable attitudes toward the black ones and act out their hostility in abusive language and debasing gestures. The black man becomes a pariah in white society. If tolerated at all, he is tolerated only because of his military skills, which are sometimes needed by the society, or for his sexual appeal to some licentious woman. In turn the black man is made to talk and act in such ways that the treatment he receives at the hands of white society seems justified in the context of the play. The same justification quite probably extended beyond the imaginary world of the theater into the real world of commerce and slavery, where brutality against the black man could be rationalized by the image of his corrupted being. As a creature judged incapable of moral discernment, deficient in human compassion, gross and brutal in his treatment of others, the black man suffered persistent dehumanization, with which slavery seemed easily reconcilable.

It is against the whole background of economic development and its inherent cultural values regarding slavery, including the psychological and historical influences on attitudes toward blackness and the black man, that the full impact of the nearly systematic literary denigration of the black man should be understood. Because there was little clamor in England against or in defense of slavery during these years, the literature of the time, so overwhelmingly disparaging of the black man, could only have had the effect of legitimating the trade by dramatizing its victims as innately base and evil, hence deserving subjugation. To say this is not to suggest that the creative literature itself so assuaged men's consciences that they gave little thought to the moral complexities of slavery. What it does suggest is that just as language often reflects reality while acting upon it as a shaping force, so the unfavorable portraits of the black man both reflected cultural attitudes and, by confirming their moral rightness, strengthened them. To return to Professor David Davis's question of whether the "literary imagination could build a bridge of sympathy and understanding across the enormous gulf that divided" white and black men, most of the evidence that lies in the creative literature of the earliest period of confrontation strongly suggests that the writers not only failed to evoke such positive feelings but rather, in ways indicative of a broad racism, widened the distance between the two peoples.

Appendix 1

Black characters in the plays, including those disguised as blacks.

Aaron, *Titus Andronicus* (Shakespeare)
Abdelazar, *The Moor's Revenge* (Aphra Behn)
Abdelmelec, *The Battle of Alcazar* (Peele)
Aethiopian women, *The Queen's Masque, The First of Blackness* (Jonson)
Africa, a nymph, *Calisto* (Crowne)
African women, *Calisto* (Crowne)
Alcade, *The Thracian Wonder* (author uncertain)
Arcanthe, disguised as a Moor, *The Lost Lady* (Berkeley)
Aron, *Titus Andronicus* (Ravenscroft)
Balthazar, *Lust's Dominion* (Dekker)
Basher Joffer, *The Fair Maid of the West*, part II (Heywood)
Beaupre, disguised as the Moor Calisto, *The Parliament of Love* (Massinger)
Calipolis, *The Battle of Alcazar* (Peele)
Calipolis, *Captain Thomas Stukley* (author unknown)
Celanta, *Old Wive's Tales* (Peele)
Eleazer, *Lust's Dominion* (Dekker)
Empress of Morocco, *The Empress of Morocco* (Settle)
Francesco, disguised as black, *The White Devil* (Webster)
Fydella, *All's Lost by Lust* (Rowley)
A little Blacka-More, *The Gentleman Dancing-Master* (Wycherly)
Lucifera, *The Prophetess* (Fletcher)
Millicent, disguised as a Moor, *The English Moor* (Brome)
Moorish guards (2), *The Island Princess* (Fletcher)
Moorish governor, *The Island Princess* (Fletcher)
Moorish king, *The Triumph of Truth* (Middleton)
Moorish woman, *Monsieur Thomas* (Fletcher)
Mullisheg, *The Fair Maid of the West*, parts I and II (Heywood)
Muly Mahamet, *The Battle of Alcazar* (Peele)
Muly Mahamat, *Captain Thomas Stukley* (author unknown)
Mulymumen, *All's Lost by Lust* (Rowley)

Nigir, *The Queene's Masque, The First of Blackness* (Jonson)
Osmin, *The Moor's Revenge* (Aphra Behn)
Othello, *Othello* (Shakespeare)
Prince of Morocco, *The Merchant of Venice* (Shakespeare)
Porus, *The Blind Beggar of Alexandria* (Chapman)
Queene of the Moors, *Masque at Whitehall* (Campion)
Symerons, a tribe of blacks, *The History of Sir Francis Drake* (D'Avenant)
Toto, *The Fair Maid of the West*, part II (Heywood)
Vangue, *Wonder of Women, Sophonisba* (Marston)
Zanche, *The White Devil* (Webster)
Zanthia, *The Knight of Malta* (Fletcher)
Zanthia, *Wonder of Women, Sophonisba* (Marston)
Zarack, *Lust's Dominion* (Dekker)

Appendix 2

A chronological list of plays containing black characters or characters disguised as blacks.

1588-89?	*The Battle of Alcazar* (Peele)
1592	*Titus Andronicus* (Shakespeare)
1596	*Captain Thomas Stukley* (Anonymous)
1596	*The Merchant of Venice* (Shakespeare)
1598	*The Blind Beggar of Alexandria* (Chapman)
1599	*Lust's Dominion* (Dekker)
1599	*The Thracian Wonder* (Author uncertain)
1600-03?	*The Fair Maid of the West*, part I (Heywood)
1604	*Othello* (Shakespeare)
1605	*The Queene's Masque, The First of Blackness* (Jonson)
1606	*Wonder of Women, Sophonisba* (Marston)
1610-14?	*Monsieur Thomas* (Fletcher)
1611	*The White Devil* (Webster)
1613	*The Triumph of Truth* (Middleton)
1614	*Masque at Whitehall* (Campion)
1616	*The Knight of Malta* (Fletcher)
1619	*All's Lost by Lust* (Rowley)
1619?	*The Island Princess* (Fletcher)
1622	*The Prophetesse* (Fletcher and Massinger)
1624	*The Parliament of Love* (Massinger)
1630	*The Fair Maid of the West*, part II (Heywood)
1637	*The English Moor* (Brome)
1637	*The Lost Lady* (Berkeley)
1659	*The History of Sir Francis Drake* (D'Avenant)
1672	*The Gentleman Dancing-Master* (Wycherly)
1675	*Calisto* (Crowne)
1677	*The Moor's Revenge* (Behn)
1686	*Titus Andronicus* (Ravenscroft)
1687	*The Empress of Morocco* (Settle)

Notes

Preface

1. David Brion Davis, *The Problem of Slavery in Western Culture* (Ithaca: N.Y.: Cornell University, 1966), p. 9.
2. Ibid., p. 478.
3. Ibid., pp. 472 ff; Wylie Sypher, *Guinea's Captive Kings: British Anti-Slavery Literature of the XVIIIth Century* (Chapel Hill, N.C.: The University of North Carolina Press, 1941), passim. Hereafter referred to as Sypher, *Guinea's Captive Kings*; Eva B. Dykes, *The Negro in English Romantic Thought* (Washington, D.C.: The Associated Publishers, Inc., 1942).

Chapter One: The Nonliterary Response

1. Margaret Trabue Hodgen, *Early Anthropology in the Sixteenth and Seventeenth Centuries* (Philadelphia, Penn.: University of Pennsylvania Press, 1964), p. 358. Hereafter referred to as Hodgen, *Early Anthropology*.
2. Winthrop Jordan, *White Over Black: American Attitudes Toward the Negro, 1550–1812* (Chapel Hill, N.C.: The University of North Carolina Press, 1968), p. 6. Hereafter referred to as Jordan, *White Over Black*.
3. Sir Sidney Lee, "The American Indian in Elizabethan England," in *Elizabethan and Other Essays*, ed. F. S. Boas (Oxford at the Clarendon Press, 1929), p. 273.
4. Edward Hall, *Henry VIII*, ed. C. Whibbley (London: T. C. and E. C. Jack, 1904), pp. 15–19.
5. Sypher, *Guinea's Captive Kings*, p. 17.
6. That differences were known to exist can be attested by Samuel Purchas, the collector of religious principles and practices of the world, who wrote with a Christian sense of urgency: "The tawny Moore, black Negro, duskie Libyan, ash-colored Indian, olive-coloured American, should with the whiter European become one *sheep-fold*, under *one great Sheepheard*." That the great "Sheepheard" must be a Christian

one, all others being false, does not deny Purchas an admirable humanity for his time. Samuel Purchas, *Purchas his Pilgrimage. Or Relations of the World and the Religions Observed in All Ages and Places Discovered. from the Creation unto This Present*, 2nd ed. (London, 1614), p. 656.

7. Richard Eden, "A Brief description of Afrika gathered by Richard Eden," in Richard Hakluyt, *The Principal Navigations Voyages Traffiques & Discoveries of the English Nation*, vol. 4 (Glasgow: James MacLehose and Sons, 1904), p. 143. Hereafter referred to as Hakluyt, *Principal Navigations*.

8. Ibid., p. 167.

9. Thomas Browne, *The Works of Sir Thomas Browne*, ed. Charles Sayle (Edinburgh: John Grant, 1912), 2:369.

10. Sypher, *Guinea's Captive Kings*, p. 26.

11. E. E. Stoll, *Othello, An Historical and Comparative Study* (Minneapolis, Minn.: University of Minnesota, 1915), p. 46.

12. David Brion Davis, *The Problem of Slavery in Western Culture* (Ithaca, N.Y.: Cornell University Press, 1966), p. 10.

13. Ibid., p. 480.

14. Sypher, *Guinea's Captive Kings*, pp. 122–128.

15. See the introduction to the Arden edition of *The Tempest*, ed. Morton Luce.

16. Hodgen, *Early Anthropology*, pp. 60–143.

17. Katherine George, "The Civilized West Looks at Primitive Africa: 1400–1800; A Study in Ethnocentrism," *Isis* 49 (1958): 64. Hereafter referred to as George, "The Civilized West."

18. Hodgen, *Early Anthropology*, p. 362. Mrs. Hodgen goes on to argue convincingly against the theory of Boas and Lovejoy, which held that primitive man received favorable treatment in most philosophical and literary works. She holds, on the contrary, that the Renaissance was primarily antiprimitivist in its outlook on newly discovered races. A study of the English literature of the period tends to confirm her views, as this study hopes to show. Mrs. Katherine B. Oakes, another modern anthropologist, has written in the same vein: "With rare exceptions seventeenth-century judgment of native African character continues to be censorious." "Social Theory in the Early Literature of Voyage and Exploration in Africa" (Ph.D. diss., University of California, 1944), p. 107.

19. Quoted by G. A. Starr, "Escape from Barbary: A Seventeenth Century Genre," *Huntington Library Quarterly* 29 (November 1965): 35–52. Starr adds that Purchas's view was shared by most seventeenth-century Englishmen. "The Moor is the anti-type of the noble savage of the New World."

20. Hakluyt, *Principal Navigations*, pp. 285–293.

21. Bernard Harris, "A Portrait of a Moor," *Shakespeare Survey* 11 1959): 92.

22. Ibid.

23. Ibid., p. 95.
24. Ibid.
25. Ibid., p. 97.
26. George, "The Civilized West," p. 62.
27. William Harrison, *An Historical Description of the Island of Britain*, in Raphael Holinshed, *Chronicles of England* (London, 1807), 1:1–42.
28. Hodgen, *Early Anthropology*, p. 152.
29. Hodgen, *Early Anthropology*, p. 407. Mrs. Hodgen points out that most cosmographers sought out similarities between foreign cultures and their own, and the degree to which such similarities were lacking was the degree to which the foreign cultures considered were inferior to the native one. This Eurocentrism, instead of bringing cultures into some kind of mutual understanding "served only to emphasize their cleavage and separation" (p. 196).
30. Jordan, *White Over Black*, p. 254.
31. Quoted by Mrs. Hodgen, ibid., p. 373.
32. Browne, *The Works of Sir Thomas Browne*, 2:386.
33. George Herbert, "A Paradox, addressed to the healthy, who think they are better than the sick," in *The English Works of George Herbert*, ed. George Herbert Palmer, 3 vols. (Boston, Mass.: Houghton Mifflin and Company, 1905), 3:403.
34. Peter Heylyn, *Cosmographie* (London, 1666), p. 45.
35. Harry Levin, *The Power of Blackness* (New York: Vintage Books, 1958), pp. 26–35.
36. Ibid., pp. 192–195.
37. P. J. Heather, "Color Symbolism," *Folk Lore* 59 (1948): 176.
38. Browne, *The Works of Sir Thomas Browne*, 2:373.
39. Ibid., p. 374.
40. Don C. Allen, "Symbolic Color in the Literature of the English Renaissance," *Philological Quarterly* 15 (January 1936): 83.
41. Jordan, *White Over Black*, p. 7.
42. See especially Shakespeare's famous antiromantic sonnet, number 130. Herrick's lines in "The Argument of His Book,"–"I write / How roses first came red and lilies white"–sums up concisely the favorite colors of the lyric poets of the period. Suckling's lines on a beautiful bride are only another example of the standards of beauty in English culture:

> Her cheeks so rare a white was on
> No daisy makes comparison
> (Who sees them is undone),
> For streaks of red were mingled there,
> Such as are on a Catherine pear,
> (The side that's next the sun.)

43. Sir Ralph Winwood, *Memorials of Affairs of State*, (1725), 2:43–44.
44. Robert Barron, *An Apology for Paris* (London, 1649), quoted by Max Andrew Nemmer, *The Dramatic Significance of Physical Distinction in*

Characters of English Renaissance Drama (Ph.D. diss., University of Pittsburg, 1961), p. 34. Hereafter referred to as Nemmer, *Dramatic Significance*.

45. Hodgen, *Early Anthropology*, p. 28.
46. Ibid., p. 281.
47. Ibid., p. 182.
48. R. R. Cowley, *Milton and the Literature of Travel* (Princeton, N.J.: Princeton University Press, 1951), p. 117.
49. Hodgen, *Early Anthropology*, p. 178.
50. Jean Bodin, *Of the lawes and customs of a Commonweale out of the French and Latin copies done into English by Richard Knolles* (London: G. Bishop, 1606). Cited in Hodgen, *Early Anthropology*, pp. 279–80.
51. Quoted by Hodgen, *Early Anthropology*, p. 179.
52. Peter Heylyn, *Microscosmus, a little description of the great world* (Oxford, 1621) 4:2. See also R. R. Cawley, *Unpathed Waters: Studies in the Influence of Voyagers on Elizabethan Literature* (Princeton, N.J.: Princeton University Press, 1940), pp. 100–104.
53. Heylyn, *Microscosmus*, 4:2.
54. Hodgen, *Early Anthropology*, p. 128. See the illustration of types of the marvelous, including a dog-headed creature.
55. Richard Bernheimer, *Wild Men in the Middle Ages, A Study in Art, Sentiment, and Demonology* (Cambridge, Mass.: Harvard University Press, 1952).
56. Ibid., p. 2.
57. Ibid., p. 121.
58. Ibid., p. 44.
59. Ibid., p. 28.
60. Ibid., pp. 34, 44.
61. Ibid., pp. 2–3.
62. Cawley, *Unpathed Waters*, p. 110.
63. J. Milton French, "Othello among the Anthropophagi," *Publication of the Modern Language Association*, 49 (September 1934): 807.
64. Cawley, *Unpathed Waters*, p. 106; French, ibid., p. 807.
65. Hodgen, *Early Anthropology*, p. 74.
66. Ibid., p. 88.
67. Ibid., p. 413.
68. Ibid., pp. 405–406.
69. John Ower, "Manichean Metaphor: The Black African in Modern Literature," *Mosaic* 2, no. 2 (Winter 1969): 1–2.
70. Levin, *The Power of Blackness*, p. 30.
71. George, "The Civilized West," p. 66. Later Christianity was to justify slavery by claiming to offer salvation to those men who were properly indoctrinated and converted to the faith.
72. Ibid., p. 67.
73. Browne, *The Works of Sir Thomas Browne*, 2:368.

74. John Josselyn, *Account of Two Voyages to New England* (1674). Cited by Jordan, *White Over Black*, pp. 245–246.
75. Cited in Lily B. Campbell, *Shakespeare's Tragic Heroes: Slaves of Passion*, (New York: Barnes & Noble, Inc., 1967), p. 60. Hereafter referred to as Campbell, *Shakespeare's Tragic Heroes*.
76. Ibid., p. 151.
77. Hodgen, *Early Anthropology*, p. 276.
78. Ibid., p. 214.
79. Hakluyt, *Principal Navigations*, 6:176.
80. Ibid., 7:262–263. In this rejection of the climatic theory there is also the implicit idea of the virtue of whiteness and the tainted or diseased nature of blackness.
81. Browne, *The Works of Sir Thomas Browne*, 2:368–380.
82. Hodgen, *Early Anthropology*, p. 234.
83. Peter Heylyn, *Cosmographie*, p. 87.
84. Hakluyt, *Principal Navigations*, 7:263–264. Also published separately in 1578, as Jordan points out.
85. Ibid.
86. Heylyn, *Cosmographie*, p. 66.
87. William Strachey, *The historie of travell into Virginia Britania* (London: Hakluyt Society, 1953), pp. 54–55.
88. Jordan, *White Over Black*, p. 24, citing Thomas Herbert, *Some Years Travels*, p. 10.
89. Ibid.
90. Hakluyt, *Principal Navigations*, 6:167.
91. Johann Boemus, *The manners, lawes, and customes of all nations* (London: Eld and Burton, 1611), p. 49.
92. Hodgen, *Early Anthropology*, p. 412.
93. Heylyn, *Cosmographie*, p. 44.
94. Hakluyt, *Principal Navigations*, 6:169–170.
95. Heylyn, *Cosmographie*, p. 67.
96. Basil Davidson, *Black Mother: The Years of the African Slave Trade* (Boston, Mass.: Little, Brown and Company, 1961), p. 57.
97. Jordan, *White Over Black*, p. 24.
98. Hakluyt, *Principal Navigations*, 6:184.
99. Heylyn, *Cosmographie*, p. 52. Meroe was a principal city in Aethiopia.
100. Richard Jobson, *The Golden Trade: Or a Discovery of the River Gambia, and the Golden Trade of the Aethiopians* (1623), ed. Charles Kingsley (Teignmouth, Devonshire, 1904), pp. 65–66. Cited in Jordan, *White Over Black*, p. 34.
101. Ibid., p. 35.
102. Johann Boemus, *The manners, lawes and customes of all nations*, pp. 34, 37.
103. Ibid.
104. Heylyn, *Cosmographie*, p. 71.

105. John Leo Africanus, *The History and Description of Africa and of the Notable Things Therein Contained...* , trans. John Pory (ca. 1600), ed. Robert Brown, 3 vols. (London: Hakluyt Society, 1896), 1:180, 187.

106. Francis Bacon, *New Atlantis: The Works of Francis Bacon*, ed. Robert L. Ellis, Douglas D. Heath, James Spedding, 15 vols. (Boston, Mass.: Brown and Taggard, 1857-74), p. 152. Cited by Jordan, *White Over Black*, p. 34.

107. John Davies of Hereford, *Microscosmos*, p. 62. Cited by Campbell, *Shakespeare's Tragic Heroes*, p. 152.

108. Samuel Purchas, *Purchas His Pilgrimes* (New York: AMS Press, 1965), 5:353.

109. Jordan, *White Over Black*, p. 40.

110. Purchas, *Purchas His Pilgrimes*, p. 356.

111. Varchi, *The Blazon of Jealousy,* trans. 1615. Cited by Campbell, *Shakespeare's Tragic Heroes*, p. 151.

112. Heylyn, *Cosmographie*, pp. 21-46. It must be noted that Heylyn tries to be objective and includes descriptions of positive traits and customs as well as these negative ones. He describes some black women as "being of a comely body, and all featured, beautiful in blackness, of delicate soft skins, and in their habit and apparel beyond measure sumptuous" (p. 21). He also notes the courtesy and industry of others, and the commendable habit of some in breeding of their maidens, who are given special training for one whole year by an "old man of best estimation" separated from society (p. 47). This attempt to see the whole truth tends to lend weight to the authenticity of his work.

113. Hakluyt, *Principal Navigations*, 6:128.

114. Sir Francis Drake, *The World Encompassed*, ed. N. M. Penzer (London: The Argonaut Press, 1926), p. 51.

115. Hakluyt, *Principal Navigations*, 6:128.

116. Purchas, *Purchas His Pilgrimes*, p. 335.

117. Hakluyt, *Principal Navigations*, 7:285-293.

118. Katherine Beverly Oakes (Katherine George), *Social Theory in the Early Literature of Voyage and Exploration in Africa* (Ph.D. Diss., University of California, 1944). Cited by Hodgen, *Early Anthropology*, p. 373.

119. Hodgen, *Early Anthropology*, p. 372.

120. Richard Lignon, *A True and Exact History of the Island of Barbados* (London: 1673), pp. 12, 15-16, 51.

121. Quoted by Davis, *The Problem of Slavery in Western Culture*, p. 450.

122. Ibid., p. 452.

123. Ibid.

124. Hodgen, *Early Anthropology*, p. 407.

125. Thomas Herbert, *Some Years Travels*, p. 10. Cited by Jordan, *White Over Black*, p. 24.

Chapter Two: A Model of Literary Response in Four Love Poems

1. Gerard Previn Meyer, in his article "The Blackamoor and Her Love," *Philological Quarterly* 18 (October 1938): 371–376, calls attention to this series of poems. He treats the problems of publication dates, authorship, and variations in editions but makes no critical commentary on any significance these poems might have for an understanding of the imaginative treatment of the black race in the early phases of its entry into the English world.

2. One extreme of the scale, the Negro as demon, is found in Elizabethan drama; the other, the Negro as noble man, is found in the drama and novel of the late seventeenth century. The latter phase of the image will not be included in this study, as it already has received adequate treatment elsewhere. See Sypher, *Guinea's Captive Kings*.

3. The dates of composition have been suggested by Dr. A. B. Grosart in his 1874 edition of the *Complete Works* (London: Privately Printed), 3:164.

4. Henry King, *The English Poems of Henry King, D. D.,* ed. Laurence Mason (New Haven: Yale University Press, 1914), p. 191.

5. Meyer, "The Blackamoor and Her Love," p. 372.

6. John Cleveland, *The Words of John Cleveland* (London, 1687).

7. Levin, *The Power of Blackness*, pp. 26–35.

8. Edward Herbert, *The Poems English and Latin of Edward, Lord Herbert of Cherbury*, ed. G. C. Moore Smith (Oxford: Clarendon Press, 1923).

9. Ibid., p. 35.

10. Ibid.

11. Ibid., p. 37.

12. Ibid., p. 38.

13. Ibid., p. 57.

14. Ibid., p. 66.

15. This argument is reminiscent of Lord Herbert's view that black is the superior color, embodying all other colors.

16. Again, this idea reminds us of Lord Herbert's poem "To a Sun-burn't Exotique Beauty." Greek mythology, of course, gives us the earliest version of this explanation of the Negro's color. *The Song of Songs* also opens with reference to the sunburned skin of the lover. The lover in this Biblical poem, however, bears little resemblance to George Herbert's unhappy girl and is hardly a possible source for his poem. In the drama, as a later chapter will show, the climatic explanation of blackness does not argue for racial equality because of the weight given to other features of the black man, such as his affiliation with demonic forces.

17. Don C. Allen, "Symbolic Color in the Literature of the English Renaissance," pp. 80–83.

18. Herbert's open-mindedness is also revealed in those lines to the healthy, quoted earlier on p. 15.

> Your state to ours is contrary,
> That makes you think us poor;
> So Black-Moores think us foule, and we
> Are quit with them, and more.
>> Nothing can see
> And Judg of things but mediocrity.

The first two lines are a succinct description of the psychological tendency to prefer oneself to what stands as a contrary—the essence of ethnocentric cultural behavior. In the last two lines Herbert has clearly eschewed such a tendency. Even on his deathbed Herbert could find an example of misjudgment by turning to the relationship between white and black people.

19. In another poem, "The Defense," a reply to his friends' ridicule of his ugly mistress, King again reflects a common attitude toward the physical qualities of Negroes. He yokes ugliness and blackness in these lines:

> Say she were foul and blacker than
> The night, or Sun-burnt African,
> If lik't by me, tis I alone
> Can make a beauty where was none.

20. Brian Morris and Eleanor Withington, eds., *The Poems of John Cleveland* (Oxford at the Clarendon Press, 1967), p. LXVII. The "unnatural alliances" here were between Englishmen and zealots and Scotch traitors.

21. John Cleveland, *The Words of John Cleveland* (London, 1687), pp. 16–17. See especially the spurious poems mentioned above: "A Relation of a Quaker that to the shame of his Profession, attempted to bugger a Mare near Colchester"; "An Old Man courting a Young Girl"; "On one that was deprived of his Testicles." In addition to these poems, one that may be authentically Cleveland's describes a deplorable mismarriage: "On an Alderman who married a very young wife." The editor of this edition certainly felt that an interracial union fitted nicely into this collection of abnormalities.

Chapter Three: Blackness in the Plays: A Variety of Aspects,
A Consistency of Opinion

1. Sir Alan C. Burns, *Colour Prejudice, with particular reference to the relationship between whites and Negroes* (London: G. Allen and Unwin, 1948); David Davis, *The Problem of Slavery in Western Culture*; Wylie Sypher, *Guinea's Captive Kings*; Harry Levin, *The Power of Blackness*; P. J. Heather, "Color Symbolism," pp. 165–183.

2. Allen, "Symbolic Color in the Literature of the English Renaissance"; Max Andrew Nemmer, *The Dramatic Significance of Physical Distinction in Characters of English Renaissance Drama* (Ph.D. diss., University of Pittsburgh, 1961).

3. Nemmer has discussed some of the broad traits of black men, such as their villainy and sexuality, but he surveys only major characters of the period. Eldred Jones, on the other hand, offers a useful series of character discussions in which he tries to come to an understanding of the character in the context of the whole play. What the present study attempts is an isolation of the factors pertaining solely to the black man's racial distinctiveness.

4. In his book *Othello's Countrymen: The African in English Renaissance Drama* (Oxford: Oxford University Press, 1965), Jones has called attention to "white" Moors in *The Battle of Alcazar*; yet there is no textual evidence, except the absence of references to their blackness, for this conclusion. This is scanty proof that Moors in the other plays were thought to be anything but black, except in those plays such as Dryden's heroic dramas where there are no references to the physical features of any of the characters. Then it is difficult to determine whether the actors darkened their skins for performance or not. Such plays are not included in this study, for although they may reflect an increase in ethnological knowledge that could distinquish among the different peoples on the African continent, they do not add to the image of the man with unmistakably black skin.

5. Alfred Harbage, *As They Liked It* (New York: Harper & Co. 1961), p. 20.

6. Max Andrew Nemmer, *The Dramatic Significance of Physical Distinction in Characters of English Renaissance Drama* (Ph.D. diss., University of Pittsburgh, 1961), p. 4.

7. Edmund Spenser, *The Poetical Works of Edmund Spenser*, eds. J. C. Smith and E. DeSelincourt (London: Oxford University Press, 1950), p. 591. For a detailed dicussion of this equation of inner beauty with outer comeliness, see Baldassare Castiglione's highly influential book *The Courtier*, translated into English in 1561. See especially Peter Bembo's argument that "outwarde beautie" is a "true signe of the inward goodnesse." Note also his belief that "beautie is a face pleasant, merrie, comely, and to be desired for goodnesse: and foulnesse a face darke, uglesome, unpleasant, and to bee shunned for ill."

8. Hill, *The Epistle of Melampus*. Cited in Nemmer, *Dramatic Significance*, p. 101.

9. William Shakespeare, *Macbeth* 1. 4. 12–15, in *The Complete Works of William Shakespeare*, ed. George Lyman Kittredge (Boston, Mass.: Ginn and Company, 1936). All future references to the works of Shakespeare will be to this edition and will be listed by the name of the play only.

10. *Twelfth Night*, 1. 2. 47–52.

11. Nemmer, *Dramatic Significance,* p. 122; see especially *The Tempest,* 1. 2. 457–459; *Measure for Measure,* 4. 2. 160–163; *Anthony and Cleopatra,* 3. 3. 32–34.

12. The degree to which the playwrights met that expectation was the degree to which they contributed to an already growing consensus about the black man. By accepting notions that were becoming widespread through hearsay and rumor, and giving dramatic tangibility to those views, the playwrights were doubtlessly reinforcing and justifying the negative responses held by many and at the same time were convincing others who perhaps had not made a cultural judgment against the black man. Of course, there were writers who departed from the general view and offered their own unique creations that faulted the stereotype, but as this study will show, they were very few and their departures were of a limited scope.

13. Philip Massinger, *The Parliament of Love,* in *The Dramatic Works of Massinger and Ford,* ed. Hartley Coleridge (London: George Routledge and Sons, 1875), 1:124. There appears to be no reference to other features of the black man in these plays, although in 1701, in a play by William Burnaby, there appears this line of ridicule: "Tho' I must own to you, at first, his Blackamore coach-man a little surpriz'd me; for his flat nose and great Collar, made me fancy they had dress'd up a Dutch-Mastiff." *The Dramatic Works of William Burnaby,* ed. F. E. Budd (London: Scholartes Press, 1931), p. 214.

14. Eldred Jones, "Africans in Elizabethan England," *Notes and Queries* 8 (1962): 302.

15. Anthony Munday and Henry Chettle, *The Death of Robert, Earl of Huntington.* Cited by Nemmer, *Dramatic Significance,* p. 98.

16. *Titus Andronicus,* 4. 2. 175. Another interesting reference to the lips of the black man is Roderigo's scornful metaphor for Othello: "What a full fortune does the thick-lips owe / If he can carry't thus" (1. 2. 66–67). Ravenscroft retained this expression about lips, although he modified other qualities.

17. *Titus Andronicus,* 2. 3. 34–35. A similar metaphorical twist to associate a physical trait with a moral value occurs in Heywood's *The Fair Maid of the West,* when Bess and Spencer have outwitted the black King of Fez and are about to sail triumphantly away from Barbarie. The cannons are ordered to be fired "To make the King tear his contorted locks / Curl'd like the knots of furies." Thomas Heywood, *The Fair Maid of the West,* part II (London: John Pearson, 1874), vol. 2.

18. *Titus Andronicus,* 5. 1. 44–45.

19. Jordan, *White Over Black,* p. 6.

20. Ibid., p. 5.

21. Nemmer, *Dramatic Significance,* p. 99.

22. *Titus Andronicus,* 5. 1. 27; 5. 1. 32.

23. Ibid., 2. 3. 72.

24. William Rowley, *All's Lost by Lust and a Shoemaker, a Gentleman*, ed. Charles Wharton Stork (Philadelphia, Penn.: University of Pennsylvania, 1910), 1. 1. 20; 1. 1. 31.

25. Thomas Heywood, *The Fair Maid of the West*, part I, ed. A Wilson Verity (London: Vizetelly & Company, 1888), 5. 2, p. 146.

26. Ibid., 5. 2, pp. 146–147.

27. Eldred Jones, *Othello's Countrymen: The African in English Renaissance Drama* (Oxford: Oxford University Press, 1965), p. 49.

28. In some plays where all the characters are Moors—as in Dryden's *The Conquest of Granada* and *Aurengzebe*—there are no racial allusions or overtones, and the characters may have been portrayed just as easily in white face as in black face. This absence of racial identification might be a sign of a change in the cultural climate of the late seventeenth century. Quakerism, for example, with its historic protest against slavery in Germantown, Pennsylvania, in 1688, and the rise of sentimentalism in England would both contribute to a broader humanitarianism which would profit the black man. And the plays that treated the Moors in a neutral tone are the probable indicators of the direction these changes were to take.

29. George Peele, *The Battle of Alcazar*, in *The Dramatic Works of George Peele*, ed. John Yoklavich (New Haven, Conn.: Yale University Press, 1961), line 297. A passage in Heywood's *The Fair Maid of the West*, part I, complicates the matter somewhat. Mullisheg, the Moorish king, orders the concubines to be collected for his harem and makes a distinction between "the loveliest of Moors / We can command and negroes everywhere" (4. 3, p. 136). But both kinds are evidently considered black.

30. Ben Jonson, *The Queen's Masques, The First, of Blackness*, in *The Works of Ben Jonson* (London: D. Midwinter, 1756), vol. 5, p. 234.

31. Thomas Campion, *Campion's Works*, ed. Percival Vivian (Oxford at the Clarendon Press, 1909), p. 152.

32. John Marston, *The Plays of John Marston*, ed. H. Harvey Wood (London: Oliver and Boyd, 1938), 1. 1, p. 10.

33. *The Merchant of Venice*, 3. 5. 42–43.

34. Thomas Dekker, *Lust's Dominion*, in *The Dramatic Works of Thomas Dekker*, ed. Fredson Bowers (Cambridge at the University Press, 1961), vol. 4, 3. 2. 245.

35. Sypher, *Guinea's Captive Kings*, pp. 105–108. See page 5 of the present study.

36. See the old Arden edition of *The Tempest* for Morton Luce's exposition of this idea, pp. XXXII–XXXVII.

37. An insight into this marriage between sin and blackness exists directly in Malcolm's comment to Macduff that inward goodness ("grace") will manifest itself in outward appearances, although not all goodly appearing things are inwardly good. Outward foulness, therefore, obviates the

possible presence of inner goodness. "Though all things foul would wear the brow of grace / Yet grace must still look so." *Macbeth*, 4. 3. 22–23. If black skin was considered foul, it could hardly be thought to mask inward beauty.

38. Dekker, *Lust's Dominion*, 2. 2. 65–69.

39. John Fletcher, *The Knight of Malta*, in *The Works of Beaumont and Fletcher*, ed. Alexander Dyce (London: Edward Maxon, 1851), 4. 2, p. 147.

40. Edward Ravenscroft, *Titus Andronicus* or *The Rape of Lavinia*, (London: F. Hindmarsh, 1687), 2. 1, p. 11.

41. Aphra Behn, *The Moor's Revenge, The Plays, Histories, and Novels of the Ingenious Mrs. Aphra Behn* (London, Pearson 1871), vol. 2, 1. 1, p. 8.

42. *Titus Andronicus*, 2. 3. 72–74. Throughout Shakespeare sin and evil are colored black by his characters. Just a few examples of many available need be quoted here. In *King John*, the Bastard denounces Herbert with what he holds to be the deepest of curses: "Thou'rt damn'd as black—nay nothing is so black / Thou art more deep damn'd than Prince Lucifer." 4. 3. 121–122. Even the color of damnation itself is black. In *King Lear* Edgar, disguised as Poor Tom, calls the "foul fiend" who is hounding him a "black angel," a synonym for devil. (3. 5. 33–34). In *Macbeth*, a play so deeply concerned with the nature of evil, the word "black" is used six times, each time as an equivalent of "evil."

43. *Titus Andronicus*, 3. 1. 206.

44. Dekker, *Lust's Dominion*, 1. 2. 191–192.

45. Ibid., 2. 2. 81.

46. Ibid., 2. 2. 89–90.

47. Ibid., 2. 3. 179.

48. Ibid., 5. 2. 169–170. In another play of Dekker's, *Patient Grissill*, the playwright confirms himself as one of the most outspoken exponents of this idea about blackness when he uses such expressions as this: "Before my soule look black with speckled sinne" and "sins black face" (lines 51 and 145).

49. In most plays containing black characters, the demonic symbolism of blackness is connected with those people. However, late in the seventeenth century Mrs. Behn, revising Dekker's *Lust's Dominion*, deliberately avoids making the connection. If she mentions black as evil— "What Devil did inspire thee / With thoughts so black and sinful," or "Thy Mother's soul was black to hers," there is no overt tie made to the color of Abdelazer's skin. Sin may be black, but Abdelazer's blackness is not invoked to symbolize his evil.

50. Elkanah Settle, *The Empress of Morocco*, (London, 1687), p. 46.

51. Ibid.

52. Dekker, *Lust's Dominion*, 5. 2. 19–20.

53. Jordan, *White Over Black*, pp. 17–20.

54. Ibid., pp. 17–18.

55. Heywood, *The Fair Maid of the West*, part I, 5. 2, p. 146.
56. Rowley, *All's Lost by Lust*, 4. 2. 43–44.
57. John Webster, *The White Devil*, ed. John Addington Symonds (New York: Hill and Wang, Inc., 1956), 5. 1, p. 90.
58. Dekker, *Lust's Dominion*, 3. 2. 164–165.
59. Jonson, *The Queen's Masques, The First, of Blackness*, pp. 238–239.
60. William Bass, *The Poetical Works of William Bass*, ed. R. Warwick (London, 1893), p. 279. Cited in Jordan, *White Over Black*, p. 11.
61. John Davies of Hereford, *Microscosmos* (London, 1603), p. 67. Cited in Campbell, *Shakespeare's Tragic Heroes*, p. 61.
62. John Crowne, *Calisto*, in *The Dramatic Works of John Crowne* (London: H. Sotheran & Company, 1873), p. 242.
63. *Anthony and Cleopatra*, 1. 2. 49–50.
64. Massinger, *The Parliament of Love*, 2. 2. 127.
65. Massinger, *The Bondsman*, 5. 3, p. 97.
66. *The Merchant of Venice*, 2. 1. 1–2.
67. Webster, *The White Devil*, 5. 1, p. 91.
68. Dekker, *Lust's Dominion*, 1. 1. 114–115.
69. Ibid., 5. 1. 180–181.
70. Ibid., 1. 1. 151–155.
71. Ibid., 1. 1. 361.
72. Ibid., 3. 2. 205–208.
73. Ibid., 5. 3. 7–11.
74. Ravenscroft, *Titus Andronicus*, 2. 1, p. 15.
75. *Titus Andronicus*, 4. 2. 67–68.
76. Ravenscroft, *Titus Andronicus*, 5. 1, pp. 38–39.
77. Ibid., 3. 1, p. 20.
78. Behn, *The Moor's Revenge*, 5. 2, p. 76.
79. Ibid., 5. 2, p. 77.
80. See endnote 59 for this chapter.
81. Jonson, *The Queen's Masque, The First, of Blackness*, p. 241.
82. Ibid., p. 244.
83. Crowne, *Callisto*, 5, pp. 321–322.
84. Ibid.
85. Webster, *The White Devil*, 5. 3, p. 104.
86. Anthony Munday, *John A Kent & John A Cumber*, eds. W. W. Greg and and Muriel St. Clare Byrne (Oxford: Oxford University Press, 1923), p. 13.
87. George Peele, *The Old Wives' Tale*, in *The Dramatic Works of George Peele*, ed. Charles Tyler Prouty (New Haven, Conn.: Yale University Press, 1961).
88. Rowley, *All's Lost by Lust*, 1. 1. 31–37.
89. Peter Hausted, *Rival Friends* (London, 1632). Cited in Nemmer, *Dramatic Significance*, p. 131.
90. Fletcher, *Monsieur Thomas*, 1. 3, 28–32.
91. William D'Avenant, *The Unfortunate Lovers* (London, 1643), 4. 2. Cited in Nemmer, *Dramatic Significance*, p. 132.

92. William Wycherly, *The Gentleman Dancing-Master*, in *The Complete Plays of William Wycherly*, ed. Gerald Weales (Garden City, N.Y.: Anchor Books, 1966), 4. 1, p. 195.

93. Richard Brome, *The English Moor* (London: John Pearson, 1873), 3. 1, p. 371.

94. Ibid., p. 38.

Chapter Four: The Devil and the Moor: "Being Hell's Perfect Character"

1. Paul Lawrence Dunbar, *The Heart of Happy Hollow* (New York: Dodd, Mead, 1904), p. 91.

2. Nemmer, *Dramatic Significance*, p. 104.

3. E. E. Stoll, *Shakespearean Studies* (New York: Stechert, 1942), p. 345. The eighteenth-century philosopher Diderot praises Samuel Richardson's probing into the human mind to its inner darkness; then, as the symbol of the demonic that he claims Richardson exposed lurking there, Diderot chooses the image of the Moor. "It is he [Richardson] who carries the torch to the back of the cave. . . . He blows upon the glorious phantom who presents himself at the entrance of the cave; and the hideous Moor whom he was masking reveals himself." Leslie Fiedler comments on this passage in Diderot: "Surely 'the hideous Moor' is a striking symbol of the demonic in ourselves." Leslie Fiedler, *Love and Death in the American Novel* (New York: Dell Publishing Company, 1966), p. 21.

4. Peele, *The Battle of Alcazar*, pp. 18–20.

5. Nemmer, *Dramatic Significance*, p. 101.

6. Jones, *Othello's Countryman*, p. 18.

7. Dekker, *Lust's Dominion*, 2. 2. 123–124. It should be noted that according to Dekker, Eleazer was meant to represent the power of cruelty and the Queen Mother, the force of lust. Yet he alone is connected with the devil. She kills her own husband, murders Eleazer's wife, plots to destroy her son after lying about his legitimacy, and is pardoned at the close of the play. Another example of Dekker's view of the association between blackness and the devil appears when Eleazer's henchmen enter smoking tobacco. In an earlier work Dekker had referred to tobacco as "filthy," "foul smelling," the "herbe of hell." *Non-Dramatic Works*, 2:207.

8. Christopher Marlowe, *Dr. Faustus*, 9 in *Elizabethan and Stuart Plays*, eds. Charles R. Baskervill, Virgil B. Heltzel, and Arthur H. Nethercot (New York: Henry Holt and Company, 1950), p. 365. In his *Tamburlaine*, Marlowe again reports black as the color of hell and deadliness. Tamburlaine, in his conquests, would allow a besieged city two chances to surrender. First he would appear before the gates dressed entirely in white and offer the city mercy and life. If refused, he would return clothed entirely in red and demand the deaths of some inhabitants while sparing others. If refused again, he would don an outfit com-

pletely of black. "Black are his colors, black pavilion; / His spear, his shield, his horse, his armor, plume, / And jetty feathers menace death and hell." 4. 1. 58–60. The city would then suffer total destruction of inhabitants and buildings.

9. William Rowley, Thomas Dekker, and John Ford, *The Witch of Edmonton*, 3. 1, in *Elizabethan and Stuart Plays*, eds. Baskervill, Heltzel, and Nethercot (New York: Henry Holt and Company, 1950), p. 1462.
10. Peele, *The Old Wives' Tale*, in *Elizabethan and Stuart Plays*, p. 240.
11. Brome, *The English Moor*, 4. 4, p. 64.
12. Rowley, *All's Lost by Lust*, 1. 1. 31–37.
13. Heywood, *The Fair Maid of the West*, part I, 4. 2, p. 129.
14. *The Merchant of Venice*, 1. 2. 143–145.
15. See Dekker's well-known lines from *Lust's Dominion*, 5. 2. 169–170, quoted in Chapter III, p. 92.
16. George Chapman, *The Blind Beggar of Alexandria* (1594–95), ed. W. W. Greg, (Oxford: Oxford University Press, 1928). When a white woman willingly chooses a black man as a lover, she almost assuredly has been portrayed as an erotic creature.
17. Fletcher, *The Prophetess*, 1. 3, p. 12.
18. Webster, *The White Devil*, 5. 1, p. 88.
19. John Marston, *Wonder of Women, Sophonisba*, ed. H. Harvey Wood (London: Oliver and Boyd, 1938), 3. 1, p. 38.
20. Fletcher, *Monsieur Thomas*, 5. 2. 30–36.
21. Ibid., 5. 2. 37–38.
22. Desdemona, of course, is the only notable exception among the portraits, and even her sexual appetite is questioned by Iago and wondered at by Othello.
23. *Titus Andronicus*, 4. 2. 64; 5. 1. 40, 45; 5. 3. 4–5.
24. Ibid., 5. 2. 85–90.
25. Ravenscroft, *Titus Andronicus*, 5. 1, pp. 51, 53.
26. Heywood, *The Fair Maid of the West*, part II, in *The Dramatic Works of Thomas Heywood* (London: John Pearson, 1874), vol. 2, 1. 1, p. 343.
27. Dekker, *Lust's Dominion*, 1. 2. 122–123.
28. Behn, *The Moor's Revenge*, 5, pp. 83–84.
29. Heywood, *The Fair Maid of the West*, part II, 1. 1, p. 350.
30. Marston, *Wonder of Women, Sophonisba*, 1. 3, p. 23.
31. Massinger, *The Parliament of Love*, 5, p. 142.
32. Fletcher, *The Knight of Malta*, 5. 2, p. 153.
33. Ibid., 2, 3, p. 134.
34. Ibid., 2, 3, p. 135.
35. Ibid., 4. 2, p. 147.
36. Ibid. Later in this chapter the point is made more emphatically that a person can be made to assume the identity imposed on him by pressures from other people.
37. Ibid., 5. 2, p. 152.

38. The following are additional references to the Moor as a devil: Alvero, Eleazer's father-in-law, has been friendly toward him until he shows aspirations to the thorne. "Peace, divell for shame," he rebukes Eleazer. When the Moor is offered the crown, Alvero confirms his judgment: "Do; do; make hast to crown him! Lords adieu. / Here hell must be when the Divel governs you." (3. 2. 243–244). When Philip hears that he may very well be the natural son of Eleazer, he sustains his belief in Eleazer's satanism: "I may be well transformed from what I am / When a black divil is husband to my dam." (4. 1. 23–24). The king of Portugal promises aid to Prince Philip with these words: "Yet shall revenge dart black confusion / Into the bosom of that damned fiend." (4. 1. 9–10). Again Philip gives us a description of what he hopes will be Eleazer's defeat: "when hell / Had from their hinges heav'd off her iron gates / To bid the damn'd Moor and divels enter" (4. 4. 8–10).

39. Dekker, *Lust's Dominion*, 5. 2. 104.

40. See Milton's *Paradise Lost*, bk. 4, 799–800; bk. 9, 412–413.

41. Dekker, *Lust's Dominion*, 4. 2. 29–34.

42. Peele, *The Battle of Alcazar*, lines 1136–38, 1160.

43. This theory of the influence of reputation on the real character of a man could be explored in a discussion of Othello, who appears to be a more fully realized example of this phenomenon. See also Zanthia's admission to being a devil as she listens to Mountferrat excoriate her bitterly (p. 131).

44. Dekker, *Lust's Dominion*, 1. 1. 1–12.

45. Ibid., 2. 3. 190–192.

46. Ibid., 2. 2. 65–69. See p. 73.

47. Ibid., 4. 2. 57–60. The vivid details of hell that seem to come easily to Eleazer's mind as though he had been there no doubt influenced the early belief that the play was actually about Satan himself and was written by Marlowe, whose known fascination for overreaching characters of huge proportions was widely recognized.

48. Ibid., 5. 3. 161–166.

49. Behn, *The Moor's Revenge*, 2. 2. p. 20.

50. Settle, *The Empress of Morocco*, p. 32.

51. Ibid.

52. *Titus Andronicus*, 5. 1. 124–150.

53. Ibid., 5. 3. 11–13.

Chapter Five: The Rites of Satan

1. Ralph Ellison, "Twentieth Century Fiction and the Black Mask of Humanity," in *Shadow and Act* (New York: Random House, 1953), p. 28.

2. Nemmer, *Dramatic Significance*, p. 101. See John Draper, *The Humors and Shakespeare's Characters* (Durham, N.H.: University of New Hampshire Press, 1945), p. 14.

3. Thomas Newton, *The Touchstone of Complexion, First written in Latine, by Levine Lemme, and now Englished by Thomas Newton* (Nosce Terpsum, 1581). Cited in Campbell, *Shakespeare's Tragic Heroes*, pp. 53–54.

4. *Titus Andronicus*, 2. 3. 38–39.

5. Nemmer, *Dramatic Significance*, p. 103. Nemmer says, "He represents evil as a planetary force of destruction that moves inexorably and often motivelessly."

6. Phineas Fletcher, *Silecides*, 1. 4. Cited in Nemmer, *Dramatic Significance*, p. 103.

7. Geoffrey Chaucer, *The Poetical Works of Chaucer*, ed. F. N. Robinson (Boston, Mass.: Houghton Mifflin Company, 1933), p. 48.

8. Nemmer, *Dramatic Significance*, p. 108.

9. In one dumb show in Peele's *The Battle of Alcazar*, Muly Mahamet and two murderers are shown smothering two young princes and strangling Muly's uncle Abdelmumen.

10. John Marston, *The Malcontent*; John Webster, *The White Devil*; Thomas Middleton and William Rowley, *The Changeling*.

11. *Richard III, Henry IV, Macbeth*; Cyril Tourneur, *The Atheist's Tragedy*.

12. Murderers and rapists: Muly Mahamet (Peele), Aaron (Shakespeare), Eleazer (Dekker), Balthazar and Zarack (Dekker), Vangue (Marston), Zanche (Webster), Zanthia (Fletcher), Mulymumen (Rowley), Fydella (Rowley), Abdelazer (Behn), Osmin (Behn), Aron (Ravenscroft). Unscrupulous and cruel blacks: Zanthia (Marston), Mullisheg and Tota (Heywood). White villains who disguise themselves as blacks: Francisco de Medici (Webster), Governor (in Fletcher's *The Island Princess*). Blacks who have killed in battle: Abdelmelec (Peele), Prince of Morocco (Shakespeare), Porus (Chapman), Symerons (Davenant). Disguised whites, but relatively innocent: Calisto (Massinger), Millicent (Brome), Arcanthe (Berkeley). Decent blacks: Abdelmelec (Peele), wife of Muly Mahamet (Peele), Prince of Morocco (Shakespeare). Noble black: Basha Joffer (Heywood); Exotic blacks: Niger, daughters of Niger (Jonson), King of the Moors (Middleton); African women (Crowne).

13. Nemmer, *Dramatic Significance*, p. 110.

14. Peele, *The Battle of Alcazar*, p. 239.

15. Ibid., pp. 197, 330.

16. Peele, *The Battle of Alcazar*, p. 305. Robert Greene, in the *Comicall Historie of Alphonsus, King of Arragon*, epitomizes Moors as "warlike" (4 Prologue, p. 1130); and Marlowe writes of them in *Tamburlaine*, part II, 3. 4. 341–342: "And Moors in whom was never pitie found / Will hew us peacemeal."

17. Marlowe, *Tamburlaine*, p. 296.

18. Yoklavich feels that Peele had confused Sebastian's "honor" with "ambition" and quotes Poleman: "Sebastian was by nature verie much given to love of armes" and "sought for no other pleasure than by

martiall matters" (p. 237). A modern evaluation notes that "the young knight-errant whose vain, headstrong, and ascetic spirit was to lead the nation to disaster, hunted, rode, and prayed, all to excess." (H. V. Livermore, *History of Portugal*, p. 253, cited by Yoklavich, p. 237.) That the young king was white and Christian goes a long way in explaining why he comes out far better than Muly.

19. Jones, *Othello's Countrymen*, pp. 53–54.
20. Ibid.
21. *Titus Andronicus*, 2. 3. 5–7.
22. Ibid., 2. 2. 114–116.
23. *Titus Andronicus*, 5. 1. 95–98.
24. Ibid., 3. 1. 203–204.
25. Ibid., 5. 1. 111–117.
26. Ravenscroft, *Titus Andronicus*, 3. 1, p. 19.
27. Ibid., 3. 1, p. 26.
28. Dekker, *Lust's Dominion*, 1. 1. 32–35.
29. Ibid., 1. 1. 194–196.
30. Ibid., 1. 1. 185–191. Beginning with Muly Mahamet the black antagonist is often seen invoking the spirit of revenge to drive himself on to further crime. Muly calls on the goddess Nemesis as the great shaper of revenge to help him to destroy his enemy Abdelmelec.

> And lastly for revenge, for deepe revenge,
> Whereof thou goddess and deviser art,
> Damnd let him be, damned and condemned to beare
> All torments, tortures, plagues and paines of hell.
>
> (4. 1. 1157–1160)

31. Ibid., 5. 3. 56–60. Note also in *Hamlet* Claudius's attempt to assuage the anger of Laertes, who has burst into the castle to revenge the death of Polonius. The king cautions Laertes to direct his vengeance only against the guilty.

> . . . is't writ in your revenge
> That swoopstake you will draw both friend and foe,
> Winner and loser.

Laertes' answer defines the scope of a white revenger: "None but his enemies" The revenge of a black man, on the contrary, is always a "swoopstake" vengeance.

32. Behn, *The Moor's Revenge*, 1. 1, p. 11.
33. For example, the criminal Mountferrat in Fletcher's *The Knight of Malta* needs to be urged to cruelty by the black Zanthia. When he appears reluctant to fight the aging Knight of Malta, Miranda, Zanthia scoffs at his weakness.

> Have you not still these arms, that sword, that heart whole?
> Is't not a man you fight with. and an old man,
> A man half kill'd already? am I not here?

> . . . never think of conscience;
> There is none to a man resolved. Be happy. (2. 3, p. 134)

34. Rowley, *All's Lost by Lust*, 5. 4. 3–5.
35. Ibid., 5. 4.
36. Sir William D'Avenant, *The History of Sir Francis Drake*, in *The Dramatic Works of Sir William D'Avenant*, (New York: Russell and Russell, 1964), p. 68.
37. Rowley, *All's Lost by Lust*, 5. 5. 40–41.
38. Ibid., 5. 5. 151–193.
39. Peele, *The Battle of Alcazar*, 2. 4. 601–606.
40. Ravenscroft, *Titus Andronicus*, p. 55.
41. Dekker, *Lust's Dominion*, 5. 3. 182–183.

Chapter Six: The Erotic Moor

1. John Davies of Hereford, *Microcosmos* (1603), p. 62. Cited in Campbell, *Shakespeare's Tragic Heroes*, p. 62.
2. Thomas Wright, *The Passions of the minde in generall*, 2nd ed., (1604), pp. 42–43. Cited in Campbell, *Shakespeare's Tragic Heroes*, p. 58.
3. Jordan points out that of all the peoples investigated by English travelers and explorers, it was only the black races who had their sexual physiology and customs fully described.
4. *The Merchant of Venice*, 3. 5. 40–57.
5. Edward Guilpin, *Skialethia* (Shakespeare Association Facsimile #2), unpaginated.
6. G. B. Harrison, *Shakespeare Under Elizabeth* (New York: Henry Holt and Company, 1933), pp. 310–311.
7. John Weever, "In Byrrham" *Epigrams*, ed. R. B. McKerrow (London: Sedgwick and Jackson, Ltd., 1911), unpaginated.
8. Francis Bacon, *New Atlantis*, in *Works of Francis Bacon*, ed. Spedding, Ellis, and Heath, 3:152. Cited in Jordan, *White Over Black*, p. 34.
9. John Day, *Law-Tricks*, or *Who Would Have Thought It*, (London, 1608), 5. 1. Cited in Jordan, *White Over Black*, p. 41.
10. Marston, *Wonder of Women, Sophonisba*, 3. 1. 61–67.
11. Ibid., 3. 1. 109–114.
12. Jones, *Othello's Countrymen*, p. 77.
13. Webster, *The White Devil*, 1. 2, p. 26.
14. Ibid., 1. 2, p. 31.
15. Ibid., 3, 1. p. 61.
16. Ibid., 5. 1, p. 90.
17. Ibid.
18. Ibid., 5. 1, p. 91.
19. Ibid., 5. 1, p. 92.
20. Ibid., 5. 1, p. 92.
21. Ibid., 5. 3, p. 103.

22. Ibid.

23. Jordan, *White Over Black*, pp. 150–152.

24. Webster, *The White Devil*, 5. 3, p. 103.

25. Ibid., 5. 3, p. 104. The same image of washing an Ethiope is used traditionally in Marston's *The Malcontent* to define the impossibility of tempering a woman's sexual appetite:

> I washed an Ethiope, who for recompense,
> Sullied my name [committed adultery and gave me horns]
> And must, I, then, be forced
> To walk, to live thus black [as a cuckold].
>
> (4. 3, p. 708.)

Although the speaker is white and the wife he speaks of is white, the black man is again obliquely linked with sexual appetite.

26. In his discussion of this play, Eldred Jones effectively explains that the contrast between Oriana and her black servant Zanthia is carried out through a play on the colors white and black. Oriana's fairness, which obviously stands for her innocence, is heightened by its comparison with Zanthia's blackness, the emblem of her evil. See Jones, *Othello's Countrymen*, p. 81.

27. Fletcher, *The Knight of Malta*, 3. 2, p. 140.

28. Ibid.

29. Ibid., 1. 1, p. 127.

30. Ibid., 1. 1, p. 127.

31. Ibid., 1. 1, p. 128.

32. Ibid., 1. 1, p. 128.

33. Ibid., 2. 3, p. 134.

34. Ibid., 1. 1, p. 128.

35. Brome, *The English Moor*, 4. 4, pp. 60–61.

36. Ben Jonson, *Volpone, Elizabethan and Stuart Plays*, eds. Baskervill, Heltzel, and Nethercot (New York: Henry Holt and Company, 1934), 3. 7. 231.

37. Massinger, *A Very Woman*, 3. 1, p. 282.

38. Ibid., 3. 1, pp. 282–283.

39. Fletcher, *The Knight of Malta*, 3. 2, p. 139.

40. Massinger, *The Parliament of Love*, 2. 3, p. 262.

41. Ibid.

42. Jonson, *Volpone*, 1. 5. 43–45.

43. *The Thracian Wonder*, in *The Dramatic Works of John Webster*, ed. William Hazlitt (London, 1851), vol. 4, 3. 3, p. 169. A possible candidate as author of this play is one William Webster, author of a tale with a similar plot.

44. William Berkeley, *The Lost Lady*, in *A Select Collection of Old English Plays*, ed. Robert Dodsley (New York: Benjamin Blum, 1964) vol. 12, 3. 1, p. 591.

45. Ibid., 3. 1, p. 592.

46. That one exception, of course, is Othello, and the normality of Desdemona's feelings toward him is certainly doubted by several characters, including Brabantio, her father, who suspects Othello of having cast a "spell" over his daughter.

47. *Two Gentlemen of Verona*, 5. 2. 11–12.

48. Ibid., 5. 2. 13–14.

49. Behn, *The Moor's Revenge*, 5. 2, p. 74.

50. Chapman, *The Blind Beggar of Alexandria*, lines 915–917.

51. Ibid., lines 1592–1594.

52. Ibid., lines 1554–1560.

53. *Titus Andronicus*, 2. 2. 15–17.

54. Ibid., 2. 2. 21–24.

55. Ibid., 2. 3. 20–29.

56. Ravenscroft, *Titus Andronicus*, 3. 1, p. 20.

57. Ibid., 5. 2, p. 51. The goat, of course, as a traditional symbol of lechery, suits the reputation of the black man in this context.

58. Dekker, *Lust's Dominion*, 1. 1. 11–17.

59. Ibid., 1. 1. 19–21.

60. Ibid., 3. 1. 1–9.

61. Behn, *The Moor's Revenge*, 5. 1, p. 70.

62. Ibid., 5. 2, 77–78.

63. Two perceptive modern black writers, Eldridge Cleaver and Malcolm X, have both alluded to the black man's intense interest today in seducing white women. Cleaver, especially, refers this obsession of the black man to centuries of oppression during which black men were forbidden on pain of torture, mutilation, or death to touch a white woman, while white men permitted themselves free access to the bodies of black women.

64. *The Merchant of Venice*, 2. 1. 11–12.

65. Dekker, *Lust's Dominion*, 5. 1. 273–278.

66. *The Merchant of Venice*, 2. 7. 78–79.

67. Behn, *The Moor's Revenge*, 5. 2. 73–76.

68. Rowley, *All's Lost by Lust*, 2. 6. 43–45.

69. Heywood, *The Fair Maid of the West*, part I, 4. 3, p. 131.

70. Ibid., 4. 3, p. 132.

71. Ibid.

72. Rowley, *All's Lost by Lust*, 5. 1, p. 133.

73. Ibid., 5. 1, p. 141.

74. Ibid.

75. Ibid., 5. 2, p. 147. The editor suggests that "moorian" is a play on the word "murrain."

76. As many as twenty to thirty years may have passed between the composition of the two parts. The dates are uncertain; see A. M. Charles, *Thomas Heywood, Playwright and Miscellanist*, (1930), p. 110; G. E. Bentley, *The Jacobean and Caroline Stage* (1941–1956), p. 568.

77. Heywood, *The Fair Maid of the West*, part II, 1. 1, pp. 347–348.

78. Ibid., part II, 1. 1, p. 354.

79. Ibid., p. 365.

80. Heywood, *The Fair Maid of the West*, part II, 3. 1, p. 385.

81. Rowley, *All's Lost by Lust*, 4. 1, 74–75.

Chapter Seven: Other Sources of Denigration: Paganism and Failure

1. Davis points out that "white Christian practice was complex. . . . we may note that paganism and religious infidelity were the prime excuses for enslaving non-Europeans." Davis, *The Problem of Slavery in Western Culture*, p. 48.

2. Jonson, *The Masque of Blackness*, p. 242.

3. Richard Crashaw, *The Poems English Latin and Greek of Richard Crashaw*, ed. L. C. Martin (Oxford at the Clarendon Press, 1957), p. 17.

4. Ibid., p. 85.

5. William Blake, "The Little Black Boy," in *Poets of the English Language*, eds. W. H. Auden and Norman Holmes Pearson (New York: The Viking Press, 1950), p. 4.

6. Thomas Middleton, *The Triumph of Truth*, in *The Works of Thomas Middleton*, ed. Alexander Dyce (London, 1840), p. 233.

7. Ibid.

8. Ibid.

9. Ibid., p. 234.

10. Webster, *The White Devil*, 5. 1, pp. 85–86.

11. Heywood, *The Fair Maid of the West*, part II, 5. 1, p. 423.

12. *Titus Andronicus*, 5. 1. 71–80.

13. Fletcher, *The Knight of Malta*, 4. 3, p. 140.

14. Ben Jonson, *Sejanus*, 5. 10, p. 937. In *Elizabethan and Stuart Plays*, eds. Baskervill, Heltzel, and Nethercot (New York: Henry Holt and Company, 1934).

15. Rowley, *All's Lost by Lust*, 2. 3. 1–9.

16. Jonson, *The Queen's Masques, The First, of Blackness*, p. 240.

17. Rowley, *All's Lost by Lust*, 1. 1, 84–88. Rowley does not allow Rodericke's Christianity to modify a judgment against his evil. Peele, on the other hand, viewed Sebastian's cause more biasedly: "as justly he intends to fight for Christ" (*The Battle of Alcazar*, 3. 1. 789) and called him "brave," "Christian," and "noble."

18. Ibid., 5. 5. 56.

19. We should recall that in the early period of African exploration very little effort was made to colonize the country and convert the natives. See Davis, *The Problem of Slavery in Western Culture*, p. 168 ff.

20. Fletcher, *The Island Princess*, 4. 5, p. 253.

21. Berkeley, *The Lost Lady*, 4. 1, p. 518.

22. Ibid., 4. 3, p. 605.

23. Hodgen, *Early Anthropology*, pp. 407–416.

24. Marlowe, *Tamburlaine*, 4. 2, p. 333.

25. Wycherly, *The Gentleman Dancing-Master*, pp. 129, 194.
26. Peele, *The Battle of Alcazar*, lines 996–1003.
27. Fletcher, *The Knight of Malta*, 1. 1, p. 128.
28. Heywood, *The Fair Maid of the West*, part II, 2. 1, p. 355.
29. Ibid., 2. 1, p. 370.
30. Ibid., 1. 1, p. 341.
31. Ibid., 1. 1, pp. 341–342.
32. Clem's verbal abuse of the black Moors fills the play. When he engages in a dancing ceremony and grows tired, he ridicules the women by decrying their uncleanliness. "Fie upon't: I am so tir'd dancing with these same black she-chimney-sweepers, that I can scarce set the best leg forward." (2. 1, p. 355). See Winthrop Jordan's reasoned conjecture about the "dirtiness" associated with the black man. (Jordan, *White Over Black*, pp. 255–257.)
33. Heywood, *The Fair Maid of the West*, part II, 2. 1, p. 356.
34. Ibid., 3. 1, p. 379. More seriously, Thomas Dekker has one of his characters employ a similar ethnocentric appeal to seduce a woman. Fernando tries to persuade Eleazer's Spanish wife to become his mistress. He argues that the Moor, because he is no Spaniard, deserves no fidelity from her.

> Maria   My husband is from hence, for his sake spare me.
>
> Fernando Thy husband is no Spaniard, thou art one
>   So is Fernando, then for thy countries sake
>   Let me not spare thee.
>   (Dekker, *Lust's Dominion*, 3. 2, 20–24).

35. Crowne, *Calisto*, p. 242.
36. It is not to claim a means to a solution to note that a knowledge of the early modes of responses to cultural confrontations aids in understanding why one society will view members of a different race so strangely even centuries later. Therefore, to sharpen our insights to black-white racial problems today, the literature of this period, especially in the most public form of art, the drama, must be an important primary source.

Chapter Eight: Some Asides on Positive Aspects of the Image of the Black Man

1. Gordon Ross Smith, "The Credibility of Shakespeare's Aaron," *Literature and Psychology* 10 (Winter 1960): 11–13.
2. *Titus Andronicus*, 4. 2. 88–92.
3. Ibid., 4. 2. 107–111.
4. Ibid., 5. 1. 53–58.
5. Ravenscroft, *Titus Andronicus*, 5. 1, p. 39.
6. Dekker, *Lust's Dominion*, 4. 2. 138–141.

7. Ibid., 4. 2. 66–70.
8. Ibid., 4. 2. 1042–1047.
9. It could be noted here that Milton permitted even Satan a moment or two of conscience when he viewed Eve living idyllically in the Garden and, overwhelmed by the beauty there, hesitated before he put his plan into operation (book 4, lines 355–392). In the case of Macbeth, Shakespeare stressed the tyrant's courage and battle prowess, and granted him an opportunity to make "violent restitution" for his crimes. No such chance is offered Eleazer, whose villainy must remain his outstanding feature.
10. Behn, *The Moor's Revenge*, 5. 1, pp. 77–78.
11. Ibid., 5. 1, p. 69.
12. Rowley, *All's Lost by Lust*, 2. 3. 20–23.
13. Fletcher, *The Island Princess*, 2, p. 237.
14. Ibid., 2, p. 238.
15. See Mark Van Doren, *Shakespeare* (Garden City, N.Y.: Doubleday Anchor Books, (1953), p. 87.
16. *The Famous Historye of the life and death of Captain Thomas Stukley*, in *Old English Drama*, Student's Facsimile Edition, no scene division or pagination.
17. Ibid.
18. *Titus Andronicus*, 4. 2. 97–103.
19. Ravenscroft, *Titus Andronicus*, 5. 1, pp. 39–40.
20. *The Merchant of Venice*, 2. 1. 107.
21. Ibid., 2. 1. 8–11.
22. Webster, *The White Devil*, 5. 6, p. 116.
23. Jonson, *The Queen's Masques, The First, of Blackness*, p. 238.
24. That black women could be thought attractive is suggested in another poem by Richard Crashaw, "Upon the faire Ethiopian sent to a Gentle-woman." The poet assumes the beauty of the Ethiopian in the word "faire," using it in both title and text. Yet he undercuts his praise by implying that she herself despises her own color because of its sharp contrast with the white hand of the mistress she has come to serve.

> Lo here the faire Chariclea! in whom strove
> So false a Fortune, and so true a Love.
> Now after all her toyles by Sea and Land
> O may she but arrive at your white hand,
> Her hopes are crown'd onely she feares that than
> Shee shall appeare true Ethiopian.

The Poems English Latin and Greek of Richard Crashaw, p. 183.
25. Dekker, *Lust's Dominion*, 2. 1. 12.
26. *The Famous Historye of the life and death of Captian Thomas Stukley*, no scene division or pagination.
27. D'Avenant, *The History of Sir Francis Drake*, pp. 54–59.
28. Their reputation for bravery could be extended even to black women, as Jonson showed when, in *The Masque of Queens*, he described the

Queen of the Aethiopians as "a woman of a most haughty spirit against enemies, and a singular affection to her subjects." Jonson, *The Masque of Queens*, p. 346.

29. Behn, *The Moor's Revenge*, 3. 3, p. 44.
30. Berkeley, *The Lost Lady*, 3. 1, p. 587. It is noteworthy that these two contrasting comments encapsulate the difference between a stereotyped response and one founded on empirical experience.
31. Ibid., 2. 2, p. 572.
32. Ibid., 2. 2, p. 572.
33. Peele, *The Battle of Alcazar*, 3. 2, pp. 244–245.
34. Ibid., p. 299.
35. Ibid., p. 335.
36. *The Merchant of Venice*, 2. 7. 76–77.
37. Heywood, *The Fair Maid of the West*, part II, 2. 1, p. 371.
38. Ibid., 2. 1, p. 371.
39. Ibid., 3. 1, p. 382.
40. Ibid.

Bibliography

Adler, Doris. "The Rhetoric of Black and White in *Othello*." *Shakespeare Quarterly* 25 (1973): 248-257.

Allen, Don,Cameron. *The Star-Crossed Renaissance*. Durham, N. C.: Duke University Press. 1941.

———. "Symbolic Color in the Literature of the English Renaissance." *Philological Quarterly* 15 (January 1936): 81-92.

Baskervill, Read, Charles; Heltzel, Virgil B.; and Arthur H. Nethercot, eds. *Elizabethan and Stuart Plays*. New York: Henry Holt and Company, 1934.

Bass, William. *The Poetical Works of William Bass*. Edited by R. Warwick Bond. London, 1893.

Beaumont, Francis, and Fletcher, John. *The Works of Beaumont and Fletcher*. Edited by Alexander Dyce. London: Edward Maxon, 1851.

Behn, Aphra. *The Plays, Histories and Novels of the Ingenious Mrs. Aphra Behn*. London: Pearson, 1871.

Berkeley, William. *The Lost Lady*, in *A Select Collection of Old English Plays*. Edited by Robert Dodsley. New York: Benjamin Blum, Inc., 1964.

Bernheimer, Richard. *Wild Men in the Middle Ages, A Study in Art, Sentiment, and Demonology*. Cambridge, Mass.: Harvard University Press, 1952.

Bethell, S. L. "Shakespeare's Imagery: The Diabolic Images in Othello," *Shakespeare Survey* 5 (1952): 62-80.

Bissell, B. H. *The American Indian in English Literature of the Eighteenth Century*. New Haven, Conn.: Yale University Press, 1925.

Blake, William. "The Little Lost Boy," in *Poets of the English Language*. Edited by W. H. Auden and Norman Holmes Pearson. New York: The Viking Press, 1950.

Bodin, Jean. *Of the lawes and customes of a commonweale out of the French and Latin copies done into English by Richard Knolles*. London: G. Bishop, 1606.

Boemus, Johann. *The fardle of facions conteining the anciente maners, customes, and Lawes, of the peoples enhabiting the two partes of the earth called Affrike and Asie*. London: Eld and Burton, 1611.

Brome, Richard. *The English Moor*. London: John Pearson, 1873.

Browne, Thomas. *The Works of Sir Thomas Browne*. Edited by Charles Sayle. Edinburgh: John Grant, 1912.

Burnaby, William. *The Dramatic Works of William Burnaby*. Edited by F. E. Budd. London: Scholartes Press, 1931.

Burns, Allan C. *Colour Prejudice, with particular reference to the relationship between whites and Negroes*. London: G. Allen & Unwin, 1948.

_____. *History of the British West Indies*. London: G. Allen & Unwin, 1965.

Campbell, Lily B. *Shakespeare's Tragic Heroes. Slaves of Passion*. New York: Barnes & Noble, Inc., 1967.

Campion, Thomas. *Campion's Works*. Edited by Percival Vivian. Oxford: Clarendon Press, 1909.

Castiglione, Baldassare. *The Courtier*. London: J. M. Dent & Sons, Ltd.

Cawley, R. R. *The Influence of the Voyagers in Non-Dramatic English Literature between 1550 and 1650, with Occasional Reference to the Drama*. Ph.D. diss., Harvard University, 1921.

_____. *Milton and the Literature of Travel*. Princeton, N.J.: Princeton University Press, 1951.

_____. "Shakespeare's Use of the Voyagers in *The Tempest*," *Publication of the Modern Language Association* 41 (September 1926): 688–726.

_____. *Unpathed Waters: Studies in the Influence of Voyagers on Elizabethan Literature*. Princeton, N.J.: Princeton University Press, 1940.

_____. *The Voyagers and Elizabethan Drama*. New York: Kraus Reprint Corporation, 1966.

Chapman, George. *The Blind Beggar of Alexandria*. The Malone Society Reprints. Edited by W. W. Gregg. London: Oxford University Press, 1928.

Cleveland, John. *The Works of John Cleveland*. London, 1687.

Cloud, Jess. "George Herbert's Black Lady: An Exploration of 'Aethiopissa ambit Cestum.'" *Seventeenth Century News* 33 (1974): 43–45.

Cowhig, Ruth. "The Importance of Othello's Race." *Journal of Commonwealth Literature* 12 (1976): 153–161.

Cox, Edward Godfrey. *A Reference Guide to the Literature of Travel*. Seattle, Wash.: The University of Washington Press, 1935.

Crashaw, Richard. *The Poems English Latin and Greek of Richard Crashaw*. Edited by L. C. Martin. Oxford at the Clarendon Press, 1957.

Crowne, John. *The Dramatic Works of John Crowne*. London: H. Sotheran & Co., 1873.

D'Avenant, William. *The Dramatic Works of Sir William D'Avenant*. New York: Russell & Russell, Inc., 1964.

Davidson, Basil. *Black Mother: The Years of the African Slave Trade*. Boston: Little, Brown and Company, 1961.

Davis, David Brion. *The Problem of Slavery in Western Culture*. Ithaca, N.Y.: Cornell University Press, 1966.

Dekker, Thomas. *The Dramatic Works of Thomas Dekker*. Edited by Fredson Bowers. Cambridge, 1961.

Drake, Francis. *The World Encompassed*. Edited by N. M. Penzer. London: The Argonaut Press, 1926.

Draper, John. *The Humors and Shakespeare's Characters*. New York: AMS Press, 1965.

Dunbar, Paul Lawrence. *The Heart of Happy Hollow*. New York: Dodd, Mead & Co., 1904.

Dust, Philip. "The Sorrow of a Black Woman in a Seventeenth-Century Neo-Latin Poem," *College Language Association Journal* 18 (1974): 516–520.

Dykes, Eva B. *The Negro in English Romantic Thought*. Washington, D. C.: The Associated Publishers, Inc., 1942.

Eden, Richard. *The Decades of the Newe Worlde*. Ann Arbor, Mich.: University Microfilms, 1966.

Ellison, Ralph. *Shadow and Act*. New York: Random House, 1953.

Evans, K. W. "The Racial Factor in *Othello*." *Shakespeare Studies*. (1969): 124–140.

Faggett, Harry L. *Black, et al. Minorities in Shakespeare's England*. Houston, Texas: Prairie View Press, 1970.

The Famous Historye of the life and death of Captain Thomas Stukely. Students' Facsimile Edition.

Fleissner, Robert F. "Herbert's Aethiopesa and the Dark Lady: A Mannerist Parallel." *College Language Association Journal* 19 (1975): 458–467.

Fleissner, Robert F. "The Magnetic Moor: An Anti-Racist View," *Journal of Human Relations* (1969): 546–566.

French, J. Milton. "Othello among the Anthropophagii." *Publications of the Modern Language Association* 49 (September 1934): 807–810.

Fuller, Thomas. *The Worthies of England*. Edited by John Freeman. London: G. Allen & Unwin, 1952.

_____. *The Holy and Profane State*.

Gardner, Helen. *The Noble Moor*. London: Oxford University Press, 1955.

George, Katherine. "The Civilized West Looks at Primitive Africa: 1400–1800; A Study in Ethnocentrism." *Isis* 49 (1958): 66–72.

Gerard, Albert. "'Egregiously an Ass': The Dark Side of the Moor. A View of Othello's Mind," *Shakespeare Survey* 10 (1957): 98–106.

Gottesman, Lillian. "English Voyages and Accounts: Impact on Renaissance Dramatic Presentation of the African," *Studies in Humanities*. Edited by William F. Grayburn. Indian University of Pa., 1970, pp. 26–32.

Greene, Robert. *The Plays and Poems of Robert Greene*. Edited by J. Churton Collins. Oxford at the Clarendon Press, 1905.

Guilpin, Edward. *Skialethia*. Shakespeare Association Facsimile, number 2, 1598.

Hakluyt, Richard. *The Principal Voyages, Traffiques & Discoveries of the English Nation*. 12 vols. Glasgow: James MacLehose and Sons, 1903–05.

Hall, Edward. *Henry VIII*. Edited by C. Whibbley. London: T. C. and E. C. Jack, 1904.

Harbage, Alfred. *As They Liked It*. New York: Harper, 1961.

Harris, Bernard. "A Portrait of a Moor." *Shakespeare Survey* 11 (1958): 89–97.

Harrison, G. B. *Shakespeare Under Elizabeth*. New York: Henry Holt and Company, 1933.

Heather, P. J. "Color Symbolism," *Folk Lore* 49 (1948): 165–183.

Heawood, Edward. *History of Geographical Discovery in the 17th and 18th Centuries*. New York: Octagon Books, 1965.

Heilman, Robert. *Magic in the Webb*. Lexington, Kty.: University of Kentucky Press, 1956.

Herbert, Edward. *The Poems English and Latin of Edward, Lord Herbert of Cherbury*. Edited by G. C. Moore Smith. Oxford: Clarendon Press, 1956.

Herbert, George. *The Latin Poetry of George Herbert*. Translated by Mark McKloskey and Paul R. Murphy.

Heylyn, Peter. *Microcosmus, a little description of the great world*. Oxford, 1621.

_____. *Cosmographie, in Four Books. Containing the Chorographie and Historie of the Whole World. . . .* London, 1666.

Heywood, Thomas. *The Dramatic Works of Thomas Heywood*. London: John Pearson, 1874.

_____. *The Fair Maid of the West*, part I. Edited by A. Wilson Verity. London: Vizetelly & Co., 1888.

Hodgen, Margaret Trabue. *Early Anthropology in the Sixteenth and Seventeenth Centuries*. Philadelphia: University of Pennsylvania Press, 1964.

_____. "Sebastian Muenster (1489–1552): A Sixteenth-Century Ethnographer." *Osiris* 2 (1954): 504–529.

Hunter, G. K. "Othello and Colour Prejudice," *Proceedings of the British Academy* (1967): 139–163.

Jarrett, Hobart. "Some Exceptional Allusions to the Negro in Non-Dramatic Literature of Seventeenth Century England," *College Language Association Journal* 6 (September 1962): 19–22.

John Leo Africanus. *The History and Description of Africa and of the Notable Things Therein Contained*. Translated by John Pory. Edited by Robert Brown. 3 vols. London: Hakluyt Society, 1896.

Jones, Eldred D. "Africans in Elizabethan England." *Notes and Queries* 8 (1962): 302.

_____. *The Elizabethan Image of Africa*. (Folger Booklets on Tudor and Stuart Civilization). Charlottesville, Va.: University Press of Va. for Folger Shakespeare Library, 1970.

_____. "The Machiavel and the Moor," *Essays in Criticism* 10 (April 1961): 234–238.

_____. *Othello's Countrymen: The African in English Renaissance Drama*. Oxford: Oxford University Press, 1965.

_____. "The Physical Representation of African Characters on the English Stage During the 16th and 17th Centuries," *Theatre Notebook* 17 (Autumn 1962): 17–21.

_____. "Racial Terms for Africans in Elizabethan Usage." *Review of National Literature* 3 (1971): 54–89.

Jonson, Ben. *The Queen's Masques. The First, of Blackness*. In *The Works of Ben Jonson*. London, 1756.

Jordan, Winthrop. *White Over Black: American Attitudes toward the Negro, 1550-1812*. Chapel Hill, N.C.: University of North Carolina Press, 1968.

King, Henry. *The English Poems of Henry King, D. D.* Edited by Laurence Mason. New Haven, Conn.: Yale University Press, 1914.

Lee, Sidney. *Elizabethan and Other Essays*. Edited by F. S. Boas. Oxford at the Clarendon Press, 1929.

Lerner, Laurence. "The Machiavel and the Moor." *Essays in Criticism* 9 (October 1959): 339-360.

Levin, Harry. *The Power of Blackness*. New York: Vintage Books, 1958.

Lignon, Richard. *A True and Exact History of the Island of Barbados*. London, 1673.

Logan, R. W. "The Attitude of the Church toward Slavery Prior to 1500." *Journal of Negro History* 17 (1932): 466-480.

Lovejoy, Arthur O.; Chinard, Gilbert; Boas, George; and Crane, Ronald S., *A Documentary History of Primitivism and Related Ideas*. Baltimore, Md.: John Hopkins Press, 1935.

Marston, John. *The Plays of John Marston*. Edited by H. Harvey Wood. London: Oliver and Boyd, 1938.

Massinger, Philip. *The Dramatic Works of Massinger and Ford*. Edited by Hartley Coleridge. London: George Routledge and Sons, 1875.

McCullough, Norman V. *The Negro in English Literature—A Critical Introduction*. Ilfracombe, England: A. A. Stockwell, 1962.

Meyer, Gerard Previn. "The Blackamoor and Her Love." *Philological Quarterly* 17 (October 1938): 371-376.

Middleton, Thomas. *The Words of Thomas Middleton*. Edited by Alexander Dyce. London, 1840.

Miller, W. E. "Negroes in Elizabethan London." *Notes and Queries* 8 (1962): 138.

Munday, Anthony. *John A Kent & John A Cumber*. The Malone Society Reprints. Edited by W. W. Gregg and Muriel St. Clare Byrne. Oxford: Oxford University Press, 1923.

Nemmer, Max Andrew. *The Dramatic Significance of Physical Distinction in Characters in English Renaissance Drama*. Ph.D. diss., University of Pittsburgh, 1961.

Novak, Maximillian E. ed. *"The Empress of Morocco" and Its Critics*. Los Angeles, Calif.: Clark Memorial Library, UCLA, 1968.

Oakes, Katherine Beverly (Mrs. Katherine George). *Social Theory in the Early Literature of Voyage and Exploration in Africa*. Ph.D. diss., University of California at Berkely, 1944.

Obaid, Thoraya Ahmed. *The Moor Figure in English Renaissance Drama* Ph.D. diss., n.p. 1974.

Ower, John. "Manichean Metaphor: The Black African in Modern Literature" *Mosaic* 2 (Winter 1969): 1-12.

Peele, George. *The Battle of Alcazar*. In *The Dramatic Works of George Peele*. Edited by John Yoklavich. New Haven, Conn.: Yale University Press, 1961.

Pieterse, Cosmo. "Shakespeare's Blacks, Moors, Blackamoors, etc." *Ba Shiru* 4 (1972): 45–62.

Prager, Carolyn. "The Negro Allusion in *The Merchant of Venice*." *American Notes & Queries* 15 (1976): 50–52.

Purchas, Samuel. *Hakluytus Posthumus or Purchas His Pilgrimes*. New York: AMS Press, 1965.

Ravenscroft, Edward. *Titus Andronicus or The Rape of Lavinia*. London: J. B. for F. Hindmarsh, 1687.

Rowley, William. *All's Lost by Lust, and a Shoemaker, a Gentleman*. Philadelphia, Penn.: University of Pennsylvania, 1910.

Rowse, A. L. *The Elizabethans and America*. New York: Harper & Brothers, 1959.

Settle, Elkanah. *The Empress of Morocco*. London, 1687.

Shakespeare, William. *The Complete Works of Shakespeare*. Edited by George Lyman Kittredge. Boston, Mass.: Ginn & Company, 1936.

Smith, Gordon Ross. "The Credibility of Shakespeare's Aaron." *Literature and Psychology* 10 (Winter 1960): 11–13.

Starr, G. A. "Escape from Barbary: A Seventeenth-Century Genre." *Huntington Library Quarterly* 29:35–52.

Stoll, E. E. *Othello, An Historical and Comparative Study*. Minneapolis, Minn.: University of Minnesota, 1915.

_____. *Shakespearean Studies*. New York: Stechert, 1942.

Strachey, William. *The historie of Travell into Virginia Britania*. London: Hakluyt Society, 1953.

Sullivan, J. P. "The Machiavell and the Moor," *Essays in Criticism* 10 (April 1961): 231–234.

Sypher, Wylie. *Guinea's Captive Kings: British Anti-Slavery Literature of the XVIIIth Century*. Chapel Hill, N.C.: The University of North Carolina Press, 1942.

Taylor, John Edward. *The Moor of Venice, Cinthio's Tale, and Shakespeare's Tragedy*. London: Chapman, 1855.

Tillyard, E. M. W. *The Elizabethan World Picture*. New York: The Macmillan Co., 1944.

Van Doren, Mark. *Shakespeare*. Garden City: Doubleday Anchor Books, 1953.

Webster, John. *The Thracian Wonder*. In *The Dramatic Works of John Webster*. Edited by William Hazlitt. London, 1857.

_____. *The White Devil*. Edited by John Addington Symonds. Hill and Wang, Inc., 1956.

Weever, John. *Epigrams*. Edited by R. B. McKerrow. London: Sedgwick & Jackson, Ltd., 1911.

Winwood, Ralph. *Memorials of Affairs of State*. 1725.

Work, Monroe N. *A Bibliography of the Negro in Africa and America*. New York: The H. W. Wilson Company, 1928.

Wycherly, William. *The Complete Plays of William Wycherly*. Edited by Gerald Weales. Garden City, N.Y.: Doubleday Anchor Books, 1966.

Index